Service Learning in Psychology

Service Learning in Psychology

ENHANCING UNDERGRADUATE
EDUCATION FOR THE PUBLIC GOOD

Robert G. Bringle, Roger N. Reeb,
Margaret A. Brown, and Ana I. Ruiz

AMERICAN PSYCHOLOGICAL ASSOCIATION
WASHINGTON, DC

Copyright © 2016 by the American Psychological Association. All rights reserved. Except as permitted under the United States Copyright Act of 1976, no part of this publication may be reproduced or distributed in any form or by any means, including, but not limited to, the process of scanning and digitization, or stored in a database or retrieval system, without the prior written permission of the publisher.

Published by
American Psychological Association
750 First Street, NE
Washington, DC 20002
www.apa.org

To order
APA Order Department
P.O. Box 92984
Washington, DC 20090-2984
Tel: (800) 374-2721; Direct: (202) 336-5510
Fax: (202) 336-5502; TDD/TTY: (202) 336-6123
Online: www.apa.org/pubs/books
E-mail: order@apa.org

In the U.K., Europe, Africa, and the Middle East, copies may be ordered from
American Psychological Association
3 Henrietta Street
Covent Garden, London
WC2E 8LU England

Typeset in Minion by Circle Graphics, Inc., Columbia, MD

Printer: Maple Press, York, PA
Cover Designer: Berg Design, Albany, NY

The opinions and statements published are the responsibility of the authors, and such opinions and statements do not necessarily represent the policies of the American Psychological Association.

Library of Congress Cataloging-in-Publication Data

Bringle, Robert G., author.
  Service learning in psychology : enhancing undergraduate education for the public good / Robert G. Bringle, Roger N. Reeb, Margaret A. Brown, and Ana I. Ruiz. — First edition.
      pages cm
  Includes bibliographical references and index.
  ISBN 978-1-4338-2079-3 — ISBN 1-4338-2079-X 1. Psychology—Study and teaching (Higher) 2. Service learning—Study and teaching (Higher) I. Title.
  BF77.B75 2016
  150.71'1—dc23
                      2015020312

British Library Cataloguing-in-Publication Data
A CIP record is available from the British Library.

Printed in the United States of America
First Edition

http://dx.doi.org/10.1037/14803-000

Contents

Foreword   *vii*
Thomas McGovern

Acknowledgments   *xi*

Introduction   3

Part I. Psychology and Civic Engagement   19

1. Psychologically Literate Citizens: Civic Learning for the Public Good   21

2. Service Learning, Civic Engagement, and Science   37

Part II. Pedagogical Approaches   53

3. Designing a Service Learning Course   55

4. Integrating Service Learning Into the Curriculum: Introductory Psychology   83

5. Integrating Service Learning Into the Curriculum: Abnormal, Health, and Community Psychology   95

6. Integrating Service Learning Into the Curriculum: Personality, Social, and Cultural Psychology   107

7. Integrating Service Learning Into the Curriculum: Developmental Psychology   119

8. Integrating Service Learning Into the Curriculum: Cognition, Learning, and Behavioral Neuroscience — 129

9. Integrating Service Learning Into the Curriculum: Statistics, Research Methods, and Research Capstone — 139

10. Future Directions: Incorporating Service Learning in Learning Communities, Interdisciplinary Courses, Online Courses, Civic Internships, and Study Abroad — 151

Part III. Faculty Engagement — **161**

11. Faculty Development for Service Learning — 163

12. The Engaged Psychology Department — 175

13. Assessment, Research, and Scholarship on Service Learning — 185

Appendix A: American Psychological Association Learning Goals and Outcomes Indicators — 201

Appendix B: American Psychological Association Learning Goals and Inferred Attributes — 203

Appendix C: Reflection Map — 205

References — 207

Index — 239

About the Authors — 255

Foreword

Thomas McGovern

In *Service Learning in Psychology: Enhancing Undergraduate Education for the Public Good*, four scholar–teachers synthesize ideals from the long history of American higher education to answer a persistent question asked by students (and their financial aid sources): What can I do with a degree in . . . ? Readers will be challenged to evaluate the epistemology, historical tradition, and pragmatic consequences of why "serving to learn, and learning to serve" should be reinstated as one hallmark of undergraduate education. Deans, department chairs across the disciplines, pre- and post-tenure faculty, graduate students striving to make a difference and to be distinct—all should have this book on their permanent shelves.

After a thought-provoking evaluation of "Psychology and Civic Engagement" (Part I), the authors use the learning outcomes framework of the American Psychological Association's *APA Guidelines for the Undergraduate Psychology Major* (Version 2.0; 2013) to organize "Pedagogical Approaches" (Part II). Beginning with a template to design service learning courses and programs in workable stages, they integrate outcomes, teaching strategies, assessment measures, and evaluation research for Introductory Psychology, core content courses, and statistics and research methods. The capstone chapter in this section is on interdisciplinary, learning community, online, civic internships, and international service learning courses. "Faculty Engagement" (Part III) offers readers a pragmatic bookend to Section I, probing issues of faculty development, departmental engagement, and the scholarship of teaching and learning for service learning. A common denominator is that civic learning is an intellectual and life-skills text that deserves adoption and constant renewal.

The authors' argument is persuasive in four ways. First, they deftly embed service learning values and principles (e.g., democracy, reciprocity, collaboration) in a longer perspective on American higher education. Second, they build on 21st-century psychology's well-researched perspectives on discipline-based knowledge, scientific methodology, and best practices pedagogy. Third, each chapter is grounded in its own well-reflected classroom and field strategies for educating psychologically literate and civically engaged global citizens. Fourth, they transfer their experiences into maps for innovative activities and professional development tool kits ready for faculty eager to use this high-impact pedagogical strategy.

HIGHER EDUCATION FOR AMERICA

The 1636 Harvard curriculum balanced liberal arts learning and vocational training in a uniquely American way. For the next 2 centuries, faculty crystallized institutional missions and incorporated new knowledge into their baccalaureate curricula. College presidents offered a moral philosophy capstone course designed to launch new graduates with Aristotle's, Cicero's, and Jefferson's classic expectations for engaged citizen leaders. The educated elite model was democratized when Abraham Lincoln in 1862 signed Justin Morrill's (a Vermont dairy farmer) Land Grant Act and legitimated vocationally oriented fields as worthy study. To educate a democracy of peoples for a democracy of vocations became a progressive era aspiration. This vision was nuanced in the early decades of the 20th century by the "Wisconsin Idea" about applying university research to community service needs as well as by the social and governmental service programs and degrees created in new municipal universities.

However, inspired by the founding of the Johns Hopkins University and its research university vision, faculty attention turned inward and the tandem development of graduate specialization and undergraduate "majors" became paramount. Service narrowed to a focus on building curricula and professional networks off and on campus versus contributing to the broader civic communities' public good.

PARADIGMS FOR DISCIPLINARY EDUCATION

The APA was founded in 1892, representing one of the new disciplines staking out intellectual and administrative territories on campus via learned societies and associations (e.g., History in 1884, Economics in 1885, Philosophy in 1901, Political Science in 1904, and Sociology in 1905). Faculty consolidated campus curricula to differentiate students' academic programs from one another, using accreditation standards and enhanced postbaccalaureate career opportunities as justifications for this specialization. Rapidly expanding new knowledge spawned more and more major field electives and fragmented the overall curriculum. Students adopted a supermarket model of course selection. Post–World War II expansion of student enrollments and the civil rights movements diversified campus demographics dramatically. Neither the multigenerational, multiethnic populations to educate nor the ubiquitous curricula structure of distribution menus attached to prescribed major field requirements (or at least area menu plans) made any common or core learning feasible.

At the end of the 20th century, transdisciplinary groups such as the Association for American Colleges and Universities convened blue-ribbon panels to recapture unifying strategies for coherence in undergraduate education. State-mandated criteria and accrediting groups' emphases on measurable learning outcomes facilitated this task. "Across-the-curriculum" strategies (e.g., writing, ethics) and critical thinking skills woven into disciplinary and professional major requirements stimulated liberal learning collaboration. Structural approaches included common first-year and senior-year experience courses, major field capstone courses, and interdisciplinary learning communities. Gradually, faculty shifted from a teaching to a learning emphasis, and they responded to pervasive calls for increased retention, graduation rates, and the public's expectations for graduates' measurable skills and knowledge acquisition.

In such a public policy and accountability context, service learning has reemerged, and with increased transformational potential. Bringle is to be appreciated as a founder and synergistic thinker for this movement and its transdisciplinary future. His coauthors—Reeb, Brown, and Ruiz—enhance his pioneering work in theoretically sophisticated, highly practical, and empirically validated ways.

NARRATIVES FOR 21ST-CENTURY CITIZENS

What can I do with a degree in . . . ? When alumni return for an anniversary reunion, they may swap stories about professors' spectacular or dreadfully dull lecture methods or perhaps recall the rigors of their statistics and/or biological bases of behavior courses. My experience has been that they are more apt to remember moments when a caring faculty member first acknowledged their gifts or how experiences as a parent, friend, work supervisor, or community citizen daily reveal the deeper meanings of the psychological concepts they learned.

Becoming a psychologically literate citizen is a lifelong learning process. The single or multiple experiences of service learning are its sine qua non laboratories. In the best traditions of the core values of classical Greek and Roman academies, the Jeffersonian and land grant and progressive eras, and GI Bill higher education, socially responsive liberal education enriches the public good.

Psychology has the wherewithal to be a "hub discipline," equal in its learning outcomes for social benefits and its global contributions for the advancements of science. These scholar–teachers make a compelling case for why service learning and civic engagement are so important and how we as faculty, partnering with diverse communities, can make it happen.

Acknowledgments

Having the American Psychological Association (APA) publish this book is extremely important to its potential to contribute to the undergraduate psychology curriculum. We are grateful to Linda Malnasi McCarter, senior acquisitions editor for APA Books, for understanding the significance of our proposal to APA's work on the undergraduate psychology curriculum. We appreciated the editorial assistance that David Becker and two anonymous reviewers provided during the revision of the book. Patti Clayton's excellent work on reflection, student learning, and democratic partnerships provided a firm foundation for developing themes that run throughout the book. She provided important input into the development of our writing and feedback on some of the writing. We extend our appreciation to her for her scholarship, insights, guidance, and feedback. Ashley Hedgepath provided input into early drafts of two chapters. Lucinda Payne, Amy Galloway, and Brian Macharg, Appalachian State University; Greg Elvers, Ron Katsuyama, and Lee Dixon, University of Dayton; and Judith Warchal, Alvernia University also read parts of the manuscript and provided feedback. Brianna Bradshear and Zachary Martin provided help to prepare the manuscript for publication.

Service Learning in Psychology

Introduction

Service learning is an educational approach in which students use knowledge and skills learned in the classroom when engaged in activities with community partners. Service learning projects can cover a wide range of activities, such as helping the homeless, tutoring children, developing informational materials (e.g., brochures), evaluating the efficacy of an organization's services, conducting research in support of social reform, and promoting awareness of social issues, such as domestic violence. Service learning is more than applied learning; it is "the integration of academic material, relevant service activities, and critical reflection in a reciprocal partnership that engages students, faculty, staff, and community members to achieve academic, civic, and personal [growth] learning objectives as well as to advance public purposes" (Bringle & Clayton, 2012, p. 105).

The integration of service learning and psychology was explored in *With Service in Mind: Concepts and Models for Service Learning in Psychology*

http://dx.doi.org/10.1037/14803-001
Service Learning in Psychology: Enhancing Undergraduate Education for the Public Good, by R. G. Bringle, R. N. Reeb, M. A. Brown, and A. I. Ruiz
Copyright © 2016 by the American Psychological Association. All rights reserved.

(Bringle & Duffy, 1998), the sixth volume in the American Association for Higher Education's monograph series "Service-Learning in the Disciplines" (Zlotkowski, 2000). Building on that work, many practitioners in the field have adopted the concept of the *psychologically literate citizen* to describe the ideal graduate who has received a full undergraduate education in psychology: "Psychologically literate citizenship describes a way of being, a type of problem solving, and a sustained ethical and socially responsive stance towards others" (Halpern, 2010, p. 21). McGovern et al. (2010) described the psychologically literate citizen as "someone who responds to the call for ethical commitment and social responsibility as a hallmark of his or her lifelong liberal learning" (p. 10). The vision for the psychologically literate citizen is an important statement for framing the centrality and value of civic development, civic learning, and civic outcomes in a way that is integrated into the undergraduate psychology curriculum. We posit that service learning is the best tool for developing psychologically literate citizens.

Along these lines, American Psychological Association (APA) educational initiatives have advocated for the inclusion of service learning in the undergraduate psychology curriculum as a means to develop the civic outcomes of students and to enhance academic learning and personal development (e.g., Halpern, 2010; McGovern et al., 2010; Reich & Nelson, 2010). To achieve this goal, service learning has to be more prevalent and intentional throughout the curriculum. This volume provides a guide for realizing this goal. We explore how service learning can enhance the undergraduate psychology curriculum in distinctive ways to produce students who are prepared to use their education to the benefit of others. We review the theory, research, and practice of service learning and link it to undergraduate psychology courses, both introductory courses and more advanced courses for those majoring in psychology. We also provide sample project designs and assignments and discuss implementation strategies.

This volume is intended to contribute to the work of those who teach psychology courses and are motivated to enrich the undergraduate learning experience for both majors and nonmajors, for those who are involved in curricular revision and faculty development activities, and for those who teach courses in cognate disciplines. APA's work on psychological education has been directed at various levels of education: high schools, 2-year institutions, 4-year institutions, graduate education programs, postgraduate education programs, and continuing education programs. Although we propose that service learning is relevant to all levels of education, we have chosen to focus on the undergraduate psychology curriculum in this volume. The material presented here can easily be adapted to other levels of education.

In the remainder of this introduction, we present a broad overview of service learning, including its benefits and defining components, rationales for pursuing it, and its efficacy. We conclude with a synopsis of the chapters in the book.

BENEFITS OF SERVICE LEARNING IN UNDERGRADUATE PSYCHOLOGY

The *APA Guidelines for the Undergraduate Psychology Major* (Version 2.0; 2013; hereafter referred to as APA Guidelines 2.0), approved by the APA Council of Representatives in 2013, identifies five goals (knowledge base in psychology, scientific inquiry and critical thinking, ethical and social responsibility in a diverse world, communication, and professional development), indicators for subordinate outcomes (see Appendix A) at the foundational level (early courses in the curriculum) and at the baccalaureate level, and personal attributes for successful demonstration of outcomes. These recent developments laid a solid foundation for an expansion of the undergraduate psychology curriculum as a basis for "doing psychology," for developing "psychological literacy," and for connecting psychology to communities.

Others acknowledge that service learning is a significant pedagogical means for advancing the learning of undergraduates in the United States (Halpern, 2010) and internationally (Bringle, Hatcher, & Jones, 2011; Cranney & Dunn, 2011). Too often, the focus is only on developing social responsibility. However, service learning can also enhance many other learning outcomes put forth by the APA Guidelines 2.0, as we explore in this volume. Although there are several high-impact pedagogies (Kuh, 2008) and alternative pedagogies for reaching learning goals (e.g., collaborative inquiry, project-based learning, integrative learning, research), we contend that service learning is the best pedagogical means for developing civic learning for the public good among undergraduate students, and we invite researchers to evaluate this assertion. In addition, service learning can enrich academic learning and students' personal growth in a manner aligned with all the goals and many of the indicators in the APA Guidelines 2.0.

Civic learning could occur by having students take courses in other disciplines (e.g., political science, philosophy, public affairs, government), but we posit that civic learning that is integrated in the undergraduate psychology curriculum better serves psychology undergraduate students, both majors and the large number of nonmajors enrolled in psychology courses. More fully integrating service learning across all levels of the psychology curriculum by making it pervasive and expected will not only enrich academic learning, civic learning, and personal growth (Ash & Clayton, 2009a, 2009b; The National Task Force on Civic Learning and Democratic Engagement, 2012) but will also develop the civic aspirations of students and promote their subsequent behavior as psychologically literate citizens in ways that contribute to the public good. Our analysis will also establish the empirical base for justifying the use of service learning, but Reich and Nelson (2010) summarized well that evidence when they concluded that a "basic reason for bringing socially responsive knowledge and service learning pedagogy into our curriculum is that in many situations they simply are a more successful way to reach our students" (p. 142).

DEFINING COMPONENTS: THE NATURE OF SERVICE LEARNING

Civic Engagement

Figure 1 illustrates how the traditional functions of the academy (i.e., teaching, research, service) can occur in the community as well as on campus. Courses can be delivered to off-campus sites in communities, researchers

INTRODUCTION

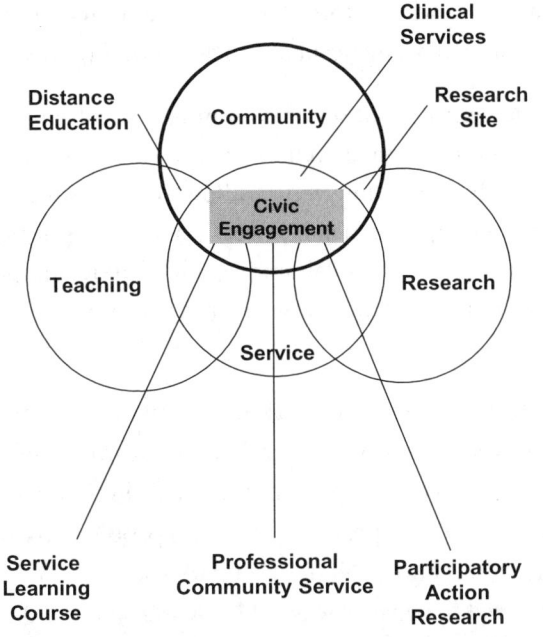

Figure 1

Civic engagement as faculty work in the community. From *Colleges and Universities as Citizens* (p. 5), by R. G. Bringle, R. Games, and E. A. Malloy (Eds.), 1999, Needham Heights, MA: Allyn & Bacon. Copyright 1999 by Allyn & Bacon. Adapted with permission.

can collect data in communities, and faculty can share professional expertise in communities. In addition, Figure 1 shows that these three areas can overlap; the intersections of (a) teaching, research, and service and (b) teaching and research can occur both on campus and in the community, although they are not shown in this diagram. Community involvement, then, is teaching, research, and/or service (and their intersections) that takes place in the community. Community involvement activities are defined by place; they can occur in all sectors of society (e.g., nonprofit, government, business) and in local, regional, national, and international locations (Bringle, Hatcher, & Clayton, 2006).

Bringle, Hatcher, and Clayton (2006) differentiated between *community involvement* and *civic engagement* in the following way:

> Civic engagement is a subset of community involvement and is defined by both location as well as process (it occurs not only in but also with the community). According to this distinction, civic engagement develops partnerships that possess integrity and that emphasize participatory, collaborative, and democratic processes (e.g., design, implementation, assessment) that provide benefits to all constituencies. (p. 258)

This differentiation between work done only in communities or for communities versus work done in and with communities represents a differentiation of approaches, epistemologies, and relationships, with the former being hierarchical, expertise-based, and problem-fixing in orientation (i.e., technocratic) and the latter being focused on community assets, collaboration, respect for diverse ways of knowing, and the development of the collective capacity of multiple constituencies (i.e., democratic; Jameson, Clayton, Jaeger, & Bringle, 2012; Saltmarsh, Hartley, & Clayton, 2009). The paradigm of democratic civic engagement defines a new approach to activities in communities that is a reciprocal, asset based, multidirectional orientation to community–campus engagement. Rather than focusing on community needs, the focus is directed at community assets as a basis for working with communities (Kretzmann & McKnight, 1993).

Because service learning is the intersection of teaching and service (Figure 1), it has dual purposes of benefiting the community and fulfilling academic learning goals. Service learning as a form of civic engagement is defined as a

> course-based, credit-bearing educational experience in which students (a) participate in mutually identified and organized service activities that benefit the community, and (b) reflect on the service activity in such a way as to gain further understanding of course content, a broader appreciation of the discipline, and an enhanced sense of personal values and civic responsibility. (Adapted from Bringle & Hatcher, 1996, p. 222)

INTRODUCTION

Civic Learning

This definition helps differentiate service learning from other types of educational experiences that take place in the community (e.g., internship, practicum, field-based instruction, cooperative education) and also differentiates it from volunteering (Furco, 1996). First, the definition identifies the unique contribution that service learning brings to higher education and to the undergraduate psychology curriculum: civic education. Unlike many internships and applied learning activities, what service learning does well, and probably better than any other pedagogy, is not just having students "serving to learn," which is applied learning, but also "learning to serve," which is referred to in the definition as "personal values and civic responsibility." What service learning should accomplish is to have students think about, critically examine, evaluate, and analyze what their role is in society with regard to civic, social, economic, and political issues and develop the skills and disposition to act on those roles. That is, students should engage in educationally meaningful community service that has relevance to and is informed by their academic studies and that also has relevance to their personal and civic lives now and in the future. They should do this as part of their studies in psychology so that they discover ways in which the content of psychology contributes to their understanding of the community issues that they encounter during their community service activities and vice versa. Civic learning is a complex category of learning. How civic learning is viewed is shaped by the course content, the community service activities, the instructor's perspective, and the community context. Civic learning can be construed as a separate area of learning with its own knowledge, skills, and dispositions, but it can also be viewed as integral to all of the learning goals in the APA Guidelines 2.0. Chapter 1 of this book examines in more detail the nature of civic learning.

Thus, unlike many practica and internships, service learning has the intentional goal of developing students' civic learning, not merely their academic learning or vocational preparation, which are the primary purposes of an undergraduate internship in psychology (Baird, 2008). However, many of the civic skills that are developed through service learning (e.g., communications skills, interpersonal skills, critical thinking, diversity, working with others, problem solving) are relevant to academic learning and to what employers value in employees (The National Task Force on Civic Learning and Democratic Engagement, 2012).

Second, unlike volunteering, service learning represents academic work in which the community service activities constitute a "text" that is interpreted, analyzed, and related to the content of a course in a way that permits a formal evaluation of learning—thus making it educationally meaningful community service. In service learning, students do not receive academic credit for engaging in community service; rather, academic credit (i.e., grades) is based on the learning that occurs as a result of the community service and connecting it to the course content. The community service activities are intentionally selected with community partners to be aligned with the educational objectives of the course and selected so that the community service is beneficial to them and those in the community who they might represent. The service may be (a) working with residents or clients of agencies (direct service), (b) working with agency staff (indirect service), (c) conducting research with the community (research), or (d) advocating for social change (advocacy; Florida Department of Education, 2009). The chapters in Part II provide examples of each type of service learning, and Chapters 1, 3, and 13 provide additional discussion of designing civic learning objectives, selecting community service activities, and assessing them.

Partnerships

This definition of service learning notes the importance of working with community members (e.g., staff at community organizations, residents, clients) to establish the basis for integrating community activities into a psychology course. Because of the commitment to and necessity of working with the community, the nature of these relationships is a central, defining component of civic engagement in general and of service learning in particular. Sigmon (1979) posited that in good service learning courses all teach, and all learn; all serve, and all are served. This changes the connotations of *service* from the expert student helping the needy community recipient to the student engaging in community work with community partners (e.g., staff, residents, clients) toward common goals. This type of relationship defines a reciprocal partnership between and among persons who are involved in service learning. Service learning educators should aspire to relationships that are guided by democratic principles characterized by the three key components of democratic processes: fairness, inclusiveness, and being participatory (Saltmarsh et al., 2009). Having democratically sound partnerships "critical for transmission of democratic practices" (Dostilio, 2012, p. 5) and critical reflection on the civic aspects of their activities are both crucial ingredients for ensuring democratic (vs. technocratic) orientations to civic involvement and developing democratic skills and democratic identities for future involvement (Bringle, Clayton, & Bringle, 2015). Chapter 1 provides additional discussion on the centrality of democratic processes to designing and implementing service learning, and Chapter 2 discusses the epistemological and methodological implications for conducting research based on democratic principles.

Reflection

This definition of service learning also identifies reflection as a key component of the pedagogy. Too often in experiential education courses students are asked to keep open-ended journals or write descriptive papers about their experiences. Well-designed reflection activities should (a) intentionally link the service experience to course-based learning objectives, (b) be structured, (c) occur regularly, (d) allow feedback and assessment, and (e) include the clarification of values (Bringle & Hatcher, 1999; Hatcher & Bringle, 1997; Hatcher, Bringle, & Muthiah, 2004). Good reflection can occur before, during, and after the community service (see Appendix C) and can result in students generating new learning and then capturing their learning for assessment (Ash & Clayton, 2009a, 2009b). Chapters in Part II present examples of reflection strategies that are aligned with learning goals so that they promote and capture learning for assessing students' academic learning, civic learning, and personal growth.

PEDAGOGICAL RATIONALES FOR SERVICE LEARNING

How can service learning enhance one, many, or all of the learning goals in the undergraduate psychology curriculum? How might the role of service learning help meet the civic learning goals of the psychologically literate citizen? There are at least four dominant rationales for service learning: disciplinary learning, student-centered learning, social justice, and democratic civic engagement (Zlotkowski & Duffy, 2010).

Disciplinary Learning

Significant work has been directed toward positioning service learning as a favored pedagogy within the disciplines (Zlotkowski, 2000). This includes the 21-volume series, "Service-Learning in the Disciplines," edited by Zlotkowski (1997–2006), with one devoted to psychology (Bringle & Duffy, 1998). Jameson, Clayton, and Ash (2013) provided an analysis of research on academic learning that has been conducted across disciplines, examining both research that measured changes across time and research that compared service learning with traditional pedagogies. Positive results for service learning are generally attained in both cases. In addition, Fitch, Steinke, and Hudson (2013) provided a similar analysis for research on cognitive outcomes for service learning. Novak, Markey, and Allen's (2007) meta-analysis found moderate effect sizes favoring service learning for knowledge, grades, and academic motivation; cognitive outcomes had a smaller but significant effect size favoring service learning. They also found that service learning produced positive and significant effects on personal and citizenship outcomes. Other meta-analyses have also found that service learning is positively associated with academic, personal, and civic outcomes, with the effect sizes ranging from small through moderate to large (Celio, Durlak, & Dymnicki, 2011; Conway, Amel, & Gerwien, 2009; Novak et al., 2007; Warren, 2012; Yorio & Ye, 2012).

INTRODUCTION

Student-Centered Learning

Barr and Tagg (1995) advocated for a paradigmatic shift from a teaching-centered orientation to a learning-centered orientation to instruction, suggesting that "a college's purpose is not to transfer knowledge but to create environments and experiences that bring students to discover and construct knowledge . . . to make students members of communities of learners that . . . solve problems" (p. 4). With factual information so readily available and with a changing knowledge base, service learning aligns well with a learning-oriented and student-oriented approach to lifelong learning after graduation. Because service learning democratizes learning, students become more active in the learning process, with community activities, community partners, and peers contributing to how learning occurs and what is learned. Zlotkowski and Duffy (2010) noted that "there are few 'right' answers in responding to community settings, students have to make inquiries, try multiple solutions, and persevere" (p. 37). Students become active coeducators in the learning process by regularly connecting through structured reflection the community activities with the course content (Ash & Clayton, 2009a, 2009b).

Social Justice

Service learning can be an effective means for approaching instruction as "education with a conscience" because it confronts students with social issues and asks them to consider both their origins and amelioration. The pioneers of service learning viewed the pedagogy as having a social justice orientation as well as a democratic emphasis (Stanton, Giles, & Cruz, 1999). The characterization of service learning as advocacy service learning or critical service learning (e.g., Mitchell, 2007; Porfilio & Hickman, 2011) carries forward the spirit for how a service learning course is designed and implemented to heighten awareness about systemic and structural characteristics that disadvantage persons. Mitchell (2007) distinguished between service learning as only a teaching strategy versus viewing it as a means for raising questions about and changing dominant conditions of privilege and oppression. Lisman (1997) viewed service learning as providing a "challenge to our overly simplistic forms of competency-based education that indirectly perpetuate the great gaps between the haves and the have-nots in our society under the false veneer of 'educational equality'" (p. 87). Brown and Riddle (2013) found that community service activities that involved direct contact in the community (vs. community service focused on community-based organizations) resulted in favorable changes in social justice attitudes.

Democratic Civic Engagement

John Dewey (e.g., 1938), an influential philosopher and past president of APA, provided philosophical, intellectual, and practical foundations for service learning by advocating for experiential education that would develop students' democratic skills and capacities for improving the human condition and the public good. Examining Dewey's contributions, Benson, Harkavy, and Puckett (2011) explained,

> Dewey theorized that education and society were dynamically interactive and interdependent. It followed, therefore, that if human beings hope to develop and maintain a particular type of society or social order, they must develop and maintain the particular type of education system conducive to it; that is to say, if there is no effective democratic schooling system, there will be no democratic society. (p. 52)

Levine's (2013) research found that simply involving students in community service activities is insufficient for developing civic learning and civic skills; they must also be involved in collaborative relationships in the civic realm. Partnerships between students and community members that have democratic qualities, (e.g., fair, inclusive, participatory; Saltmarsh et al., 2009) are critical and necessary to allow civic lessons to be fully developed and academic learning to be clarified. Bowman's (2011) meta-analysis found that face-to-face interactions with diverse groups resulted in favorable and significant effects on civic attitudes, behavioral intentions, and behaviors, compared with classroom-based educational experiences and cocurricular activities.

INTRODUCTION

EFFICACY OF SERVICE LEARNING

How can students be prepared for active civic lives? Through what pedagogical means can this be accomplished? The treatment of pedagogy in the chapters of Halpern (2010) is largely traditional. When service learning is mentioned, it is only aligned with the APA Guidelines 2.0 Goal 3, Ethical and Social Responsibility in a Diverse World. This reflects one of the strengths of service learning but leaves unexplored how service learning can enhance learning associated with the other four APA goals. Good service learning contains factors that are known to help students achieve in-depth understanding of content: (a) active learning, (b) frequent feedback from others (e.g., instructors, other students, community members), (c) collaboration with others, (d) cognitive apprenticeship (i.e., mentored relationships in which students can discuss and learn generalization of principles, transfer of knowledge between theory and practice, and analysis of perplexing circumstances), and (e) practical applications that involve students in tasks that have real consequences with a safety net as a buffer against high-stakes mistakes (Marchese, 1997).

A growing body of research supports the breadth of outcomes for service learning. Meta-analyses have provided a consistent picture of significant effect sizes for service learning over other pedagogies for academic, civic, and personal outcomes (Bowman, 2011; Celio et al., 2011; Novak et al., 2007; Warren, 2012; Yorio & Ye, 2012). Eyler's (2011) review of the research literature concluded that service learning contributes to political interest and efficacy, a sense of connectedness to community, social responsibility, future intent to participate in community life, and life skills. Beyond learning outcomes, service learning—as is the case with all high-impact pedagogies (Kuh 2008)—has a positive effect on students' persistence in higher education (Bringle, Hatcher, & Muthiah, 2010; Lockeman & Pelco, 2013), particularly with minority and marginalized students (Lockeman & Pelco, 2013). Astin and colleagues' (Astin & Sax, 1998; Astin, Sax, & Avalos, 1999; Sax & Astin, 1997) longitudinal analyses of students found that service learning led to political and community involvement 5 years after graduation, especially when reflection was a strong component of their experiences. Not all service learning courses produce all of these outcomes, and poorly designed service learning may not result in a learning advantage, but the empirical research supports the efficacy of high quality service learning.

OVERVIEW OF THE BOOK

This volume is divided into three major parts. The first part explores the intersection of psychology and civic engagement. Because civic learning is an underappreciated and underdeveloped component of the undergraduate psychology curriculum, the nature of civic learning is further explored in Chapter 1. Service learning also confronts traditional approaches to epistemology because it decentralizes authority from the expert to a broader array of constituencies. Students in service learning become aware that they can learn not only from the instructors but also from peers and community partners who can be cogenerators of knowledge as well as coeducators. Chapter 2 explores the nature of this paradigmatic expansion of epistemology and its implications for not only teaching with service learning but also conducting participatory community action research.

Because service learning is not a familiar pedagogy, the second part of the book provides concrete guidance for designing service learning courses. Specific examples are presented for integrating service learning into common courses in the psychology curriculum (e.g., Introductory Psychology, core content courses, research and statistics courses, capstone courses) as well as some evolving opportunities for psychology instructors to use service learning (learning communities, interdisciplinary courses, online courses, civic internships, international service learning). Chapters 3 through 10 each provide examples of how partnerships can be established to support service learning and how students can be involved in community-based activities. In addition, each chapter gives examples for how instructors can structure regular reflection activities to enable students to understand with increasing cognitive complexity the connections between (a) service activities and (b) academic learning, civic learning, and personal growth.

INTRODUCTION

The final part of the book, consisting of Chapters 11 through 13, presents information and resources for how faculty can be supported to develop service learning courses. This includes suggestions for faculty development activities, thinking of community engagement and service learning from the perspective of the department, and assessing the outcomes of involving students and faculty in civic engagement activities that include service learning. Service learning courses can open up unique opportunities to expand work with community partnerships, including research on teaching and learning and engaged scholarship (e.g., disciplinary research).

CONCLUSION

Reich and Nelson (2010) concluded that commitment to service learning in the undergraduate psychology curriculum is not widespread and that most emphasis is still on Altman's (1996) foundational knowledge rather than socially responsive knowledge. Psychology and the teaching of psychology have much to gain from a more systematic integration of service learning throughout the curriculum. Research leads to the conclusion that service learning can provide "value added" to reaching learning outcomes identified by the APA Guidelines 2.0. To the degree that psychology instructors aspire to being scholar educators who design instruction on the basis of the science of teaching and learning, the empirical base that supports service learning's capacity to augment academic learning, civic learning, and personal growth of students should attract additional attention. The subsequent chapters of this volume address the value added by service learning and provide guidance for realizing the full spectrum of outcomes that are associated with the psychologically literate citizen (McGovern et al., 2010). The analysis of theory, research, and practice associated with service learning is presented to establish it as the best pedagogy for producing civic-minded psychology students, graduates, and citizens.

PSYCHOLOGY AND CIVIC ENGAGEMENT

1

Psychologically Literate Citizens: Civic Learning for the Public Good

Why do we need more than a vocational education? In part, because we live more than a vocational life: we live a larger civic life and we have to be educated for it.
—Mathews, 1995, p. 70

For almost 400 years of U.S. history, the heart of higher education's purpose has been to serve the public good (Ehrlich, 2000; Fitzgerald & Primavera, 2013; Hartman, 2013; Kezar, Chambers, & Burkhardt, 2005; Saltmarsh & Hartley, 2011; Saltmarsh & Zlotkowski, 2011). Traditional definitions of *public good* consist of objectives that promote general human well-being, such as peace, order, prosperity, justice, and community (Douglass, 1980). Higher education's role as a servant of the public

http://dx.doi.org/10.1037/14803-002
Service Learning in Psychology: Enhancing Undergraduate Education for the Public Good, by R. G. Bringle, R. N. Reeb, M. A. Brown, and A. I. Ruiz
Copyright © 2016 by the American Psychological Association. All rights reserved.

good evolved from preparation of students for public service and the clergy during the earliest phases of American higher education to also offering, beginning in the 19th century, vocational and professional training in such disciplines as agriculture, medicine, and engineering. Tied to increasing industrialization of the country and the need for professionally trained citizens, the U.S. Congress and state legislatures provided funding to certain colleges and universities in the form of land grants (Association of Public and Land Grant Universities, 2012; Sternberg, 2010). The post–World War II era saw an explosion of federally funded research within universities in domains related to defense, health, and the sciences—all areas of national interest that benefited the public directly or indirectly. Also, the student population expanded to include returning soldiers, women, people of diverse backgrounds, and nontraditionally aged students. As these trends have demonstrated, higher education has been responsive to society's issues and the ethos of each era, and its purpose has been to benefit not only the individual students it serves but also the broader public good as well. The Truman Commission on Higher Education reaffirmed the civic mission of higher education by identifying the following three goals as preeminent among all other goals: "Education for a fuller realization of democracy in every phase of living. Education directly and explicitly for international understanding and cooperation. Education for the application of creative imagination and trained intelligence to the solution of social problems" (as cited in Association of American Colleges and Universities' Liberal Education and America's Promise Initiative, n.d., para. 1).

Yet since the 1960s, the intensely market-oriented environment began a shift in higher education toward emphasis on individual gain and entrepreneurship, which had the net effect of commodifying and corporatizing higher education (Kezar et al., 2005). The commodification of higher education has led to a tension among the multiple purposes of education. Chief among these are the seemingly competing purposes of education for economic goals (e.g., careers, economic development) and education for civic goals (citizenship, public good). *A Crucible*

Moment: College Learning and Democracy's Future (The National Task Force on Civic Learning and Democratic Engagement, 2012) called for a pervasive "civic reform movement" (p. 8) to transform institutions of higher learning so that they "prepare students for careers and citizenship, rather than only the former" (p. 10). The report argued, "It is all the more important that civic learning be integrated into the curriculum" (p. 10) and that integrating civic engagement can contribute to local and global economic growth and more generally to the quality of life in communities. In that book, the U.S. Department of Education reinforced the necessity of producing both well-prepared employees and citizens: "To fulfill America's promise in our global society, our education system at all levels, from early learning through higher education, must serve our nation *both* [emphasis added] as its economic engine and its wellspring for democracy" (foreword by Kanter and Ochoa, in The National Task Force on Civic Learning and Democratic Engagement, 2012, p. v).

The process of reexamining purpose within the academy has also occurred within psychology as scholars assessed psychology's role in furthering public interests (M. B. Smith, 1990); examined the tension between scientific and professional psychology (Sarason, 1988); confronted the lack of an overarching purpose in the discipline (Schneider, 1990); appraised psychology's underlying values, morals, and assumptions (Prilleltensky, 1997); and challenged the current model of undergraduate instruction (Altman, 1996; McGovern et al., 2010; Reich & Nelson, 2010). These analyses point toward the need for education in psychology to be concerned with the public good and to be sensitive to pressing social issues such as justice, peace, the alleviation of suffering, and the promotion of human flourishing to complement the prestige-oriented culture in academic psychology that is heavily weighted toward basic research. The American Psychological Association (APA) Public Interest Directorate (see Exhibit 1.1) and the Society for the Study of Social Issues also provide important perspectives and resources relevant to the public good.

> **Exhibit 1.1**
>
> **American Psychological Association Public Interest Directorate**
>
> A. General statement of the American Psychological Association (APA) Public Interest Directorate:
>
> > The APA Public Interest Directorate fulfills APA's commitment to apply the science and practice of psychology to the fundamental problems of human welfare and the promotion of equitable and just treatment of all segments of society through education, training, and public policy.
>
> B. Major objectives of the Public Interest Directorate:
>   1. Promote aspects of psychology that involve solutions to the fundamental problems of human justice and equitable and fair treatment of all segments of society.
>   2. Encourage the utilization and dissemination of psychological knowledge to advance equal opportunity and to foster empowerment of those who do not share equitably in society's resources.
>   3. Increase scientific understanding and training in regard to those aspects that pertain to, but are not limited to, culture, class, race/ethnicity, gender, sexual orientation, age, and discrimination, and support improving educational training opportunities for all persons.
>
> C. General issue areas of the APA Public Interest Directorate:
>   1. Aging (e.g., elder abuse and neglect)
>   2. Children, youth, and families (e.g., early mental health interventions)
>   3. Individuals with disabilities (e.g. disability employment resources)
>   4. Ethnic minority affairs (e.g., racism and discrimination)
>   5. HIV/AIDS (e.g., Behavioral and Social Science Volunteer Program)

> **Exhibit 1.1**
>
> **American Psychological Association Public Interest Directorate (*Continued*)**
>
> 6. Lesbian, gay, bisexual, and transgender issues (e.g., stress and health among sexual minorities)
> 7. Socioeconomic status (e.g., homelessness)
> 8. Violence (e.g., intimate partner and domestic violence)
> 9. Women's issues (e.g., empowering girls and women)
> 10. Work, stress, and health (e.g., work and unemployment stress)
>
> Note. Adapted from *About the Public Interest Directorate*, by the American Psychological Association, 2015. Retrieved from http://www.apa.org/pi/about/index.aspx. Copyright 2015 by the American Psychological Association.

CIVIC LEARNING AND PSYCHOLOGY

Ernest Boyer (1990) stated that the aim of education

> is not only to prepare students for productive careers, but also to enable them to live lives of dignity and purpose; not only to generate new knowledge, but to channel that knowledge toward humane ends; not merely to study government, but to help shape a citizenry that can promote the public good. (p. 160)

Reich and Nelson (2010) provided a historical account for the ways in which these themes have been present in psychology, including how psychologists have taken different perspectives on the salience of civic engagement in the discipline. They concluded, though, that only a small proportion of psychologists is involved in civic engagement related to social issues. With regard to undergraduate education, Altman (1996) proposed that the undergraduate psychology curriculum should support three learning domains: foundational knowledge (i.e., the core content and methods of psychology), professional knowledge (i.e., knowledge of the practice of psychology), and socially responsive knowledge. The purposes of the latter include, "first to educate students in the problems of society; second, have them experience and understand first-hand social issues in their community; and third, give students the experience and skills to act on social problems" (pp. 374–375).

Civic engagement in general and service learning in particular provide opportunities for psychology departments to enhance academic learning, civic learning, and personal growth by engaging in teaching, research, and professional service focused on contributing to the public good. Service learning can help students and instructors define for themselves what it means to participate in and create a more democratic society by having the pedagogy reflect democratic processes (i.e., being inclusive, participatory, and fair; Saltmarsh, Hartley, & Clayton, 2009). Service learning presents a means to establish partnerships with local agencies, schools, nonprofit organizations, and government agencies that reflect democratic values of working with community partners. Not all educators, including instructors of psychology courses, are interested in civic learning for their students, neither in each course in the curriculum nor as an area of work for themselves and their teaching, research, or professional service. However, psychology educators do presumably recognize civic learning and preparation for a civic life as an important broad educational goal of a college education for their students, and this is reflected in the *APA Guidelines for the Undergraduate Psychology Major* (Version 2.0; 2013; hereafter referred to as APA Guidelines 2.0). How this is achieved can linger for many educators as a largely unresolved matter (Abes, Jackson, & Jones, 2002), and it is underdeveloped for much of the contemporary undergraduate psychology curriculum (Altman, 1996; Reich & Nelson, 2010). There is, to be sure, public value in educating psychologically literate students (Cranney & Dunn, 2011; Halpern, 2010), but more must be done to develop psychologically literate citizens who are both motivated and well-prepared to actively contribute to their communities and the public good throughout their lives (McGovern et al., 2010). Altman's (1996) call for directing more attention toward socially responsive knowledge, in contrast to the dominant emphasis on foundational knowledge, is an example of understanding the civic value added through service learning.

Too often, it is assumed that civic education, if it is achieved at all, is accomplished through a diffuse approach that is largely unintentional, haphazard, and ill defined (e.g., through general education courses or elective courses). In contrast, considering how civic education can be a pervasive and expected part of the curriculum has received considerable attention in higher education (Ehrlich, 2000; Fitzgerald & Primavera, 2013; Hartman, 2013; Kezar et al., 2005; The National Task Force on Civic Learning and Democratic Engagement, 2012; Saltmarsh & Hartley, 2011) and within a variety of disciplines (e.g., Zlotkowski, 2000), but only marginally within psychology (e.g., Altman, 1996; Bringle & Duffy, 1998; Chew et al., 2010; McGovern et al., 2010; Osborne & Renick, 2006; Ozorak, 2004; Reich & Nelson, 2010). For example, most of the chapters in Halpern (2010) and Cranney and Dunn (2011) do not mention service learning as a means for reaching academic or civic outcomes, with only isolated exceptions (Charlton & Lymburner, 2011; Chew et al., 2010; Sokol & Kuebli, 2011). We are advocating that psychology instructors approach civic education more deliberately for all students enrolled in psychology courses and for students majoring in psychology. Rather than letting civic learning happen elsewhere and by accident, intentionally building service learning into the breadth and depth of the undergraduate psychology curriculum allows instructors and students to consider how civic dimensions of psychology can be examined, analyzed, developed, understood, and acted on then and in the future.

CONCEPTUAL FRAMEWORKS FOR CIVIC LEARNING

Civic learning is a multifaceted category of learning and it does not have a universal definition. How civic learning is viewed is shaped by the discipline, course content, the community service activities, the instructor's perspective, and the community context. It is also shaped by the political, social, economic, and historical contexts of communities, a region, and a nation. This diversity of interpretations of civic learning is a strength because it does not require any particular definition of civic learning. Furthermore, a service learning course and community service experiences can be designed to address a range of context- or discipline-specific conceptualizations. Civic learning is typically viewed as being composed of knowledge, skills, and dispositions (values, attitudes, or motives) to equip students to participate actively in public life within a diverse democratic society (Battistoni, 2013).

Knowledge

In addition to a focus on the academic forms of civic knowledge (dates and places of events, definitions, knowledge of government), civic knowledge includes deeper knowledge of public and social issues and knowledge of their underlying causes (Battistoni, 2002, 2013). Battistoni (2013) detailed how civic knowledge can also encompass knowledge of civic responsibilities, knowledge of democratic participation, knowledge of how to work on public tasks, and knowledge of social connections to institutions in civil society. Civic knowledge is not confined to the academy, and service learning emphasizes an epistemology that views civic knowledge as being widely distributed among instructors, students, residents, and staff of community-based organizations, as well as elsewhere in communities (see Chapter 2). This broader view of civic knowledge allows students and community members to become cocreators of knowledge, rather than simply relying on the expertise of textbooks or professors (Dostilio et al., 2013; Fretz & Longo, 2010). It also acknowledges that many individuals, not only instructors, can assume the role of coeducators of students, and service learning students should develop through regular, structured reflection an appreciation for how others contribute to their learning. With regard to the content knowledge of the undergraduate curriculum, service learning provides a basis for instructors and students to explore with community partners the civic aspects of the spectrum of psychology's knowledge. The community service activities also provide opportunities for students to observe, test, evaluate, analyze, and appreciate the relevance of psychology's content to community issues. The chapters in Part II provide illustrations for integrating community service experiences into specific courses.

Skills

Battistoni (2002) delineated a set of civic skills that educators from different disciplines or professions can instill as part of preparing students for active participation in democratic public life. This set of civic skills includes critical thinking; communication and deliberation (speaking and listening); public problem solving; civic judgment; civic imagination and creativity; teamwork, coalition building, and collective action; community organizing; and organizational analysis. Psychology instructors should be able to readily connect these civic skills to the academic content of courses. Although Battistoni's framework for civic learning in the disciplines aligns particular orientations to specific disciplines or professions, his list can also stimulate psychology instructors to identify civic learning goals that are associated with many if not all of the outcome indicators in APA Guidelines 2.0.

Civic professionalism is professional work with a civic purpose reflected in knowledge of the civic traditions and values of the professions, including the skills of public problem solving and civic judgment. Service learning in psychology courses can help students clarify career paths and consider how their careers and professional skills can contribute to the public good (e.g., types of career, type of work within a career, type of employer). Service learning can also contribute to skills employers value (e.g., communication, critical thinking, application, problem solving, ethical behavior, innovation, use information, understand global context; The National Task Force on Civic Learning and Democratic Engagement, 2012).

Social responsibility is responsibility to the larger society, including knowledge of public issues that are associated with an area of work, political knowledge of issues, and organizational analysis. Service learning in the psychology curriculum can enhance students' sensitivity to difficult issues in communities, develop a sense of self-efficacy to contribute (Reeb, Folger, Langsner, Ryan, & Crouse, 2010), and result in lifelong habits of civic engagement.

Social justice involves bringing one's values to bear on social problems and using knowledge of the principles of social justice, civic judgment, collective action, and cross-cultural competencies. Walker (2000) contended that some types of service activities are "Band-Aids" to social issues (e.g., charity-oriented community service), but service learning can be used to challenge social institutions and teach students advocacy skills that can be focused on addressing the root causes of social injustice. In psychology courses, service learning that is supported by appropriate critical reflection can be directed toward a social justice orientation by engaging students in face-to-face direct service with marginalized and disenfranchised populations (Bowman, 2011; Brown & Riddle, 2013). Wang and Rodgers (2006) found that service learning courses with a social justice emphasis resulted in more complex cognitive development than service learning courses without a social justice orientation. In addition, the service learning course with a social justice focus should incorporate reflection activities that regularly and intentionally structure this type of analysis (Mitchell, 2008; Porfilio & Hickman, 2011).

Connected knowing or the *ethic of caring* is concern for the future of the public world using the knowledge of others and their perspective of the world, critical thinking, coalition building, and exercising good communication skills. Service learning in psychology courses can lead to developing enhanced empathy, sensitivity to diverse populations, more accepting attitudes toward others, collaborative skills, and lifelong habits of civic engagement.

Public leadership involves citizens as servant–leaders using the knowledge of collaborative leadership, community building, and good communication skills. Service learning in psychology courses can lead to the development of leadership skills that have a servant leadership orientation with civic dimensions directed toward the public good (Greenleaf, 2002).

Public intellectuals are thinkers who contribute to public discourse using knowledge from literature and arts, civic imagination, and creativity. Service learning courses in psychology can produce psychologically literate citizens who use their disciplinary background to analyze and evaluate alternative approaches to social issues, provide psychologically informed commentary to others about social issues, and construct new approaches based on psychological principles and research.

Engaged or *public scholarship* is citizenship through participatory community action research that uses knowledge of how to conduct scholarly research and how it can contribute to communities, accompanied by organizational analysis and public problem solving. Service learning with a focus on conducting participatory community action research can provide a basis for developing an appreciation for how psychology's research tools and knowledge base can contribute to shaping improvements for the public good (see Chapter 2).

Values

One of the definitional outcomes of well-designed service learning is having students examine and develop values associated with civic engagement. Battistoni (2013) noted that many educators are hesitant to approach the subject of civic values as legitimate learning goals. This may be why some proponents of civic engagement use the seemingly more neutral terms *attitudes*, *dispositions*, or *motivation* to describe this area of civic learning (Battistoni, 2002). Saltmarsh (2005) presented the *key democratic values* that are important to service learning as engaging in relationships with community partners that are participatory, fair, and inclusive—values he believed can be widely agreed on and shared.

CIVIC LEARNING AS COLLABORATION

John Dewey, who served the APA as a president, made it clear that democratic capacity and moral development are contingent on face-to-face interactions in the public sphere. Action (e.g., community service), then, is necessary but not sufficient for the development of democratic skills. Dewey (1916) stated, "Society must have a type of education which gives individuals a personal interest in social relationships" (p. 99). Levine's research demonstrated that deliberation through collaboration is necessary to develop civic attitudes and skills in students. Keen and Hall (2009) found that sustained dialogue across boundaries of perceived difference that occurs during service produces positive outcomes. In addition, reflection was also important, including reflection with people students served, the people they served alongside, their supervisors at the service site, the college staff, and their peers.

THE CIVIC-MINDED GRADUATE

To provide an integrated conceptualization of civic learning outcomes, Steinberg, Hatcher, and Bringle (2011) proposed that a *civic-minded graduate* (CMG) represents the integration of civic learning with academic learning and describes students who are dedicated to engaging actively in their studies to pursue a career or community involvement that addresses issues in society for the public good. Civic mindedness is viewed as distinct from a self-orientation, family orientation, or corporate or profit orientation. The CMG construct is composed of a set of knowledge outcomes, dispositions, skills, and behavioral intentions. The core elements of the CMG that can be fostered through an undergraduate educational experience that includes service learning are:

- *Academic knowledge and technical skills.* In receiving a college education, CMGs will have acquired advanced knowledge and skills in at least one discipline that is relevant to their involvement in community issues.
- *Knowledge of volunteer opportunities and nonprofit organizations.* CMGs will understand ways they can contribute to society, particularly through nonprofit organizations and volunteering.
- *Knowledge of contemporary social issues.* CMGs have an understanding of the complex issues encountered in modern society, both at the local and national levels.
- *Listening and communication skills.* To help solve problems in society, CMGs have the ability to communicate well with others. This includes written and spoken proficiency as well as the art of listening to divergent points of view.
- *Diversity skills.* CMGs have a rich understanding of, sensitivity to, and respect for human diversity in the pluralistic society in which they live. This is presumed to be fostered by students' interactions with persons in the community who are different from themselves in terms of racial, economic, religious, or other background characteristics.
- *Consensus-building skills.* CMGs can collaborate with others, including those who differ from themselves.

- *Valuing civic involvement.* These students value helping others and being active in their communities.
- *Self-efficacy.* CMGs have a realistic view that their action will produce the desired results.
- *Social trusteeship of knowledge.* CMGs develop a sense of responsibility to use their knowledge to the benefit of the public good.
- *Behavioral intentions leading to civic behavior.* CMGs have intentions to be involved in community service in the future.

The work on CMG encompasses a coherent conceptual framework, measurement, guide to interventions, developmental theories, and a basis for assessment and research. As such, it provides a model for approaching civic development at different levels of analysis (individual, course, major, institution) and across time (Bringle & Steinberg, 2010; Bringle, Studer, Wilson, Clayton, & Steinberg, 2011; Steinberg et al., 2011). CMG also provides a basis for conceptualizing and operationalizing the "citizen" in *psychologically literate citizen.*

CIVIC LEARNING IN PSYCHOLOGY

The APA Guidelines 2.0 identify five major goals (knowledge base in psychology, scientific inquiry and critical thinking, ethical and social responsibility in a diverse world, communication, and professional development) and indicators for subordinate outcomes at the foundational level (early courses in the curriculum) and at the baccalaureate level. These guidelines (see Appendix A) provide a framework for considering how to enhance the psychology curriculum with service learning to develop connections between psychological academic learning and civic learning and personal growth.

Each one of the goals and many of their subordinate indicators can have civic dimensions. Service learning, through structured reflection, can contribute to students' understanding of psychology content (see the Introduction for research support for this conclusion and others that follow). It is also especially well aligned with how psychological content can inform understanding of social issues and public policy as well as interpersonal and intercultural issues in Goal 1 (Knowledge Base in Psychology). With regard to Goal 2 (Scientific Inquiry and Critical Thinking), service learning activities and reflection can contribute to critical thinking, especially about the relevance of psychological research tools and content to answering questions about civic aspects of social issues, including what psychological research has to offer to different levels of analysis (e.g., intrapersonal, interpersonal, group, systemic, sociocultural). Goal 3 (Ethical and Social Responsibility in a Diverse World) identifies personal and professional values that afford interactions with diverse groups (e.g., racial, ethnic, gender, class) and that are important to understanding psychological knowledge, social issues, and civic behavior. Service learning activities can provide opportunities for students and instructors to critically examine these factors, consider how existing approaches help or hinder progress toward the public good, and develop greater sensitivity to issues of power, privilege, and discrimination. Service learning in psychology can also enrich civic learning for Goal 4 (Communication) by providing opportunities to communicate with diverse persons (e.g., abilities, cultural perspectives) and develop sensitivity to, appreciation of, and respect for them. Finally, for Goal 5 (Professional Development), service learning in psychology courses can help students clarify career plans, understand unfamiliar communities, develop effective skills that can be attractive to employers, and consider how interest in the public good might shape their career path. One of the clearest ways that students can manifest a civic orientation is by choosing a service-based career or by manifesting civic dimensions to a career in any field.

Subsequent chapters of this book provide additional discussion of civic learning within the psychology curriculum, including chapters in Part II on how to design service learning courses and concrete examples of service learning in frequently offered psychology courses. They also illustrate how civic learning outcomes can be developed for the goals in the APA Guidelines 2.0. Part of the innovative and creative work in which instructors can engage is adapting these materials and examples to their particular course goals and community context. Those instructors who successfully do so will discover that service learning makes teaching more rewarding to them and more meaningful to students.

CONCLUSION

Lagemann's (1989) analysis of the role of Thorndike and Dewey in higher education led her to conclude, "I have often argued to students, only in part to be perverse, that one cannot understand the history of education in the United States during the twentieth century unless one realizes that Edward L. Thorndike won and John Dewey lost" (p. 185). Lightfoot's (2013) analysis of the contrast between Thorndike and Dewey noted that Dewey's emphasis on the centrality of community praxis for developing rationally, morally, and civically grounded students was displaced by Thorndike's focus on quantifying learning, the view that moral development followed intellectual achievement, and the nondemocratic perspective that there is an inevitable and meaningful hierarchy within society based on intellectual and academic superiority. Consequently, the role of civic education in the psychology curriculum warrants a counternormative adjustment that increases its salience. Bringle, Clayton, and Plater (2013) noted, "A focus on private gain (credentialing for employment) may displace public good (educating for citizenship) as the primary raison d'etre of the academy—to the detriment of our students, our communities, and our democracy" (p. 6). Civic learning can enhance and enrich academic learning and skills that are valued by employers (The National Task Force on Civic Learning and Democratic Engagement, 2012). The fundamental questions being posed are, What does it mean to want to prepare students, nonmajors and psychology majors, to be civic minded, civically oriented persons who have been informed by whatever psychology courses they have taken as undergraduates and are prepared to be civically engaged in the future for the public good? How well does the undergraduate psychology curriculum accomplish this aspiration? Could it do better?

Bronfenbrenner (1979) lamented,

> In the United States, it is now possible for a person eighteen years of age, female as well as male, to graduate from high school, college, or university without ever having cared for, or even held, a baby; without ever having looked after someone who was old, ill, or lonely; or without ever having comforted or assisted another human being who really needed help. No society can long sustain itself unless

its members have learned the sensitivities, motivations, and skills involved in assisting and caring for other human beings. (p. 53)

Community service activities that are integrated into psychology courses bring students into partnerships that have democratic qualities that can lead to empathy, understanding, social responsibility, and gratitude. These activities also help students develop democratic and civic skills. Coupling educationally meaningful community service with psychology course content through critical reflection provides what might be the most powerful way of engaging students in their academic work and developing students' civic identity (Bringle, Clayton, & Bringle, 2015). For, as Huber and Hutchings (2010) note, "when faculty from different disciplinary communities teach their fields using a civic lens, both the concept of citizenship and even the field itself (as taught and learned) are subject to change" (p. x).

2

Service Learning, Civic Engagement, and Science

This chapter explores how the values and processes of service learning pedagogy are aligned with approaches to epistemology that incorporate multiple perspectives. Research paradigms have an underlying philosophy of science characterized by an ontological perspective and an epistemological approach. *Ontology* refers to the nature of reality, whereas *epistemology* refers to the methodology used to build knowledge and to the relationship between the researcher and reality. What many consider to be traditional academic research has been shaped by positivism, but alternative philosophies of science compete for inclusion. For example, Gibbons et al. (1994) described a new (Mode 2) production of knowledge that recommends the pursuit of research within a context of social accountability, application, and transdisciplinarity.

Alongside this philosophical shift, Ernest Boyer's (1990) *Scholarship Reconsidered* broadened the view of scholarship to include the scholarship of discovery (traditional research), the scholarship of integration (putting

---

http://dx.doi.org/10.1037/14803-003
Service Learning in Psychology: Enhancing Undergraduate Education for the Public Good, by R. G. Bringle, R. N. Reeb, M. A. Brown, and A. I. Ruiz
Copyright © 2016 by the American Psychological Association. All rights reserved.

facts in perspective or making connections across disciplinary and stakeholder perspectives), the scholarship of application (use of knowledge in socially responsive ways), and the scholarship of teaching (not only transmitting knowledge but also transforming and extending it). One interpretation of Boyer's work is that the scholarship of engagement is a particular way of conducting each of those four types of scholarship. That is, there can be engaged discovery, engaged integration, engaged application, and engaged teaching. Boyer (1996) challenged higher education to bring new dignity to the scholarship of engagement, and one means for accomplishing this is for it to be more inclusive, participatory, and fair. Further, he recommended "connecting the rich resources of the university to our most pressing social, civic, and ethical problems, to our children, to our schools, to our teachers, to our cities" (pp. 19–20).

The first section of this chapter connects service learning and epistemology to engaged scholarship in the form of participatory community action research (PCAR). The second section provides a review of alternative philosophies of science (positivism, relativism, pragmatism, realism, and postpositivism). In addition, the new (Mode 2) production of knowledge (Gibbons et al., 1994) is presented as a basis for recent recommendations regarding engaged scholarship (Van de Ven, 2007). The third section describes PCAR as it relates to service learning. In the fourth section, the benefits of PCAR service learning are highlighted, such as its potential to (a) support, enhance, and expand university-related community research; (b) support the pursuit of the American Psychological Association's (APA's) *APA Guidelines for the Undergraduate Psychology Major* (Version 2.0; 2013); and (c) facilitate advocacy service learning that emphasizes a social justice perspective to community engagement.

CONNECTIONS AMONG SERVICE LEARNING, ENGAGED SCHOLARSHIP, AND PARTICIPATORY COMMUNITY ACTION RESEARCH

Minkler and Wallerstein (2003) defined PCAR as follows:

> A collaborative approach to research that equitably involves all partners in the research process and recognizes the unique strengths that

each brings... [PCAR] begins with a research topic of importance to the community with the aim of combining knowledge and action for social change to improve community. (p. 6)

Terms used interchangeably with PCAR include *community-based research*, *community action research*, and *participatory action research*. Engaged scholarship, service learning pedagogy, and PCAR share a historical perspective that higher education's purpose is to serve the public good (see Chapter 1), an emphasis on democratic processes (participatory, inclusive, and fair; Saltmarsh, Hartley, & Clayton, 2009), and a commitment to asset-based community development (Kretzmann & McKnight, 1993). Van de Ven (2007) highlighted service learning as a major tool of civic engagement, noting, "Service learning is perhaps the most widely diffused form of engaged scholarship" (p. 8).

PCAR, which we show as reflecting new epistemological approaches that incorporate multiple perspectives (Gibbons et al., 1994), represents a vehicle for engaged scholarship and service learning pedagogy. Minkler and Freudenberg (2010) noted that PCAR has emerged as a central "movement for a more engaged scholarship" due to the "growing recognition that the complexity of... today's health and social problems... make them poorly suited to traditional outside expert-driven research and interventions" (p. 275). PCAR represents one distinct type of community activity incorporated in service learning courses (see Chapter 3). Strand, Cutforth, Stoecker, Marullo, and Donohue (2003) contended, "[PCAR], when used as a teaching strategy, is an exceptionally effective form of service learning... appropriate for a variety of... curricular levels" (p. 137), and the "promise of service learning as a pedagogy [is] truly realized in the principles and practices of [PCAR]" (p. 121). According to Porpora (1999), "PCAR represents one of the more advanced forms of service learning" and perhaps the "highest stage of service learning" (p. 121). Part II of the present book contains specific examples of PCAR as a form of service learning that can enhance academic learning, civic learning, and personal growth in students working in communities. Before a full discussion of PCAR service learning, the implications of alternative philosophies of science for engaged scholarship are presented.

PHILOSOPHIES OF SCIENCE, ENGAGED SCHOLARSHIP, AND SERVICE LEARNING

Traditional Approaches

Van de Ven (2007) argued that a review of alternative philosophies of science for engaged scholarship and service learning is instructive because a researcher's philosophy of science is a critical choice—it serves as a foundation, with major implications for the types of questions asked, the methods used, and interpretative approaches used. Thus, "it is better to choose a philosophy of science than to inherit one by default" (p. 36). We will review several traditional philosophical perspectives that provide a basis for comparing and contrasting them with PCAR.

Positivism assumes (a) a single objective reality, (b) a researcher who is independent of the subject, and (c) a researcher who is capable of examining the subject without influencing it. With a detached approach, the positivist incorporates procedures to prevent values or biases from influencing outcomes, because such influences are viewed as threats to validity. In positivism, a hypothesis is developed from research and theory, and systematic techniques are used to test it. Despite the influence of positivism, "social science cannot be objective, rational, and cumulative, because language, culture, social norms, political ideologies mental biases, and selective perception constitute the inputs and processes of science" (Van de Ven, 2007, p. 37). In reaction to positivism, alternative paradigms have been developed.

Relativism denies absolute truth (i.e., truth is relative to differences in perception), and some relativists (e.g., social constructivists) view reality, including the interpretation of research results, as socially constructed. Thus, no researcher is capable of stepping outside sociolinguistic constructs or sociopolitical positionality to view research findings in an objective way. There is no privileged frame of reference and knowledge development involves transformation of a *Weltanschauung* (a comprehensive image of the world and humanity's relation to it) that requires a productive interplay among multiple perspectives, disciplines, models, and methods.

Pragmatism, like positivism, accepts that "there are real things, whose characteristics are entirely independent of our opinions" (Pierce, 1878/1997,

p. 21). But similar to relativism, pragmatism holds that "our sensations are as different as our relations to the objects" and we must "ascertain by reasoning how things really are" (p. 21). Science involves systematic observations accompanied by interpretive reasoning. When theories compete, the pragmatist adopts the theory with the most adaptive consequences. "Theories thus become instruments, not answers to enigmas" (James, 1907/1996, p. 32); or as Lewin (1952) noted, "There is nothing so practical as a good theory" (p. 169). Dewey's pragmatism (instrumentalism) was committed to the development of theories that "give intelligent direction . . . in search for ways to make the world more one of worth and significance, more homelike, in fact" (Dewey, 1946, p. 20).

According to *realism*, reality exists independent of our minds, and empirical approaches are used to test hypotheses derived from theoretical models of reality. Realism accepts the existence of unobservable entities in reality that remain beyond accurate perception, accompanied by a philosophical stance that theories roughly capture the unobservables. Through an iterative process, models are modified in light of research findings and are increasingly closer approximations of reality, though we can never completely comprehend reality. "We cannot know that our current theories are true, but they are truer than earlier theories, and [will be] replaced by something more accurate in the future" (Chalmers, 1999, p. 238).

Although positivism has been called the inherited view (Putnam, 1962), there was a shift to *postpositivism* in the middle-to-late part of the 20th century (Trochim & Donnelly, 2006). Postpositivism (also called *critical realism*; Trochim & Donnelly, 2006) is a "middle ground between positivism and relativism" (Van de Ven, 2007, p. 61): Postpositivism accepts an objective reality but also holds that the research process is influenced by the researcher's values and biases. All observation is fallible (value laden), and though objectivity is pursued to control biases, full objectivity is impossible. Postpositivism breaks with positivism by recommending theoretical and methodological triangulation (discussed later) to develop increasingly accurate models of reality. By emphasizing multiple perspectives and methods, postpositivism provides a bridge from traditional philosophies of science to a new approach to knowledge production (Gibbons et al., 1994), which is reviewed next and shown to coincide with recent recommendations for engaged scholarship and service learning (Van de Ven, 2007).

Mode 2 Production of Knowledge: A New Approach to Epistemology

In *The New Production of Knowledge*, Gibbons et al. (1994) concluded that "a new form of knowledge production is emerging alongside the traditional, familiar one" and that this new model "affects not only what knowledge is produced but also how it is produced" (p. vii). *Mode 2* retains some aspects of positivism (e.g., testing hypotheses in systematic or controlled research) but is influenced by pragmatism (e.g., conducting research in a context of application and social accountability), relativism (e.g., viewing knowledge as a construction derived from multiple perspectives and methods), and realism (e.g., evolving frameworks to guide research). Thus, in contrast to traditional research (referred to as *Mode 1*), Mode 2 is a socially distributed knowledge production system (Gibbons et al., 1994), meaning that it is "both supplied by and distributed to individuals and groups across the social spectrum" (p. 14). Mode 2 is becoming increasingly influential, but there have been several criticisms of the approach (e.g., Hessels & Van Lente, 2008). Mode 2 has five primary attributes, each of which coincides with recent recommendations regarding engaged scholarship (Van de Ven, 2007). This discussion is pertinent to the use of service learning pedagogy in the psychology curriculum, because PCAR service learning is a form of engaged scholarship, and it has values and principles that coincide with those of Mode 2 epistemology.

First, Mode 2 knowledge is *produced in the context of application*. Mode 1 knowledge can have practical applications, but application is viewed as distinct from knowledge production, and knowledge transfer is a prerequisite for application. In contrast, Mode 2 does not recognize a sharp distinction between knowledge production and application; that is, a project guided by Mode 2 begins with an intention for it to be useful to society (Gibbons et al., 1994). Likewise, each phase of engaged scholarship and PCAR service learning (conceptualization, planning, implementation, and evaluation) is aligned with Van de Ven's (2007) recommended emphasis on the concept of *relevance*, the degree to which an activity "addresses the pragmatic situation or issue for which it was intended" (p. 67).

Second, Mode 2 knowledge production is *transdisciplinary*; that is, it uses a range of theoretical perspectives and methods (across disciplines) in an "evolving framework to guide problem solving" (Gibbons et al., 1994, p. 5). In the Mode 2 approach, "discoveries lie outside the confines of any particular discipline" and so "new knowledge produced in this way may not fit easily into any one of the disciplines that contributed to the solution" (p. 5). Likewise, for engaged scholarship (including PCAR service learning), Van de Ven (2007) referred to *conscious pluralism*; that is, engaging faculty and service learning students from various disciplines, as well as community partners who contribute a variety of perspectives and methods for reflecting on, understanding, or addressing a particular community issue. For a discussion of interdisciplinary (transdisciplinary) service learning, the reader is referred to Chapter 10.

Third, Mode 2 knowledge is characterized by *heterogeneity of skills and organizational diversity*, with knowledge production sites beyond the university (e.g., community agencies, nonprofit organizations, government agencies)—all linked in a communication network (Gibbons et al., 1994). With regard to engaged scholarship, Van de Ven (2007) recommended that stakeholders from various perspectives engage in multimedia interactions (e.g., written reports, online interactions, presentations, face-to-face interactions), referred to as *knowledge translation boundary conversations*. Van de Ven's review of studies identifying the effective elements of communication indicated that research findings are more likely to be adopted if they are (a) perceived as yielding advantages over other approaches; (b) explicit, simple to understand, observable, and testable; (c) presented as part of a persuasive argument; and (d) reflect at least some views held by the audience. In brief, persuasion involves (a) *logos*, "internal consistency or clarity of the argument"; (b) *pathos*, "power to stir the emotions, beliefs, values, knowledge, and imagination"; and (c) *ethos*, "credibility, legitimacy, and authority of the speaker" (p. 243). These attributes are pertinent to the dissemination of findings of PCAR service learning projects to community stakeholders.

The fourth attribute of Mode 2 is *reflexivity and social accountability*, which "permeate the whole knowledge production process" (Gibbons et al., 1994, p. 7). In all phases of research, there is reciprocity among stakeholders in decision making, with a concern regarding the social significance of the research from the beginning. In discussing reflexivity in engaged scholarship, Van de Ven (2007) drew three interrelated conclusions: (a) "entanglements with partisanship, politics, values, and ethics are inevitable" (p. 290); (b) researchers cannot know their "own assumptions... and viewpoint" until engaging with others (p. 291); and (c) partners must be "reflexive by making clear whose... interests are served in a study" (p. 290). These conclusions inform (a) the implementation of PCAR service learning projects and (b) reflection (see Chapter 3, this volume) about service learning projects.

Finally, Mode 2 knowledge production incorporates *multidimensional criteria for quality control*. Quality control is not limited to one discipline's peer review; instead, it "incorporates a diverse range of intellectual interests as well as other social, economic or political ones" (Gibbons et al., 1994, p. 8), such as social acceptability, cost-effectiveness, and sustainability. Van de Ven (2007) provided recommendations for considering multiple perspectives within the context of engaged scholarship. These recommendations, as reviewed later, are pertinent to (a) interpretation of PCAR service learning projects and (b) reflection exercises for PCAR service learning students.

To consider multiple perspectives across disciplines, stakeholders, and settings, Van de Ven (2007) recommended *triangulation*. In psychology, triangulation is often used to examine multiple methods (e.g., multitrait–multimethod matrix; Campbell & Fiske, 1959); however, in engaged scholarship, triangulation more broadly examines perspectives across disciplines, stakeholders, and settings to identify themes of convergence as well as contradictory information (Van de Ven, 2007). When convergence occurs among multiple sources, "this reliability provides confidence in having a valid representation of the problem domain" (Van de Ven, 2007, p. 285). When contradiction occurs, it could mean (a) there is bias in at least one informational source, (b) there are errors or outliers in at least one source, or (c) "different... sources tap different dimensions or domains of... the phenomenon" (p. 285). Thus, the examination of contradictions across informational sources may identify different dimensions of an issue, generate insights that promote an integrative explanation, prevent acceptance of myopic conclusions, or reveal conflicting values or interests among stakeholders. In these examinations, Van de Ven recommended *arbitrage*—a strategy that involves "assigning different weights to different perspectives at different times in different situations" (Friedman, 2000, pp. 23–24). To develop an integrative theory from information obtained across sources, Van de Ven recommended a strategy called *consilience*, "a 'jumping together' of knowledge by linking facts and fact-based theory across disciplines to create a common groundwork of explanation" (Wilson, 1999, p. 7).

PARTICIPATORY COMMUNITY ACTION RESEARCH

General Description

Strand et al. (2003) emphasized three guiding principles for PCAR: (a) collaboration; (b) validation of multiple sources of knowledge, different methods, and various forms of dissemination; and (c) social action to pursue social justice. Strand et al. (p. 9) compared PCAR with traditional academic research (Table 2.1). PCAR processes are captured by the often-cited quote in community psychology, "nothing about me, without me" (G. Nelson, Ochocka, Griffin, & Lord, 1998, p. 881), and are well aligned with new perspectives on engaged scholarship (Van de Ven, 2007) and the Mode 2 research approach (Gibbons et al., 1994). Shared attributes include production of knowledge in a context of application, emphasis on social accountability, recognition of multiple knowledge-production sites beyond the university, co-ownership of data, emphasis on collaboration among multiple stakeholders, multiple modes for disseminating research tailored to different audiences, recognizing beneficiaries of research beyond academic researchers, and incorporating multiple perspectives in examining, interpreting, and integrating research findings.

The nature of partnerships is integral to well-implemented PCAR, and Strand et al. (2003) identified 10 principles of community–campus partnerships, which fall into three categories: (a) *principles guiding*

Table 2.1
A Comparison of Traditional Academic Research and Community-Based Research

	Traditional academic research	Community-based research
Primary goal of the research	Advance knowledge within a discipline	Contribute to betterment of a particular community, social change, social justice
Source of the research question	Extant theoretical or empirical work in a discipline	Community-identified issue or need for information
Who designs and conducts the research?	Trained researcher, perhaps with the help of paid assistants	Trained researchers, students, community members in collaboration
Role of researcher	Outside expert	Collaborator, partner, and learner
Role of community	Object to be studied ("community as laboratory") or no role at all	Collaborator, partner, and learner
Role of students	None, or as research assistants	Collaborators, partners, and learners
Relationship of the researcher(s) and the participants–respondents	Short term, task oriented, detached	Long term, multifaceted, connected
Measure of value of the research	Acceptance by academic peers (publication, for example)	Usefulness to community partners and contribution to social change
Criteria for selecting data collection methods	Conformity with standards of rigor, objectivity, researcher-control; preference for quantitative and positivistic approaches	The potential for drawing out useful information, sensitivity to experiential knowledge, conformity to standards of rigor, and accessibility; open to a variety and combination of approaches
Beneficiaries of the research	Academic researchers	Academic researcher, students, community
Ownership of the data	Academic researchers	Community

Table 2.1
A Comparison of Traditional Academic Research and Community-Based Research (*Continued*)

	Traditional academic research	Community-based research
Mode of presentation	Written report	Varies widely and may take multiple and creative forms (for example, academic publications, video, theater, written narrative)
Means of dissemination	Presentation at academic conference, submission to journal	Any and all forums where results might have impact: media, public meetings, informal community settings, legislative bodies, and others

Note. From *Community-Based Research and Higher Education: Principles and Practices* (p. 9), by K. J. Strand, N. Cutforth, R. Stoecker, S. Marullo, and P. Donohue, 2003, San Francisco, CA: Jossey-Bass. Copyright 2003 by John Wiley & Sons, Inc. Adapted with permission.

partnership initiation—sharing a world view, agreeing about goals and strategies, and possessing trust and mutual respect; (b) *principles guiding partnership processes*—sharing power, communicating clearly and listening carefully, understanding and empathizing with each other, and remaining flexible; and (c) *principles guiding partnership outcomes*—satisfying each other's interests and needs, obtaining enhanced organizational capacities, and adopting long-range social change perspectives. These guiding principles, which align with Mode 2 knowledge production (e.g., social accountability, multiple criteria for quality control) are known to yield benefits that enhance the likelihood of success with regard to implementation, productivity, and sustainability of PCAR projects (e.g., Reeb & Folger, 2013; Reeb, Snow, et al., 2014; Stoecker, Tryon, & Hilgendorf, 2009; Strand et al., 2003; Van de Ven, 2007; Wandersman & Florin, 2000). These include

- increasing the commitment that community members have to the research process, findings, and use because the research represents their own social change agenda;

- maximizing a research program to fit with community values, assets, and needs;
- enhancing the quality of data collection and validity of measures by incorporating language, perspectives, special knowledge, and experiences of community members;
- increasing community investment and trust, reflected in higher response rates, greater validity of data, greater commitment to research, and improved project sustainability;
- empowering all research team members through shared expertise and growth;
- highlighting the democratization of the research process; and
- ensuring that results are owned by both the community and research team and thereby have implications for social change, policy change, or program change.

PCAR Service Learning

Students become involved in PCAR in different ways, such as through independent study, a research assistantship (paid or volunteer), or a service learning course. Service learning emphasizes a connection between community activities and course content, regular and structured reflection, civic learning, and assessment of student learning and community outcomes (Introduction and Chapter 3). The benefits of service learning on students' academic learning, civic learning, and personal growth are well documented (Introduction); undergraduate students involved in a PCAR-related service learning course are likely to have similarly enhanced educational experiences while contributing to significant community benefits.

As part of the orientation to PCAR, service learning participants (i.e., students, community partners) should be educated on the APA (2010) *Ethical Principles of Psychologists and Code of Conduct*, especially for the protection of human research participants. If the community organization has a code of conduct (see Exhibit 3.1, pp. 67–69, for an example), faculty and students should be familiar with it. The *Service Learning Code of Ethics*

(Chapdelaine, Ruiz, Warchal, & Wells, 2005) and PCAR ethical principles (Centre for Social Justice and Community Action, Durham University, & National Co-ordinating Centre for Public Engagement, 2012) are also valuable resources. Finally, as a requirement for PCAR service learning, faculty and students involved in PCAR should complete training for conducting research, such as the Collaborative Institutional Training Initiative Program (2014; Social and Behavioral Research Investigators Course) or its equivalent. If community partners are directly involved in research activities, they should also complete the research ethics training.

BENEFITS OF PCAR SERVICE LEARNING

Students involved in a PCAR service learning course may pursue any particular type (or combination of types) of service learning (see Chapter 3), including (a) direct, (b) indirect, (c) research, and (d) advocacy. Chapter 10 describes an interdisciplinary PCAR service learning project at a homeless shelter (Reeb, Glendening, Farmer, Snow, & Elvers, 2014). The project examines (a) student outcomes (academic learning, civic learning, and personal growth), (b) outcomes for persons who are homeless (e.g., self-sufficiency, employment, housing retention), and (c) agency outcomes (improved social climate of shelter). This project incorporates the defining features of PCAR as delineated in Table 2.1. Service learning students provide direct service (e.g., GED training), indirect service (e.g., development of educational brochures or media for shelter guests), research (e.g., data collection, dissemination of findings), and/or advocacy (e.g., assisting a nonprofit organization with antistigma projects). Some students participate in multiple types of activities (concurrently), some participate in them sequentially, and others focus on one type. Undergraduate service learning students from various majors worked alongside graduate students, faculty, and community partners to implement this project, playing key roles in providing activities to (a) enhance self-sufficiency or coping of persons experiencing homeless and (b) improve the shelter's social climate (previously a prison).

PCAR Service Learning Supports the Pursuit of APA Learning Goals

PCAR service learning supports the pursuit of all five APA (2013) learning goals, many indicators, and associated personal attributes (Appendixes A and B). For the sake of illustration, consider a PCAR service learning project in an agency serving clients with mental illness. Students' understanding of mental illness from course content would be augmented through interactions with clients and staff, contributing to the pursuit of Goal 1 (Knowledge Base in Psychology) and associated personal attributes (e.g., being conversant about psychological phenomena). Students assisting with design, data collection, analysis, or disseminating results would contribute to APA Goal 2 (Scientific Inquiry and Critical Thinking) and accompanying personal attributes (e.g., being precise, systematic, logical). Students grappling with understanding disadvantages faced by individuals with mental illness in society (e.g., social stigma, lack of access to services) would contribute to APA Goal 3 (Ethical and Social Responsibility in a Diverse World) and related personal attributes (e.g., being tolerant, respectful, sensitive, fair-minded). If students are producing brochures or media for purposes of education or dissemination of research findings, this would enhance APA Goal 4 (Communication) and associated personal attributes (e.g., being comprehensible, precise). PCAR requires collaboration and teamwork, and so PCAR service learning contributes to APA Goal 5 (Professional Development) and related personal attributes (e.g., being collaborative). Because PCAR projects frequently focus on underserved populations, PCAR would enhance diversity initiatives and APA's strategy of infusing sociocultural factors into each of the five learning goals.

PCAR Service Learning Facilitates Advocacy Service Learning Initiatives

PCAR can facilitate advocacy service learning, which Mitchell (2008) referred to as *critical service learning*:

> There is an emerging body of literature advocating a "critical" approach to community service learning with an explicit social justice

aim. A social change orientation, working to redistribute power, and developing authentic relationships are most often cited in the literature as points of departure from traditional service-learning.... Critical service learning programs encourage students to see themselves as agents of change, and use the experience of service to address and respond to injustice in communities. (pp. 50–51)

Consistent with the Mode 2 emphasis on conducting research in the context of application, PCAR service learning provides experiential opportunities to work on projects that address parts of APA's (2014b, 2014c) Public Interest Directorate (see Exhibit 1.1), which applies "the science and practice of psychology to the fundamental problems of human welfare and social justice and the promotion of equitable and just treatment of all segments of society through education, training and public policy" (APA, 2014c, para. 1). The APA Public Interest Directorate can inform service learning projects, including PCAR, and serve as a valuable resource to guide reflection exercises. Also, as students work with faculty, graduate students, and community professionals, they have the opportunity to observe, reflect on, and learn about evidence-based practices.

PCAR also provides opportunities for students to engage in activities that are related to public policy. As students engage in these activities and augment their knowledge regarding public policy through structured reflection, they become better prepared and empowered for participating in public policy as postgraduate citizens. Minkler and Freudenberg (2010) provided a comprehensive discussion of using PCAR to effect change in public policy, concluding that

> [PCAR] can be an important tool in efforts to move from data gathering and interpretation to the use of findings in ways that ... influence the lives of a large number of people. Policy-focused [PCAR] can identify, make visible, and legitimize issues so that they ... are placed on the public's agenda. It can ... help partnership members bring the attention of ... mass media to long ignored issues—or newly uncovered problems—based on findings that are both newsworthy and grounded in strong evidence. (pp. 290–291)

Minkler and Freudenberg reviewed (a) conceptual models in the policy making process, (b) key steps in using PCAR in public policy initiatives, (c) key considerations and opportunities for campus–community partners to pursue policy changes, and (d) barriers and challenges in policy focused PCAR. Finally, *psychopolitical validity* (Prilleltensky, 2008), a central concept in community psychology, may be helpful in guiding and evaluating PCAR service learning projects. Psychopolitical validity incorporates two criteria in evaluating a community project: Type I, *epistemic*, which "demands that psychological and political power be incorporated into community interventions," and Type II, *transformative*, which "requires that interventions move beyond [alleviative or] ameliorative efforts and towards structural change" (Prilleltensky, 2008, p. 116). In this respect, psychopolitical validity coincides with the emphasis on social accountability and multiple criteria for quality control in Mode 2 production of knowledge.

CONCLUSION

Service learning, when combined with PCAR, has the potential to support, enhance, and expand university-related engaged scholarship initiatives. PCAR service learning has all of the ingredients necessary to (a) enhance academic learning, civic learning, and personal growth in students; and (b) make significant sustainable contributions to the community—not only alleviative or ameliorative contributions but also contributions representing transformative change, such as empowering community organizations and community members, as well as public policy changes that pursue goals related to social justice. Careful consideration of PCAR principles, as well as the guiding principles of Mode 2 production of knowledge, will enhance the likelihood of success with regard to the implementation, productivity, and sustainability of PCAR service learning projects.

TWO

PEDAGOGICAL APPROACHES

3

Designing a Service Learning Course

Shulman (1998) suggested that "teaching begins with a vision of the possible or an experience of the problematic" (p. 6) and that "every course is inherently an investigation, an experiment, a journey motivated by purpose and beset by uncertainty" (p. 5). Creating a vision of what is possible in a service learning course involves considering not only student and instructor attributes, course content, and institutional mission but also factors inside and outside the classroom. A course integrating service learning leads to a more permeable classroom in which insights gained from community experiences flow easily into the content of the course, and in which course content is related to settings outside the classroom (L. R. Sandy, 1998). Such permeability can create deeper learning experiences

---

Donna K. Duffy contributed to the writing of this chapter.

http://dx.doi.org/10.1037/14803-004
Service Learning in Psychology: Enhancing Undergraduate Education for the Public Good, by R. G. Bringle, R. N. Reeb, M. A. Brown, and A. I. Ruiz
Copyright © 2016 by the American Psychological Association. All rights reserved.

but may also increase uncertainty during a course. Formulating an effective course design can maximize student learning, instructor growth, and benefits to communities.

Incorporating any new strategy into a course is a learning process for an instructor, and it may be helpful to consider the first attempt to use service learning as a pilot course. Instructors can become overwhelmed by trying to do too much too soon and may benefit from the advice to "start small rather than not at all" (Duffy, Barrington, West, Heredia, & Barry, 2011). For example, an instructor could start by having students involved in limited community service, small projects, or team-based approaches to the community service component of a course. An instructor could also choose to have the service learning component be an option in a course, with an alternative assignment (e.g., writing a research paper) for other students. Initially, the service learning option could be capped to make it more manageable. Experience could then lead to revisions and subsequent expansion.

Principles of good practice can guide, at a general level, the design, implementation, and assessment of service learning courses (Franco, Duffy, Baratian, Hendricks, & Renner, 2007; Heffernan, 2001; Howard, 2001; Jacoby, 2014). Research supports the conclusion that service learning courses promote academic learning and critical thinking and contribute to civic knowledge, skills, dispositions, and personal growth (see Introduction, this volume; Billig & Eyler, 2003; Brandenberger, 2013; Bringle & Steinberg, 2010; Clayton, Bringle, & Hatcher, 2013a, 2013b; Conway, Amel, & Gerwien, 2009; Eyler & Giles, 1999; Felten & Clayton, 2011; Novak, Markey, & Allen 2007). In this chapter we discuss the rudiments of course design, working with community partners to develop community activities that are consistent with learning objectives and community benefits, designing effective reflection using the DEAL (describe, examine, and articulate learning) model for critical reflection (Ash & Clayton, 2004, 2009a, 2009b; Jameson, Clayton, & Bringle, 2008), and assessing outcomes. Subsequent chapters in Part II of this volume focus on enhancing specific psychology courses with service learning.

TYPES OF SERVICE LEARNING COURSES

Service learning courses can involve four distinct approaches to the types of community activities by students (e.g., Florida Department of Education, 2009): (a) direct service learning, (b) indirect service learning, (c) research service learning, and (d) advocacy service learning. Which is most appropriate for a course will be the result of considering learning objectives and discussions with community partners about what best fits their circumstances.

In *direct service learning*, students are engaged in interactions with clients of a community organization or residents in a community. Examples of direct service learning include students tutoring youth, providing support to elderly persons at a community center, or assisting community members who are experiencing mental illness or homelessness.

Indirect service learning involves students working behind the scenes to increase, enhance, or direct resources to support an organization, neighborhood, or government office to address an issue in the community. Examples include fundraising, developing resource materials (e.g., brochures, instructional aids, web pages), or facilitating access to services (e.g., augmenting the collaboration between a homeless shelter and a health clinic).

In *research service learning* students use psychological methods (e.g., design, measurement, data analysis) in community-based activities. For example, students could collaborate with community partners to develop an assessment instrument and/or conduct a program evaluation. Alternatively, the research could be participatory community action research wherein a team of individuals (faculty, students, and community partners) collaborate to conduct research that contributes to solutions and social transformation (see Chapters 2 and 9).

Students in *advocacy service learning* apply psychological content to examine root causes of social issues and encourage transformative change in communities (e.g., increasing public awareness concerning an issue, changing policy, advocating for client rights, changing infrastructure to improve access to services). Activities could include conducting presentations in the community to increase awareness of a policy issue, obtaining support for a social change initiative, and assisting community members who are working for a cause (e.g., letters, e-mails, telephone calls, and face-to-face meetings with government officials or legislators).

Although these distinctions identify service learning activities that fit each type, service learning can involve activities across multiple categories, especially for ongoing partnerships embedded within a broad program of engaged service and engaged scholarship. For example, students from different service learning courses can contribute to different stages of a long-term community partnership in the following ways: (a) transforming a homeless shelter to provide integrated services (e.g., health care; mental health care; job training, placement, and support; legal services; supportive housing); (b) evaluating the efficacy of the shelter (e.g., whether it decreases recidivism and/or increases employment); (c) promoting the homeless shelter as a model for other shelters; (d) examining the efficacy of transferring the model to other shelters; (e) designing a secure data base across area shelters; and (f) working with community members to advocate for public funds to establish integrated shelters.

The most frequent approach has been to develop service learning on a course-by-course basis, typically by integrating community service activities and reflection into an existing course. Such curricular revision can intentionally focus on particular types of courses taught by psychology instructors. For example, service learning can be integrated into

- first-year success seminars to help entering students adjust to college;
- orientation to major courses;
- themed learning communities, which are clusters of courses that cohorts of students take, one or more of which has a service component (see Chapter 10);
- Introductory Psychology (see Chapter 4);
- courses in the major (see Chapters 5–9);
- capstone courses taken by graduating seniors, which integrate material across the discipline (see Chapter 9);
- civic internships, which are career-oriented service learning courses (see Chapter 10);

- participatory community action research courses, in which students conduct community research that provides useful information to the community (see Chapters 2 and 9);
- international service learning courses (Chapter 10);
- honors courses; and
- online courses (Guthrie & McCracken, 2010; Strait & Sauer, 2004; see also Chapter 10, this volume).

An additional approach to curricular development of service learning occurs at the departmental level rather than at the course level. This changes the unit of analysis and the focus of discussion and includes more instructors in developing an engaged curriculum. As a result, curricular issues are considered from the beginning of the major to the capstone experience, and sequences of courses can be coordinated. Chapter 12 provides more details about this approach. Another approach focuses on developing interdisciplinary certificates, minors, and majors aligned with community engagement and composed of multiple service learning courses, including psychology courses (Butin, 2010). These may have titles such as *community-based leadership, public leadership, nonprofit sector,* or *community service studies.* These innovations are intentional, coherent, and sequenced curricula that involve a number of instructors within and across departments.

DESIGNING, IMPLEMENTING, AND ASSESSING SERVICE LEARNING

Designing, implementing, and assessing service learning courses are ongoing processes that are shaped by institutional resources, specific course objectives, and priorities and goals of community partners. The following sections summarize key issues to consider.

Resources

Professional staff in a center for community engagement or office of service learning (or a similarly named unit) on campus are important resources to learn about course redesign, community resources, suggestions for implementation, and assessment. These professional staff members interact with faculty from many disciplines on service learning and civic engagement initiatives. Institutions sometimes focus on specific initiatives or themes (e.g., sustainability), and aligning a project with them may provide additional resources (e.g., colleagues, community partners, seed grants). Similarly, the American Psychological Association (APA) establishes public education campaigns with supporting materials. Exploring the APA Public Interest Directorate (see Exhibit 1.1) and division websites can expand the context and resources available for service learning in a specific course. Campus Compact has a syllabus file that provides examples of service learning courses (http://www.compact.org). Bringle and Duffy's (1998) edited volume provides guidance and examples of service learning courses in psychology.

Reframing and Adding Course Objectives

Halpern and Hakel (2003) noted, "Varying the conditions under which learning takes place makes learning harder for learners but results in better learning" (p. 39). As students move beyond the classroom, instructors have the opportunity to reframe learning objectives to capture the richness and complexity of the learning opportunities in community settings. Service learning can contribute to all five broad goals and the indicators listed in the *APA Guidelines for the Undergraduate Psychology Major* (Version 2.0; APA, 2013; hereafter referred to as APA Guidelines 2.0): knowledge base in psychology, scientific inquiry and critical thinking, ethical and social responsibility in a diverse world, communication, and professional development (see Appendix A). Considering issues, observations, insights, questions, and perplexing dilemmas presented in community settings can encourage instructors to rethink and expand learning objectives initially and continue revisions and adjustments as a course evolves (Duffy, 2004). The APA Guidelines 2.0 assist in formulating learning objectives related to academic learning of course content, civic learning, and personal growth. However, the goals and associated indicators are broad and operate at the metacourse level (i.e., foundational level, baccalaureate level). Course learning objectives tailored to a particular course and to particular community service activities have to be much more specific.

Table 3.1 presents a heuristic incorporating the broad APA (2013) goals and the three domains of learning objectives in service learning courses (i.e., academic learning, civic learning, and personal growth; Ash & Clayton, 2009a, 2009b) that can be used to develop more specific learning objectives that best fit the course goals at both the foundational and baccalaureate levels. The academic, civic, and personal domains are relevant to all five goals. No single course will attend to all outcomes in the APA Guidelines 2.0, so specific learning objectives can be developed for those outcomes that are most pertinent to the course goals that are being enriched through service learning. One of the assets of a service learning-enhanced course is how service learning not only enriches academic learning but also how additional learning objectives can be developed for civic learning and personal growth. The work of psychologists is rich in examples of civic responsibility or the "active participation in the public life of a community in an informed, committed, and constructive manner with a focus on the common good" (Gottlieb & Robinson, 2002, p. 16). Course objectives can be developed that focus on the various ways psychology can contribute to the public good, how the science of human behavior can help students develop a broader understanding of social issues, and how students can be more active in communities and contribute to the public good (see Chapter 1 for a more detailed discussion of civic learning in psychology courses). The syllabus should incorporate a rationale for the service learning component of the course that articulates how the service learning activities contribute to and enhance academic learning, civic learning, and personal growth.

Reciprocal Partnerships

Because service learning highlights the commitment to and necessity of working with the community, not just in it, and for, or on behalf of, the community, the nature of relationships involved in service learning is a central, defining dimension of the pedagogy. Robert Sigmon (1979), one of the pioneers of service learning, noted that in good service learning all

Table 3.1

Framework for Generating Learning Objectives for a Service Learning Course From APA Guidelines 2.0

Service learning	APA goals				
	Knowledge Base in Psychology	Scientific Inquiry and Critical Thinking	Ethical and Social Responsibility in a Diverse World	Communication	Professional Development
Academic learning	Goal 1.1a: Use basic psychological terminology, concepts, and theories in psychology to explain behavior and mental processes.	Goal 2.1c: Use an appropriate level of complexity to interpret behavior and mental processes.	Goal 3.3E: Apply psychological principles to a public policy issue and describe the anticipated institutional benefit or societal change.	Goal 4.3b: Recognize that culture, values, and biases may produce misunderstandings in communication.	Goal 5.1D: Apply relevant psychology content knowledge to facilitate a more effective workplace in internships, jobs, or organizational leadership opportunities.

Civic learning	Goal 1.3A: Articulate how psychological principles can be used to explain social issues, address pressing societal needs, and inform public policy.	Goal 2.5D: Evaluate the generalizability of specific findings based on parameters of the research design, including caution in extending western constructs inappropriately.	Goal 3.3B: Develop psychology-based strategies to facilitate social change to diminish discrimination practices.	Goal 4.3C: Interact sensitively with people of diverse abilities, backgrounds, and cultural perspectives.	Goal 5.1E: Adapt information literacy skills obtained in the psychology major to investigating solutions to a variety of problem solutions.
Personal growth	Goal 1.3d: Predict how individual differences influence beliefs, values, and interactions with others, including the potential for prejudicial and discriminatory behavior in oneself and others.	Goal 2.1E: Use strategies to minimize committing common fallacies in thinking that impair accurate conclusions and predictions.	Goal 3.3c: Explain how psychology can promote civic, social, and global outcomes that benefit others.	Goal 4.2b: Deliver brief presentations within appropriate constraints (e.g., time limit, appropriate to audience).	Goal 5.4d: Assess strengths and weaknesses in performance as a project team member.

Note. Adapted from *APA Guidelines for the Undergraduate Psychology Major* (Version 2.0), by the American Psychological Association, 2013. Retrieved from http://www.apa.org/ed/precollege/undergrad/index.aspx. Copyright 2013 by the American Psychological Association.

teach and all learn, all serve and all are served. This type of relationship in which students and instructors work with community partners, defines a reciprocal partnership between the persons who are involved in service learning. Instructors can improve reciprocity by making these relationships more interdependent, enhancing communication, and involving the community partners as coeducators (e.g., Jacoby, 2014; M. G. Sandy & Holland, 2006; Stoecker, Tryon, & Hilgendorf, 2009).

There are at least five constituencies who typically are involved in service learning courses: (a) students, (b) staff at community-based organizations, (c) faculty, (d) campus administrators (e.g., service learning staff, executive leaders, dean, or department chair), and (e) residents of communities or clients served by community-based organizations (Bringle, Clayton, & Price, 2009; Clayton, Bringle, Senor, Huq, & Morrison, 2010). These are not the only five constituencies, but these are particularly relevant to the design, implementation, and assessment of most service learning courses. All of these stakeholders can be considered partners who contribute to the development of a service learning course before it is implemented. Instructors designing and revising service learning courses should consider how they can incorporate each of these partners and how they can improve relationships to enhance service learning course outcomes for the various partners (not just students). Each of these relationships should be guided by democratic principles. Saltmarsh, Hartley, and Clayton (2009) identified the following three key components of democratic processes: that they are fair, inclusive, and participatory.

Reciprocity is sometimes used to convey minimal commitment to mutual benefit through the exchange of resources; that is, each person benefits and the exchanges are equitable. This type of reciprocity is a transactional relationship. *Transactional relationships* are short term and project based, with limited and planned commitments that work within an existing system; the parties maintain their separate identities, and they have their own goals (Clayton et al., 2010). Transactional relationships may be acceptable, and they are rather common. However, a higher level is achieved when a relationship has transformational qualities. In *transformational partnerships*, persons come together with a longer term perspective on how their goals merge and develop, how they revise their own goals and identities, and how they develop new systems to work together (Clayton et al., 2010).

Developing and improving reciprocal partnerships in service learning creates a broad, aspirational picture of partnerships that is complex, multifaceted, and challenging, but nevertheless enriching to the educator and others. In contrast to "community placements," service learning partnerships involve multiple persons; thus, each person can have particular goals and outcomes, and democratic processes should be incorporated in each relationship. Furthermore, the development of these partnerships must be nurtured as part of developing a service learning course—both before it is offered and as the course continues to be offered and improved. This highlights the role that each person (faculty, staff, students, community constituencies) can assume as codeveloper, colearner, coeducator, and cogenerator of knowledge (Dostilio et al., 2013). More interesting, though, is thinking about the transformational learning of each partner, not only students. Ultimately, the extent to which instructors enact engagement in democratic ways and toward democratic ends will depend on how well they have a shared commitment to relationships that are at least mutually beneficial and possibly transformational. This provides interesting possibilities for the psychology curriculum to evolve in powerful and meaningful ways through service learning partnerships.

Orienting Students

As students consider course options during the registration period, the registration website may (a) make it clear that a course has a service learning requirement or option and (b) invite students to contact the course instructor for more details regarding the service learning activity. Instructors may also choose to communicate with students registered in the course, describing the service learning expectations and activities to help students make an informed decision about enrolling in the course. On some campuses, professional staff from an office of service learning (or its equivalent) can help instructors with student orientation, community partnerships, and other resource materials.

Service learning as a pedagogical approach is counternormative to traditional instruction (Clayton & Ash, 2004; Howard, 1998). For example, service learning has students engage in collaborative activities in the community in which they actively participate in determining the learning that is occurring and reflect on those experiences with regard to the academic content of the course, the civic and community context of their activities, and their own personal development. Asking students to be responsible for their learning (rather than being solely dependent on the instructor), to be active rather than passive, and to be reflective can be sources of surprise, frustration, and disillusionment for some students (Ash & Clayton, 2004). Instructors have to be deliberate in presenting a rationale for this different pedagogy and in orienting students to a different set of expectations for their behavior and their roles in the classroom and in the community. Students should receive pertinent information about expected roles for themselves and key individuals, applicable legal issues (e.g., reporting suspected physical abuse), rules and policies of the community organizations, logistical matters (e.g., transportation, resources that are available to them), proper conduct (e.g., norms for speech, dress, behavior), and when to notify someone about emerging issues that warrant professional attention (Chapdelaine, Ruiz, Warchal, & Wells, 2005).

Students often benefit from two orientations to a community activity: one in the class and another at the agency. The in-class orientation may include representatives of partner organizations who discuss their organization's mission, reinforce expectations, and answer questions. During the on-site orientations, students should learn more about the organization's background and mission, receive a tour, obtain information on policies, and meet key staff members. Some instructors use a written contract, letter, or memorandum of understanding that outlines expectations for the instructor, student, and agency staff. On some campuses, an office of service learning may be available to assist in creating connections to the community and providing sample agreement forms and orientations.

A code of conduct for students may be presented and explained (see Chapdelaine et al., 2005). Some organizations have a formal code of conduct (see Exhibit 3.1 for an example). In addition, to demonstrate the

Exhibit 3.1

Code of Conduct

1. I will be conscious of the fact that everything I do, directly or indirectly, has the potential to reflect upon St. Vincent de Paul as a whole. I will hold myself to the highest possible standard of conduct reflective of the work that I do, always striving to avoid even the appearance of impropriety.
2. I will recognize the worth, dignity and uniqueness of all persons, and will at all times treat clients, customers, staff, and fellow volunteers with respect, regardless of race, color, sex, sexual orientation, age, religion, national origin, marital status, political belief, mental or physical disability, military status, status as a veteran or any types of discrimination based on personal characteristics, conditions or status.
3. I will at all times clearly distinguish between statements made by me as a private individual and statements representing St. Vincent de Paul and/or statements that could be mistakenly interpreted as representing St. Vincent de Paul.
4. I will at all times conduct myself in a professional manner while in public places and particularly at times when customers, clients, and/or supporters of St. Vincent de Paul are present.
5. I will at no time aid or abet a client and/or anyone else in any form of illegal activity, or participate in any illegal activity that would directly or indirectly reflect adversely on the agency's integrity, or expose the organization to any negative publicity. I will never knowingly contribute to enabling a client's irresponsible behavior, or put my own safety or the safety of others at risk.
6. I will at all times avoid relationships or commitments that conflict or may conflict with the interests of St. Vincent de Paul.
7. I will avoid any romantic attachments and/or sexual relationships with clients, customers, and/or residents, whether they are temporary or long-term participants in an agency program or activity.

(continues)

Exhibit 3.1

Code of Conduct (*Continued*)

8. I understand that, as a St. Vincent de Paul volunteer, I am not permitted to invite clients or residents into my home for any reason, nor am I permitted to spend the night in a client or resident's quarters.
9. I will actively work to expand choices and opportunities for all people with special regard for disadvantaged or oppressed groups of people.
10. I will avoid exploitation of professional relationships for personal gain. I will at no time accept monetary gifts from customers, clients, or residents without prior approval of the program manager.
11. I will not purchase from or sell any merchandise or services to clients, customers, or residents, nor will I engage in their hire for personal projects.
12. I will at no time engage in activities designed to proselytize or convert a customer, client, or resident to a particular religion, belief, or church.
13. I will actively work to prevent practices that are inhumane or discriminatory against any person or group of persons.
14. I will respect the privacy of customers, clients, and residents and hold in confidence all information obtained in the course of providing professional services, to include:
    a. I will not disclose confidential information regarding any facet of the program of its participants without prior approval from senior management;
    b. I will not acknowledge to anyone outside the agency that an individual is a participant, client, customer, resident or recipient of any agency program or services;
    c. I will not discuss or reveal confidential information regarding fellow volunteers or St. Vincent de Paul employees; and
    d. I will make no statements to the media.

> **Exhibit 3.1**
>
> **Code of Conduct (*Continued*)**
>
> 15. I will at no time use profanity, vulgarity, obscenities, or discriminatory slurs against or involving customers, clients, residents, or fellow volunteers.
> 16. I will not be under the influence of drugs and/or alcohol while volunteering or while acting as a representative, actual or perceived, of the agency.
>
> *Note.* From "Code of Ethics for Volunteers," by the Society of St. Vincent de Paul, Dayton, OH. Retrieved from http://www.stvincentdayton.org/docs/code-of-ethics.pdf. Reprinted with permission.

general relevance of the organization's code of conduct, the instructor, staff representative, and students can examine the thematic similarities between it and APA's (2010) *Ethical Principles of Psychologists and Code of Conduct*. If the course incorporates research (see Chapters 2 and 9, this volume), the protection of human research participants is warranted, and students and others involved in the research (e.g., community partners) should complete the Collaborative Institutional Training Initiative Program (2014; Social–Behavioral–Educational track) or an equivalent.

Students have to be prepared for community-based service learning activities. The preparation should include a clear understanding of appropriate activities that are aligned with their knowledge and skills on the basis of their educational background and experience. Service learning students can benefit from a clear understanding of what behaviors and activities are inappropriate in the setting and whom to consult when there is ambiguity about roles, expectations, risk management, and behaviors. Preparation can also include orientation to the community and/or community organization, understanding relevant organizational policies, training that may be required (e.g., CPR training), and knowledge of relevant laws (e.g., privacy, confidentiality, reporting abuse). In addition to ethical safeguards for service learning students involved in community-based research, there are other ethical concerns that arise (e.g., assuring competence, avoiding multiple relationships), especially in any situation in which students directly interact with clients at an agency or residents in communities.

Reflection

Effective reflection is structured around learning objectives in the domains of academic learning, civic learning, and personal growth (Table 3.1) and their intersections (see Figure 3.1) to generate learning that is aligned with the goals in the APA Guidelines 2.0. Bringle and Hatcher (1999) posited that the strongest reflection links the service experience to course content, is guided, occurs regularly, involves feedback to the learner to enhance the learning, and helps clarify values. Hatcher, Bringle, and Muthiah (2004) found empirical support that regular reflection, structured reflection, and reflection that focused on personal values were independently related to the reported quality of service learning courses. There are a variety of reflection activities that can encompass qualities of good reflection and support student learning. For example, students can engage in structured group discussions (e.g., see http://civicreflection.org), do class presentations, analyze an ethical case study on the basis of course material and a critical incident at their service site, or write a research paper detailing how the psychology literature expands on their understanding of a critical incident. Appendix C presents an array of reflection activities for prior to beginning community service activities, during the course, and at the end of the course. These can be conducted individually, with other students, using a course management system, or with community partners (Eyler, 2002). The remainder of this section details how reflection can be structured to generate new learning, deepen the learning, and then capture the learning.

The DEAL model for critical reflection (Ash & Clayton, 2004, 2009a, 2009b; Jameson et al., 2008) incorporates the following steps in critical reflection: (a) *describe* the experience objectively and in detail; (b) *examine* the experience from personal, civic, and/or academic perspectives framed by learning objectives; and (c) *articulate learning* that has resulted.

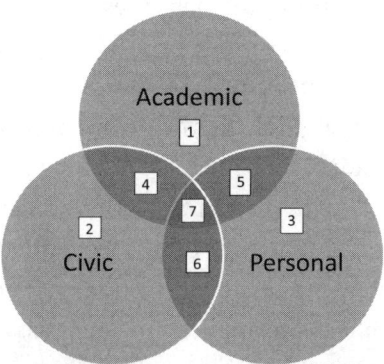

Figure 3.1

Learning domains that community service can enhance. 1 = Community service illustrates or informs a deeper understanding of an academic concept, theory, or research finding (e.g., students learn to differentiate the use of positive reinforcement, negative reinforcement, and punishment while they reflect on their observations of an elementary teacher's interaction with children in the classroom). 2 = Community service contributes to civic growth in ways that are not necessarily related to the course content (e.g., students increase their knowledge of the nonprofit sector or better understand the dynamics of power and privilege, but these are not topics in the psychology course). 3 = Community service contributes to personal growth in ways that are not necessarily related to the course content (e.g., students clarify personal values or career plans, but these are not topics in the psychology course). 4 = Community service connects academic content to civic learning (e.g., the course content covers intergroup contact theory and students learn better approaches for interacting with diverse groups in the community on the basis of the theory and research presented on the intergroup contact theory as well as better learning the material on intergroup contact hypothesis). 5 = Community service connects academic content to personal growth (e.g., the course presents information on nonverbal communication and students analyze nonverbal cues at the site and become more aware of their nonverbal cues that they are displaying at the service site). 6 = Community service contributes to civic learning and personal growth in ways that are not necessarily related to the course content (e.g., students become more knowledgeable about a community issue and more empathetic toward those persons associated with the community issue, but the community issue is not a specific topic in the psychology course). 7 = Community service connects academic content to civic learning and personal growth (e.g., the course content on stigma influences how students conduct their service activities, the power of stigma in their interactions and the interactions of others, their awareness of their own attitudes and prejudices, and their understanding of the course material on stigma).

Critical reflection in this model begins with a detailed description of what happened during the community activities. This description may be in response to general prompts or may be guided by a particular focus that follows in the subsequent prompts.

In the examine stage of DEAL, the prompts (e.g., for written reflection, for group discussion) can be specific learning objectives derived from the APA Guidelines 2.0 with respect to academic learning, civic learning, and/or personal growth. One tool that is available for writing examine prompts and that facilitates assessment is Bloom's (1956) taxonomy (knowledge or recall, comprehension, application, analysis, synthesis, evaluation), which we use for illustration. A revision of Bloom's taxonomy is also available (L. W. Anderson & Krathwohl, 2001). Using Bloom's taxonomy to structure examine prompts from lower to higher order reasoning supports students in making meaning of their experiences through critical reflection up to whatever level is desired for a particular reflection activity. In our examples, the different levels are focused on the following:

- Knowledge: Identify relevant knowledge (concepts, theories, research findings, personal attributes, community issues).
- Comprehension: Demonstrate understanding of knowledge.
- Application: Connect the relevant knowledge to the service experiences.
- Analysis: Examine components by identifying causes and consequences and by comparing and contrasting components.
- Synthesis: Develop new ways or perspectives and propose alternative solutions.
- Evaluation: Make judgments about the material and defend proposals.

In the third stage of the DEAL model, students articulate what they have learned through their community experiences and the process of describing and examining. Academic learning, civic learning, and personal growth can occur with reference to course material (Sections 1, 4, 5, and 7 of Figure 3.1) or can occur independent of academic content (Sections 2, 3, and 6 of Figure 3.1). Tables 3.2, 3.3, and 3.4 contain three illustrations for how reflection prompts based on learning objectives can be developed for three different areas of Figure 3.1 using the DEAL model. The examples use

Table 3.2
Sample DEAL Model Reflection Prompts

Learning domain	Academic learning (Section 1 of Venn diagram in Figure 3.1)
APA learning outcome	Indicator 1.3D: "Explain how psychological constructs can be used to understand and resolve interpersonal and intercultural conflicts" (APA, 2013, p. 19).
Course-specific learning objective	Students will accurately and effectively use appropriate constructs from attribution theory when critically examining an interpersonal interaction at their service site.
DEAL/describe (objectively)	▪ Describe a particular interaction that was interesting to you (e.g., because it was supportive, or contentious, or difficult). ▪ When did interpersonal interactions take place? Where did it take place? ▪ Who else was there? Who was not there? ▪ What did you do? What did others do? What actions did you take? What did you communicate? ▪ Who did not speak or act? Did you or others laugh, cry, make a face, complain, criticize, argue, and so forth?
DEAL/Examine (Six levels are based on Bloom's [1956] taxonomy)	Knowledge: From research on attribution theory, identify elements (e.g., theories, constructs, research findings) that are relevant to the interaction. Comprehension: Define, in your own words, each of these elements so someone outside this course will understand them. Are there any other elements that might be relevant? If so, identify them and explain them in your own words. Application: Explain how each of these elements of attribution theory is relevant to the interaction. Which components of the interaction illustrate an element?

(continues)

Table 3.2
Sample DEAL Model Reflection Prompts (*Continued*)

	Analysis: What aspects of the interaction shaped its nature and course? How might implicit attributions made by one of the parties (including you) reflect an attributional bias or one of the other elements? Which type of bias? What elements? What evidence do you have to support your conclusions? What was the cause of the bias (e.g., motivation, cognitive, interpersonal)? How did early interactions shape later interactions in terms of attributional elements? What were the consequences of the interaction? Are there components of the interaction that were inconsistent with attributional elements (e.g., self-serving bias, actor–observer differences)? If so, why do you think that occurred?
	Synthesis: How would you use any of these attributional elements to improve interactions like this one? On the basis of your attributional analysis, what might you or others do in the future to improve interactions like this one? Imagine what would happen during the interaction if one of the elements that you have identified was not present or if the opposite of it occurred? Would it have improved the interaction? Why or why not? Develop guidelines for more effective interactions in the future based on the elements of research on attributions.
	Evaluation: What is missing from your analysis of this interaction that was important to its course but is not understood in terms of the elements of research on attribution theory? What are the strengths and weaknesses of your attributional analysis of the interaction? How would you justify your analysis to an outsider (e.g., what sorts of evidence would you present, what conclusions would you draw, what are the limitations of your analysis)? What do you now think are the most important elements of research on attribution theory for interpersonal communications? What are the implications of your analysis for future interactions between these persons?
DEAL/articulate learning	As a result of completing this reflection, ▪ I learned that . . . ▪ I learned this when . . . ▪ This learning matters because . . . ▪ In light of this learning, in the future I will . . .

Note. APA = American Psychological Association; DEAL = describe, examine, and articulate learning model for critical reflection (Ash & Clayton, 2004, 2009a, 2009b; Jameson, Clayton, & Bringle, 2008).

Table 3.3
Sample DEAL Model Reflection Prompts

Learning domain	Academic learning, civic learning, and personal growth
APA learning outcome	Indicator 5.1D: "Apply relevant psychology content knowledge (Section 7 of Venn diagram in Figure 3.1) to facilitate a more effective work-place in internships, jobs, or organizational leadership opportunities" (APA, 2013, p. 33).
Course-specific learning objective	Students will use course material to understand effective work behaviors, including effective work behaviors for themselves in the community.
DEAL/describe (objectively)	▪ Consider a specific set of work behaviors at the organization that you and others engaged in. When did these experiences take place? ▪ Where did they take place? ▪ Who else was there? Who wasn't there? ▪ What did you do? What did others do? What actions did you or they take? What did you or they communicate? ▪ Who did not speak or act? Did you or others laugh, cry, make a face, complain, criticize, argue, and so forth?
DEAL/examine (Six levels are based on Bloom's [1956] taxonomy)	Knowledge: From this course (or chapter), identify elements (e.g., constructs, theories, and research findings) that are relevant to your understanding of and analysis of these work behaviors, others who were present, and yourself. Comprehension: Define, in your own words, each of these elements so someone outside this course will understand them. Are there any other elements that might be relevant? If so, explain them in your own words. Application: Explain how each of these elements is relevant to what you have observed and experienced. How do these elements help you understand the work environment, the workers' behavior, and your behavior? Which are the most relevant elements and why? Which are relevant to your behavior in this situation? Which are not? With regard to these elements, how have you or others changed?

(continues)

Table 3.3
Sample DEAL Model Reflection Prompts (*Continued*)

Analysis: What is the main purpose or mission of the organization? How does the type of organization (e.g., non-profit, government, for profit) influence the work environment and the workers' behaviors? What motivates these employees? What distracts them? What are the major sources of satisfaction and what are the major sources of stress for these employees? What do you think caused these employees to choose this work environment? What matters most to them? How is the work environment shaped by them and how does the work environment help determine their behavior? Now answer each of those questions for yourself as someone in this work environment. Would you like to work in this environment? Why or why not? What strengths and assets do you have that would be compatible with this work environment? What is it about you that is inconsistent with this work environment? (Identify course elements that are relevant to each of these answers.)

Synthesis: If you worked in this environment, how would you try to change it? Do you think you could change it? Why or why not? How would you modify what this organization is trying to do (i.e., its purpose or mission)? What would you add? What would you eliminate or reduce? Would any of those changes make it a better work environment for you? For the current employees? Are there different kinds of employees that you think would be better suited for the current work environment? For your improved work environment? (Identify course elements that are relevant to each of these answers.)

	Evaluation: In what ways do you think this organization is contributing to the public good? To what degree do you like the purpose or mission of this organization? Is its purpose something that you care about? Why or why not? How do you think the employees at this organization would agree or disagree with your analysis? What about the general public or special interest groups? Which perspective is more valid? Why? What have you found personally relevant from the course material that has influenced your approach to your current and future work? What from the community site has influenced your approach to your future work? How effective do you think this organization is? What evidence would you propose collecting to evaluate its effectiveness? Would the evidence be convincing to you? To staff? To those outside the organization (e.g., funders, government officials, groups who are interested in the mission of the organization)?
DEAL/articulate learning	As a result of completing this reflection, - I learned that . . . - I learned this when . . . . - This learning matters because . . . - In light of this learning, in the future I will . . .

Note. APA = American Psychological Association; DEAL = describe, examine, and articulate learning model for critical reflection (Ash & Clayton, 2004, 2009a, 2009b; Jameson, Clayton, & Bringle, 2008).

Table 3.4
Sample DEAL Model Reflection Prompts

Learning domain	Civic learning and personal growth (Section 6 of Venn diagram in Figure 3.1)
APA learning outcome	Indicator 5.4B: "Describe problems from another's point of view with respect to sociocultural factors" (APA, 2013, p. 35).
Course-specific learning objective	Students will identify and critically examine sociocultural origins for a marginalized person at their service site and demonstrate empathy for the individual.
DEAL/describe (objectively)	▪ When did you become aware of a marginalized person at your community organization? Where did this take place? ▪ Who else was there? Who was not there? ▪ What did you do? What did others do? What actions did you or we take? What did you or we communicate? ▪ Who did not speak or act? Did you or others laugh, cry, make a face, complain, criticize, argue, and so forth?
DEAL/examine (Six levels are based on Bloom's [1956] taxonomy)	Knowledge: What factors do you think are relevant to why this person is in this status? List three factors that influence how or why others view the person the way they do. List three factors that influence their point of view toward the person's life and world. Are there any social factors? Are there any cultural factors? Are there any other types of factors (e.g., interpersonal, economic, social services, personality, mental health)? Comprehension: Define in detail and in your own words, each of these factors that you have identified. Which is most important? Why? Are there any other factors that are relevant? If so, identify and define them in your own words. Application: What convinced you that these factors shaped the individual's point of view? What about the point of view of others? What did you see in this person's behavior and that of others that supports your inference that these factors are important? Are their social factors (e.g., how others treat the person, talk to the person) that support the person's status? If so, what are they and how are they important? Are their cultural factors? If so, what are they and how are they important? In your experience, why do you think you identified these factors? How might your biases influence your analysis? Would someone else identify other factors?

	Analysis: What are the consequences of this person's status? Have you ever felt the same way that this person might feel? How did you feel? What caused your feelings? What did you do? How does this person cope? How did you cope? How does your analysis of these circumstances for that person and yourself make you feel about the individual you identified and the feelings each of you experience? What are the similarities and differences between that person's position and your experience?
	Synthesis: Who defines this person in this status and who does not? Why? What might be done to help this individual with the circumstances? How might the person's status be elevated to others? What can you do to help this individual? What might you do to help others in a similar situation? How would you construct an intervention (e.g., publicity campaign, a group meeting, change in policy) to lessen the effects of this type of marginalization and stigmatization?
	Evaluation: What is your opinion of this individual? On the basis of what you have seen at the service site, what additional interpretations do you have of this person and the circumstances? How have your thinking, feelings, and behavior changed over time with respect to this person? How do you feel about your view of this person compared to how others' view this person? What do you think and feel about the social and cultural factors that resulted in this person's status? Are they valid? Are they justified? Should they change? Why or why not? What social programs might be developed to help with these issues you have surfaced? Would it work? Why or why not?
DEAL/articulate learning	As a result of completing this reflection, ■ I learned that . . . ■ I learned this when . . . ■ This learning matters because . . . ■ In light of this learning, in the future I will . . .

Note. APA = American Psychological Association; DEAL = describe, examine, and articulate learning model for critical reflection (Ash & Clayton, 2004, 2009a, 2009b; Jameson, Clayton, & Bringle, 2008).

learning objectives based on the APA Guidelines 2.0, but they can be tailored to a particular course and community service activity (see other chapters in Part II for examples). Note that there can be different levels of expectation for different learning objectives within a course, given the nature of the course material and the community activities. Also, a particular course might only aspire to an intermediate level of Bloom's (1956) taxonomy (e.g., early courses in the curriculum only expect learning to progress to the application or analysis stage). In any case, reflection should include prompts to the desired level to scaffold learning to reach the desired end state.

Assessing Student Learning Outcomes

Depending on the nature of the course, the type of community service activity, and the instructor's purpose for having a community service activity, greater emphasis may be placed on assessing academic learning, civic learning, or personal growth. Assessment may be based on self-report scales, measures recommended in the APA Guidelines 2.0, or other measures of outcomes. When learning objectives are framed according to specific levels of Bloom's (1956) taxonomy or some other framework and when reflection using the DEAL model (or some other model) has guided students to make meaning of their experiences, their learning can be assessed with reference to those criteria. For example, did the articulated learning include the specific concepts and demonstrate an understanding of the concept? How did the articulated learning show that understanding of the concept was related to the community service, that the community service enhanced additional understanding of the concept, and that it is valued as a basis for specific goals in the short term and long term (Ash & Clayton, 2009a, 2009b)?

Thus, within the DEAL model, reflection products that contain demonstrations of students' academic learning, civic learning, and personal growth can be assessed according to levels of Bloom's (1956) taxonomy and feedback can be given to students on drafts and final products. Students can engage in successive activities focused on a particular learning objective (e.g., group discussions, followed by a written product that receives peer feedback, followed by a revised written product that receives the instructor's feedback). This approach incorporates specifying a set of learning objectives, having standards, and using progressive reflection to generate learning (through reflection prompts), to deepen learning (through formative assessment or feedback), and to document learning (through summative assessment or grading and reporting outcomes; Clayton & Ash, 2004). The DEAL model also provides rubrics for critical thinking that can be applied to reflection products and can be the basis for additional feedback (Ash & Clayton, 2004, 2009a, 2009b). There is more discussion of assessment in Chapter 13.

CONCLUSION

The important goals for the psychology curriculum are defined in the APA Guidelines 2.0, and students can have the opportunity to find ways to make these ideas their own through service learning. Having students think about civic issues with reference to the course content during a semester is an important step in helping them to uncover new insights and to move beyond simply preparing for the next multiple-choice examination. Confronting an ill-defined situation may spark questions in students regarding how a community works and ways they can make a contribution. Such questions are at the core of becoming a psychologically literate citizen focused on the public good.

4

Integrating Service Learning Into the Curriculum: Introductory Psychology

This chapter presents the rationale for enriching introductory psychology courses with service learning. Introductory psychology has an estimated annual enrollment of around 1.5 million students (Steuer & Ham, 2008). Although almost all psychology majors take introductory psychology (Stoloff et al., 2010), most students in the course are not psychology majors (Stoloff, 2010). For those nonmajors, introductory psychology may be their only psychology course.

CONTENT OF THE INTRODUCTORY PSYCHOLOGY COURSE

Gurung, Ansburg, Alexander, Lawrence, and Johnson (2008) noted that the nature of introductory psychology is confounded by several factors: definition of the field, variability in the content of textbooks (Zechmeister &

---

http://dx.doi.org/10.1037/14803-005
Service Learning in Psychology: Enhancing Undergraduate Education for the Public Good, by R. G. Bringle, R. N. Reeb, M. A. Brown, and A. I. Ruiz
Copyright © 2016 by the American Psychological Association. All rights reserved.

Zechmeister, 2000), variability in how introductory psychology is taught (Homa et al., 2013; Wolfle, 1942), and discrepancy in how the field is viewed as separate areas versus as an integrated discipline (Gurung et al., 2014). They did not recognize this variability as an asset for either instructors (e.g., teaching to their strengths) or for students' outcomes (e.g., students learning more or better from enthusiastic instructors teaching about areas of expertise).

Gurung et al. (2014) recommended that introductory psychology courses have, as their common core, (a) the scientific method; (b) at least two topics from each of the following four areas: biological (e.g., neuroscience, sensation, consciousness, motivation), cognitive (e.g., cognition, memory, perception), development (e.g., learning, life-span development, language), social and personality (e.g., social, personality, intelligence, emotion, multicultural, gender), and mental and physical health (e.g., abnormal, health, therapies); (c) coverage of ethics, diversity, variations in human functioning, and applications for each of the topics covered; and (d) an integration module. This presents a daunting task for an instructor of introductory psychology.

In addition, Gurung et al. (2014) recommended a nationally coordinated assessment of introductory psychology courses and a laboratory with the introductory psychology course for increasing scientific literacy. Although they recommended that every introductory psychology course have a laboratory (most do not), an experiential component of integrated community service may be a more appropriate alternative because a service learning component can make the content of the introductory psychology course more relevant to the lives of both nonmajors and majors. They also proposed recommendations for faculty development that put an emphasis on the input side of the teaching versus learning continuum (e.g., attending teaching conferences, reading literature on teaching, attending workshops). Their discussion of faculty development largely ignored alternative forms of faculty development (see Chapters 11 and 12, this volume) and research that exists on the relationship between faculty development activities and changes in teaching behaviors, classroom performance, and students' learning outcomes (e.g., Chism, Palmer, & Price, 2013).

RATIONALE FOR SERVICE LEARNING IN INTRODUCTORY PSYCHOLOGY

Can a single course about psychology have any relevance to contemporary lives of students? Historically, how much relevance the psychology curriculum should have for the lives of students has been a matter of contention. On the one hand, Wolfle (1942) noted,

> To give them some knowledge of why we all do the things we do, to increase, even by a little, their ability to face personal conflict is, personally and *socially*, one of the most valuable contributions the course can make. Granting that the chances of failure are frequently large, the possibility of some success justifies the effort. (p. 690, emphasis added)

On the other hand, others have questioned the appropriateness and capacity of Introductory Psychology to fulfill the goal of personal relevance (e.g., Muenzinger, 1939; Skaggs, 1927).

Service learning can contribute to unique learning outcomes and attributes identified in the American Psychological Association's *APA Guidelines for the Undergraduate Psychology Major* (Version 2.0; APA, 2013). As a high-impact pedagogy (Kuh, 2008), service learning can enhance the introductory psychology course by augmenting student motivation, curiosity, and self-directed learning. Community service also confronts students with perplexing circumstances that do not conform readily to available solutions. If there is proper preparation, orientation to the site, and support, then students can develop the capacity to cope "with complexity and ambiguity" (APA, 2013, p. 19), be flexible in their thinking (p. 19), tolerate ambiguity (p. 23), be adaptable (p. 36), and be resourceful in meeting the challenges they encounter (p. 36). Thus, service learning provides a powerful means to link academic course content to contemporary issues in society and to the personal lives of students (e.g., values, attitudes, career plans, empathy).

Stoloff (2010) noted that many of the students in introductory psychology might be first-year students with unrealistic academic expectations about college workload, studying, class attendance, and persistence on assignments. High-impact practices (Kuh, 2008) such as service learning have the advantage of enhancing first-year student motivation and persistence (Bringle, Hatcher, & Muthiah, 2010; Lockeman & Pelco, 2013). Good service learning experiences should enhance students' sense of self-efficacy and confidence (APA, 2013, p. 36). Furthermore, service learning almost always places students in contact with persons who differ from themselves. When properly designed, these experiences can reduce stereotypes and result in more empathic responses by students, resulting in greater respect, sensitivity, and tolerance (APA, 2013, p. 28). Most central to the purposes of involving students in service learning is their civic development and civic learning. In addition to "serving to learn," "learning to serve" can result in greater generosity, the intention to be more civically engaged in the future (APA, 2013, p. 28), and a greater sense of social responsibility (p. 36; see also Chapters 1 and 3, this volume).

Service learning is predicated on the importance of having students be reflective (APA, 2013, p. 36) about their experiences. Service learning students can reflect on the relevance of the course and the service to the skills, knowledge, and credentials that are required for various careers. Service in schools and community organizations can allow students to observe careers that can be entered with a baccalaureate degree (APA, 2013, pp. 65–66). Regular, structured reflection can also be focused on the civic aspects of the community service (e.g., why social issues exist, what they can do to contribute to alleviating social issues) and on their personal development (e.g., how they can become more capable of contributing, how careers can be civically oriented; see Chapter 3).

Students can make presentations either in class or to community partners or produce written products (e.g., final reports, brochures, web pages) for a variety of purposes that are comprehensible and articulate (APA, 2013, p. 31) and that are relevant to different audiences (p. 31). Products presented to community partners have the additional benefit that they can be significant for the organization and its clients. If this work is done by groups of students or with community partners, the community service supports the development of collaborative skills (APA, 2013, p. 23, 36).

Large lecture introductory psychology courses can face a challenge for implementing service learning. If they have accompanying discussion or recitation sections, these sections can provide the opportunity to organize and implement service learning. Alternatively for large, lecture-only courses, service learning might be offered as an option, either instead of an alternative assignment (e.g., research paper, participation in a laboratory section; Kretchmar, 2001) or for additional academic credit (e.g., some students enroll in an additional one credit hour for the service learning component and receive a separate grade for that credit).

DESIGNING SERVICE LEARNING COURSES FOR LEARNING OUTCOMES

There are many ways to integrate community service activities into introductory psychology courses. The examples in Table 4.1 can be used in the introductory psychology course. The identification of community service activities with community partners must be well aligned with the

Table 4.1
Examples of Service Learning Projects in Introductory Psychology

Course theme in Introductory Psychology	Type of service learning	Example project	Examples of activities
Analyzing behavior	Direct	Tutor and mentor in public school classrooms.	Tutor one-on-one or small groups, read with students, assist with homework.
	Indirect	Assist a nonprofit organization with activities.	Doing background research, writing and designing presentation or brochures, assisting with fundraising.
	Research	Implement a study of a critical issue on campus (e.g., date rape).	Data collection, data analysis, reports to relevant offices, assistance in the implementation of an intervention.
	Advocacy	Develop activities on campus for a critical issue.	Research issue, talk to experts on campus and in the community, develop materials, organize other students.

course's learning objectives (at least most of them, if not all) and benefit all constituencies. Chapter 3 provides guidance for developing community partnerships and specific learning objectives (i.e., academic learning, civic learning, personal growth). All constituencies should understand the rationale for the community service component.

As one example, college students can be in elementary school classrooms to help teachers with classroom activities, assist students with assignments and activities, tutor one-on-one or in small groups, and provide additional assistance as needed. Students in introductory psychology who tutor youth in schools, particularly public schools, have rich opportunities to connect their tutoring to many if not all topics in the course through reflection activities. Some illustrations follow and each of these can be developed into reflection prompts on the basis of the DEAL (describe, examine, and articulate learning) model for critical reflection (Ash & Clayton, 2004, 2009a, 2009b; Jameson, Clayton, & Bringle, 2008) and Bloom's (1956) taxonomy (see Chapter 3, this volume).

Learning

How have you used learning principles when tutoring? Give examples of how the teacher is using different types of reinforcement and punishment. What are the strengths and deficiencies of the different contingencies for the teacher? For the students? Develop a plan for future tutoring that is based on learning principles. What are the components of observational learning and how can social learning principles be used in the classroom? See Table 4.2 for an example of how this area can be developed as a specific learning objective for academic learning, civic learning, and personal growth using the DEAL model and Bloom's (1956) taxonomy (see Chapter 3, this volume).

Development

Analyze which stages the schoolchildren are at for different stage theories (e.g., Freud, Piaget, Kohlberg, Erikson). Is there any variability among the children? Why or why not? How are maturational processes illustrated in

Table 4.2
Sample DEAL Model Reflection Prompt

Learning domain	Academic learning, civic learning, and personal growth (Section 7 of Venn diagram in Figure 3.1)
APA learning outcome	Indicator 1.1a: "Use basic psychological terminology, concepts, and theories in psychology to explain behavior and mental processes" (APA, 2013, p. 18).
Course-specific learning objective	Students will accurately identify and use terminology, concepts, and theories from the learning chapter with reference to their community activities and their own lives.
DEAL/describe (objectively)	<ul><li>When did these experiences take place? Where did they take place?</li><li>Who else was there? Who was not there?</li><li>What did you do? What did others do? What actions did you or others take? What did you or they communicate?</li><li>Who did not speak or act? Did you or others laugh, cry, make a face, complain, criticize, argue, and so forth?</li></ul>
DEAL/examine (Six levels are based on Bloom's [1956] taxonomy)	Knowledge: Identify key concepts, theories, and research results from the learning chapter that are relevant to your community service activities at the public school.
	Comprehension: Describe each of these elements in your own words so that someone not familiar with psychology can understand each of them.
	Application: Identify the connections between each of these elements and your community service activities. How did you observe each of them occurring and who demonstrated the learning element (e.g., by the teacher, by students, by yourself)? Give multiple examples. How do you think each of these elements applies your own behavior in the school (i.e., how have you used these elements)? Give multiple examples.
	Analysis: Which of these elements is most relevant to your activities at the public school? What are the similarities and differences between the application of these elements to elementary school students and to you as a college student? Identify circumstances in the elementary students' lives that complicate or inhibit their performance in school. Do the same for yourself.

(continues)

Table 4.2
Sample DEAL Model Reflection Prompt (*Continued*)

	Synthesis: Which elements might you use in the future to obtain better results from your community activities? Which of these might you use to improve your own performance at the school or your behavior as a college student? On the basis of your analysis of the role of these elements in how elementary students learn and perform, what changes will you make in your work with them? With the teacher? What positive and negative outcomes might occur if you make these changes? How might learning principles be used to increase parental involvement in their elementary students' schoolwork? What recommendations would you make to college students who work at this school in the future? What changes might you make in your studying based on learning theory? Describe how assisting elementary students has helped you study better. How might you design a self-improvement program based on learning theory for yourself? What do you think the results would be if you implemented such a program? What are the impediments to you implementing a program based on learning principles to improve your studying?
	Evaluation: What do you think are the best or most effective ways to help students with their schoolwork and what are the least effective ways? What evidence do you have to support your evaluations? What does the teacher in the classroom think are the best ways? Do you agree? Why or why not? In what ways does the learning chapter assist you in your evaluation (give examples)? Do you think you can use the information on learning to improve your own studying and performance? Why or why not?
DEAL/articulate learning	As a result of completing this reflection, • I learned that . . . • I learned this when . . . • This learning matters because . . . • In light of this learning, in the future I will . . .

Note. APA = American Psychological Association; DEAL = describe, examine, and articulate learning model for critical reflection (Ash & Clayton, 2004, 2009a, 2009b; Jameson, Clayton, & Bringle, 2008).

the children's development and behavior (e.g., social, intellectual, physical, social, moral)? What attributes of temperament are present? How do they vary among children? How are they related to your work with each child?

Stress and Coping

Analyze your first day at the school in terms of the concepts presented in the course textbook chapter on stress and coping. Which of these applied: major life event, daily hassle, conflict (which type), primary and secondary appraisal, frustration, optimism, general adaptation syndrome, fight-or-flight reaction? What coping strategies did you use? What coping strategies do you see the classroom teacher using? The children? Compare and contrast the various coping strategies that you see and do not see in terms of their relative effectiveness for the individual dealing with stress.

Social Psychology

Analyze attributions from multiple perspectives. What are the attributions (e.g., internal or external, stable or unstable) about your service activities in the classroom by the teacher, the students, your classmates, and your friends? Which of these illustrate the fundamental attribution error? What are the presumed stereotypes, attitudes, and prejudice of the general public about poor performance of public school children? How can these attitudes be changed (e.g., in university students, in the general public)? What examples of social influence (e.g., conformity, obedience, group think, social facilitation) do you see operating among the school children? How might more prosocial behavior and less aggressive behavior be promoted in the school or classroom using the theories and research in the textbook and lectures?

Personality

How might different theories of personality (e.g., psychodynamic, humanistic, cognitive, behavioristic) be used to analyze the behavior of elementary students (e.g., misbehavior in the classroom, motivation for school work)? What key concepts from each theory are relevant? How might each theory be used to design interventions to improve student behavior?

Personal Growth

Students can be asked to relate their observations and activities to their own lives, their values, their future plans, and how the experiences have changed them. The focus can include a self-evaluation of personal skills and attributes and setting goals for professional development.

Civic Growth

Civic growth can be facilitated by asking students to respond to DEAL model reflection prompts (see Chapter 3) about the social factors that are implicated in the lives of the elementary school students (e.g., poverty, family issues, neighborhood factors) and the difficulties faced in educating young children. What assumptions (attitudes, stereotypes, beliefs) did you have at the beginning of the semester about your school (e.g., teachers, students, learning)? Which assumptions were supported and which were refuted by your experience? What is the role of community service and involvement in your life now and in the future? What future goals do you have for levels and types of community service? Why?

Assessment

Formative and summative assessment of outcomes in any educational enterprise is important to monitoring implementation, determining how well objectives were met, and providing feedback for various purposes (e.g., grades, improvement, representation of teaching to external audiences). Chapters 3 and 13 provide information for structuring assessment that can be used in introductory psychology courses. Traditional methods for assessing academic learning (e.g., multiple-choice examinations, essay examinations) can be complemented with other approaches to assess additional learning objectives (e.g., civic learning and personal growth) and feedback from community partners about community benefits.

CONCLUSION

Introductory psychology courses provide the most powerful and pervasive leverage point for educating students about the nature of psychology. Service learning provides the most important way that the introductory psychology course can motivate students, increase the likelihood of course completion, achieve academic learning outcomes, and augment learning with civic learning and personal growth. Although the prevalence of service learning in introductory psychology courses is not known, based on Campus Compact reports (e.g., Campus Compact, 2013) and syllabus files (e.g., http://www.compact.org) we estimate it to be low. Its underutilization in the face of strong empirical evidence about the efficacy of service learning is unfortunate and should be corrected in the future. Although the recommendation of the APA working group on the introductory psychology course (Gurung et al., 2014) is that every course should have a laboratory component, an experiential component of integrated community service may be a more appropriate alternative. A service learning component will make the introductory psychology course more relevant to the lives of both nonmajors and majors, and laboratories can be a component of later courses in the curriculum.

5

Integrating Service Learning Into the Curriculum: Abnormal, Health, and Community Psychology

The courses discussed in this chapter are subdisciplines related to clinical psychology that share several features: They (a) incorporate theory, research, and applied components (i.e., scientist–practitioner perspective); (b) promote well-being; (c) explore causes of maladjustment; (d) express concern for social justice; and (e) yield interventions to address maladjustment or improve well-being. The first section reviews evidence that service learning can enrich the outcomes of these courses. The second section provides examples of service learning activities and projects around a theme for each course. The third section provides a detailed example of a structured approach to reflection in an abnormal psychology course.

http://dx.doi.org/10.1037/14803-006
Service Learning in Psychology: Enhancing Undergraduate Education for the Public Good, by R. G. Bringle, R. N. Reeb, M. A. Brown, and A. I. Ruiz
Copyright © 2016 by the American Psychological Association. All rights reserved.

SERVICE LEARNING

General Benefits of Service Learning

The Association of American Colleges and Universities has identified service learning as a high-impact educational practice (Kuh, 2008). Benefits of service learning pedagogy include enhanced academic learning, civic learning, and personal growth (see Introduction, this volume). Service learning facilitates pursuit of all five learning goals delineated in the American Psychological Association's *APA Guidelines for the Undergraduate Psychology Major* (Version 2.0; APA, 2013; see Appendix A, this volume). Service learning supports diversity goals and infuses sociocultural factors in the curriculum, supporting the argument that "the preferred manner of tackling diversity goals is incorporated in the context of the major" (APA, 2013, p. 38). These benefits are particularly relevant for courses in abnormal, health, and community psychology, given the course themes (e.g., social stigma) and populations involved (e.g., people with mental illness).

Service learning also provides experiential opportunities to become familiar with APA's (2014a, 2014b) Public Interest Directorate (see Exhibit 1.1, this volume), which "applies psychology to the fundamental problems of human welfare and social justice and the promotion of equitable and just treatment of all segments of society through education, training and public policy." APA's Public Interest Directorate provides a resource for a psychology curriculum developing psychologically literate citizens, particularly in regard to abnormal, health, and community psychology courses. Because these courses emphasize the application of psychology, service learning allows students to observe and support assessment, intervention, and research activities representing best practices, evidence-based practices, and professional competencies (Dalton & Wolfe, 2012; Masters, France, & Thorn, 2009).

Service Learning in Abnormal, Health, and Community Psychology: Documented Benefits

Reeb, Sammon, and Isackson (1999) compared service learning students with non–service learning students on course-related learning in abnormal psychology. Service learning students (mentors for troubled youth in the juvenile justice system) completed written reflection exercises to connect course concepts to community work. Examinations focused on course concepts (vs. focusing on service) and consisted of 45 multiple-choice items (90%) and one essay (10%), with multiple-choice items computer scored and essays graded by an instructor blind to group membership. Early in the semester, examination performance was similar across groups, but service learning students showed superior performance during the remainder of the semester. Service learning pedagogy in abnormal psychology also promotes students' civic learning, including social responsibility (Reeb et al., 1999) and community service self-efficacy (Reeb, Folger, Langsner, Ryan, & Crouse, 2010), and helps achieve community goals (e.g., positive role models, empowers clients) according to community partners (Reeb et al., 1999). Similar outcomes are reported for service learning in community psychology (e.g., Curwood, Munger, Mitchell, MacKeigan, & Farrar, 2011; O'Sullivan, 1993) and health psychology (e.g., Kaugars, 2011; Sgoutas-Emch, 2013) courses. Beneficial outcomes are more likely when there is an emphasis on collaboration among students, faculty, and community partners, with all parties engaging in structured reflection exercises.

EXAMPLES OF SERVICE LEARNING PROJECTS

Abnormal Psychology

Coping and social support are central to understanding the management of and recovery from mental disorders. Lazarus and Folkman (1984) defined *coping* as "constantly changing cognitive and behavioral efforts to manage specific external and/or internal demands that are appraised as taxing or exceeding the resources of the person" (p. 141). Cobb (1976) defined *social support* as information enhancing one's perception of being "cared for and loved, esteemed, and a member of a network of... communication and... mutual obligations" (p. 300). Ralph (2005) noted that "recovery is active coping rather than passive adjustment.... Recovery is not accomplished alone; the journey involves support and partnership" (p. 131). Recovery from mental illness does not mean "cured"; instead, it involves coping with, compensating for, and seeking social support in hopeful attempts to transcend symptoms in pursuit of a meaningful and productive life (Corrigan & Ralph, 2005). According to longitudinal research (Calabrese & Corrigan, 2005), recovery is more common than often believed and service learning can highlight this theme. Table 5.1 provides examples of different types of service learning activities and projects in abnormal psychology courses around the theme of coping and social support in managing mental illness. Other course themes could be developed in a similar manner.

Health Psychology

Concern regarding inadequate health care access for individuals who are homeless or living in poverty is a theme pertinent to health psychology (Taylor, 2015). People experiencing homelessness are at extreme risk for health problems and are disadvantaged in obtaining health care (Weinreb, Gelberg, Arangua, & Sullivan, 2007). "Reducing persistent health disparities among the . . . homeless requires a broad strategy that can address . . . social and environmental conditions that result in adverse health outcomes" (Weinreb et al., 2007, p. 198). Approximately 25% to 40% of single homeless individuals have a diagnosable mental disorder (Snow & Reeb, 2013), and "most have a history of alcohol and/or drug abuse and/or dependence (60–80 percent)" (Toro & Janisse, 2004, p. 245), which further magnifies (a) the need for health care and (b) the obstacles to obtaining it. Table 5.1 illustrates different types of service learning projects involving this theme of improving access to health care for this population. Other service learning themes could also be developed for this course.

Community Psychology

Decreasing the social stigmatization of individuals with mental illness is a theme in community psychology. *Social stigma* includes several components (Snow & Reeb, 2013): stereotypes, labeling, prejudice, power differential, separation, status loss, and discrimination. One result of

Table 5.1
Examples of Service Learning in Abnormal, Health, and Community Psychology Courses

Course theme in Abnormal Psychology	Type of service learning	Example project	Examples of activities
Enhance coping with mental illness	Direct	Provide direct service to enhance a day treatment program for mental health clients.	Develop a stress management intervention (relaxation training) and assist in implementing it with clients.
	Indirect	Fundraise for a day treatment program to enhance support group sessions for clients with chronic mental illness.	Prepare and distribute fundraising brochure, organize a fundraising event, and collect funds, with the purpose of enhancing a support group (arrange outside speaker) or improving support group access (arrange transportation).
	Research	Assist with a research project to evaluate an intervention to enhance coping, stress management, and social support for clients at a mental health agency.	Collaborate with staff to develop research questions, identify psychometric instruments, collect data, analyze data, and write summaries to disseminate findings to different audiences (including agency staff).
	Advocacy	Assist a nonprofit organization (National Alliance on Mental Illness) with a project to improve social climate of an agency's setting to make it more conducive to developing coping skills.	Develop or conduct presentations to increase awareness of the potential of recovery from mental illness or provide ideas for making an agency setting more conducive to recovery (e.g., improving social climate of the setting).

(continues)

Table 5.1
Examples of Service Learning in Abnormal, Health, and Community Psychology Courses (*Continued*)

Course theme in Health Psychology	Type of service learning	Example project	Examples of activities
Improve health care access for people experiencing homelessness	Direct	Provide direct assistance to individuals in a homeless shelter to educate them on health care options and health care access.	Work one-on-one with shelter guests to (a) explain the Affordable Care Act and Medicaid Expansion or (b) teach them computer skills to access these programs.
	Indirect	Develop educational materials for a homeless shelter regarding health care options and access.	Develop materials (brochures or media) or arrange guest speakers to educate clients on (a) the Affordable Care Act and Medicaid Expansion, (b) how to apply for these programs, or (c) how to access health resources (e.g., free clinics) in their own community.
	Research	Assist with research examining the efficacy of a program that connects clients at a homeless shelter to health care access.	Collaborate with staff to determine (a) the extent to which clients participate in the program and (b) if the program is effective in connecting clients to services, analyze data, and write summaries to disseminate findings to different audiences (including shelter staff).
	Advocacy	Assist a nonprofit organization to influence local, state, or national decisions affecting health care access. Examples of organizations include Community Catalyst, Families USA, Health Care for America Now, Enroll America.	Assisting a nonprofit organization in educating the public (e.g., presentations), community organizing, or lobbying (e.g., letters to local shelters, homeless solutions boards, or state representatives) to advocate for (a) resources to improve health care access in shelters or (b) extend a successful model to other shelters.

Course theme in Community Psychology	Type of service learning	Example project	Examples of activities
Reduce social stigma toward mental illness	Direct	Develop or implement a program to reduce self-stigma (i.e., the internalization of public stigma).	Work with clients (one-on-one and/or discussion groups) to make them aware of (a) social stigma, (b) the risk (and consequences) of self-stigma, and (c) methods to prevent self-stigma (e.g., ways to continue working to strengthen coping skills and social support).
	Indirect	Assist a mental health agency to develop an anti-stigma program for family members of individuals with mental illness.	Develop materials (brochures or media or arrange guest speakers to work with families focused on (a) mental illness myths, (b) dangers of stigma and self-stigma, (c) the potential of recovery, and (d) ways to support a loved one with mental illness who encounter social stigma.
	Research	Assist a nonprofit organization (e.g., Mental Health America, National Alliance on Mental Illness) with a research project to examine effects of an anti-stigma program.	Collaborate with a nonprofit organization staff to develop research questions, collect data, analyze data, write summaries, and disseminate findings to different audiences (academic, mental health agency staff).
	Advocacy	Assist a nonprofit organization (e.g., Mental Health America, National Alliance on Mental Illness) in developing, implementing, and/or managing an anti-stigma campaign.	Conduct library research to inform an anti-stigma campaign that combines education and contact strategies and assist with the presentations for the public, family members of clients, and staff of mental health agencies.

being stigmatized is *self-stigma*—the internalization of public stigma, often leading to a loss of self-esteem, blaming oneself, and feeling shame (Corrigan, 2000). Corrigan and O'Shaughnessy (2007) identified three stigma-reducing strategies. *Protest strategies* involve (a) economic boycotts of producers (e.g., newspaper) of stigmatizing output or (b) a moral (or shame) protest (e.g., rebuking organizations with stigmatizing views). Anecdotal claims that protest is beneficial are not supported by research, and protest may result in attitude rebound (i.e., worsening of stigmatizing attitudes). *Education strategies* (e.g., public service announcements) decrease stigma by debunking myths with facts. *Contact strategies* reduce stigma by facilitating constructive social interaction between citizens and stigmatized group members. Overall, "a strategy that combines contact and education . . . may be best" (Snow & Reeb, 2013, p. 128). Table 5.1 illustrates different types of service learning projects involving the theme of decreasing mental illness stigma, representing one of many potential service learning themes for this course.

ILLUSTRATIVE SERVICE LEARNING EXAMPLE: HEALTH PSYCHOLOGY

In the example presented earlier for service learning in health psychology, the types of service learning activities (see Table 5.1) are interrelated and can build on one another and contribute to improving health care access for individuals who are homeless. Each specific example has merit as a separate service learning project. Nevertheless, in either (a) an advanced undergraduate course or (b) a sequence of courses involving collaboration among undergraduate students, graduate students, faculty, community partners, and clients, a broad service learning project could integrate the four types of service learning in Table 5.1.

Such a multifaceted service learning project would support the pursuit of all five APA (2013) learning goals and associated personal attributes (see Appendixes A and B, this volume). To work successfully with individuals who are homeless, students must be familiar with problems related to homelessness (e.g., trauma, mental illness, substance abuse); thus, the project would contribute to the pursuit of APA Goal 1 (Knowledge Base in Psychology) and related personal attributes (e.g., being conversant about psychological phenomena). Service learning work on a program evaluation of a project's benefits for health care access would contribute to the pursuit of Goal 2 (Scientific Inquiry and Critical Thinking) and related personal attributes (e.g., being systematic). Service learning students working on this type of project would become familiar with such issues as poverty and social stigma, thus contributing to the pursuit of Goal 3 (Ethical and Social Responsibility in a Diverse World) and pertinent personal attributes (e.g., being sensitive, fair minded). The project also would contribute to the pursuit of Goal 4 (Communication)—especially in activities related to media development (i.e., "Exhibit effective presentation skills for different purposes"; p. 30) and direct assistance to clients completing applications for health care (i.e., "Interacting effectively with others"; p. 31)—and related personal attributes (e.g., being respectful, prepared, precise, flexible). Finally, the project involves teamwork (collaborating with faculty, community partners, and clients) and management skills and therefore would contribute to the pursuit of Goal 5 (Professional Development) and related personal attributes (e.g., being collaborative).

AN EXAMPLE OF USING STRUCTURED REFLECTION

Chapter 3 of this volume provides a discussion of reflection, guides for developing reflection prompts (Tables 3.1–3.4 and Figure 3.1), and a DEAL model for reflection (Ash & Clayton, 2004, 2009a, 2009b) that incorporates Bloom's (1956) taxonomy to (a) encourage students to reflect in increasingly complex ways and (b) provide a basis for instructors to assess the quality of reflection and learning. The DEAL model contains the following components: (a) describe the experience objectively; (b) examine the experience from personal, civic, and/or academic perspectives; and (c) articulate learning acquired from the service learning activities and related reflection.

Table 5.2 provides a sample of structured reflection prompts based on the DEAL model for direct service learning: working to improve coping skills at a day treatment program. In brief, the structured reflection prompts

Table 5.2
Sample DEAL Model Reflection Prompt

Learning domain	Academic learning and personal growth (Section 5 of Venn diagram, Figure 3.1)
APA learning outcome	Indicator 1.3c: "Correctly identify antecedents and consequences of behavior and mental processes" (APA, 2013, p. 19).
Course-specific learning objective	Students will use research and theory on coping to do a situational analysis: (a) identify antecedents of maladaptive coping; (b) describe the coping exhibited by a client, student, staff member, or volunteer; (c) analyze consequences of the maladaptive coping; (d) identify strategies to improve coping skills; (e) propose strategies for all parties to collaborate in making the setting more conducive to adaptive coping; and (f) apply their learning in ways that improve personal coping skills.
DEAL/describe (objectively)	<ul><li>In general, what happened at the organization that is relevant to coping? What was the maladaptive coping?</li><li>Specify the situational antecedents.</li><li>When did the maladaptive coping take place?</li><li>Who exhibited the maladaptive coping (student, faculty, staff, or client)?</li><li>What were the negative consequences?</li><li>What did the person do after perceiving the negative consequences? What did you or others do? What did you or others communicate?</li><li>Who did not speak or act? Did you or others have emotional reactions (verbal or nonverbal)?</li></ul>
DEAL/examine (Six levels are based on Bloom's [1956] taxonomy)	Knowledge: Identify the specific components of the coping process on the basis of theories and research. Comprehension: In your own words, fully explain the specific components of the coping process, the major theories of coping, and research findings related to coping. Do this in a way that would allow someone outside of this course to understand these different elements. Application: Identify each specific component of your own coping in some situation (e.g., at the community-based organization). Connect the course content on coping to specific instances of maladaptive coping that you observed. Can you identify a "vicious cycle"; that is, did the coping lead to negative consequences that, in turn, contributed to an environment wherein maladaptive coping is even more likely? What other elements of the course content are relevant?

Table 5.2
Sample DEAL Model Reflection Prompt (*Continued*)

	Analysis: Identify interconnections among the antecedents of coping, the actual coping, the consequences of coping, and the resultant environmental situation. In other words, explain how the coping (problem-focused or emotion-focused) was maladaptive in that it did not "match" the situation (high vs. low levels of instrumental control in the situation). Would the coping, although maladaptive in this situation, be adaptive in others? (If so, explain and give examples.) What were the antecedents and consequences of your own coping?
	Synthesis: What specific changes in the person's coping do you recommend and what specific changes in the situation would alter the observed patterns? Given your overall understanding, provide recommendations for how clients, students, agency staff, and volunteers could collaborate to develop and implement an intervention that (a) improves coping with difficult situations in this setting and (b) modifies the setting to make it more conducive to adaptive coping for everyone. How could you improve your own coping?
	Evaluation: What are the strengths and weaknesses of your analysis and recommendations? Are there aspects of coping that you did not consider? Will you be able to apply recommendations to improve your own coping, or will there be obstacles in doing this? What are the obstacles and how could you overcome them? What evidence would you cite to justify your recommendations to someone outside of class? Did your analysis identify weaknesses in coping theories?
DEAL/articulate learning	As a result of completing this reflection, • I learned that . . . • I learned this when . . . • This learning matters because . . . • In light of this learning, in the future I will . . .

Note. APA = American Psychological Association; DEAL = describe, examine, and articulate learning model for critical reflection (Ash & Clayton, 2004, 2009a, 2009b; Jameson, Clayton, & Bringle, 2008).

in Table 5.2 require students to (a) conduct an in-depth situational analysis of maladaptive coping (exhibited by a client, student, staff member, or volunteer at a day treatment program for clients with mental illness), (b) develop and recommend strategies for improving coping and preventing maladaptive coping in the situation, and (c) consider the analysis and recommendations not only for the day treatment program but also for their own personal growth with regard to coping skills in daily living.

Reflection exercises based on the DEAL model can be used to assess demonstrated learning for academic, civic, and personal domains. The civic-minded graduate construct provides additional procedures for assessing civic learning (see Chapter 1, this volume; Bringle & Steinberg, 2010; Steinberg, Hatcher, & Bringle, 2011). Validated measures of constructs associated with a service learning project's purpose are also useful. For example, if the service learning project in abnormal psychology focused on coping, pre- to postsemester assessment of coping (e.g., Multidimensional Coping Inventory; Endler & Parker, 1990) could identify changes in students' coping repertoire. Assessment of community service self-efficacy (e.g., Community Service Self-Efficacy Scale; Reeb et al., 2010) could identify changes in the confidence of students in understanding or improving their coping or the coping of others in applied settings.

CONCLUSION

To some extent, students can learn the course content of abnormal, health, and community psychology in the classroom, but service learning allows students to (a) apply the theory and research from these courses to make community contributions and (b) reflect on experiences in ways that augment their academic learning, civic learning, and personal growth. As noted earlier, these courses share the feature of incorporating theory, research, and applied components; therefore, service learning plays a critical role in these courses by augmenting learning, expanding learning, and examining how psychology can support the public good.

6

Integrating Service Learning Into the Curriculum: Personality, Social, and Cultural Psychology

Human behavior is a function of the person and the environment. This chapter examines three courses in the psychology curriculum that further students' understanding of these seminal factors: Personality Psychology (focus on the person), Social Psychology (focus on the immediate social environment), and Cultural Psychology (focus on the person and environment at the level of culture). The integration of service learning into these courses is discussed and recommended as a way to enhance student engagement; contribute to communities; foster students' academic, civic, and personal growth; and meet the learning goals in the American Psychological Association's *APA Guidelines for the Undergraduate Psychology Major* (Version 2.0; 2013). Service learning's contributions to advancing student growth are presented for each course, and an in-depth example is provided of service learning integrated into a social psychology course.

---

http://dx.doi.org/10.1037/14803-007
Service Learning in Psychology: Enhancing Undergraduate Education for the Public Good, by R. G. Bringle, R. N. Reeb, M. A. Brown, and A. I. Ruiz
Copyright © 2016 by the American Psychological Association. All rights reserved.

PERSONALITY PSYCHOLOGY AND SERVICE LEARNING

The field of personality psychology emphasizes theory and basic research more than applied or engaged research (Esses & Dovidio, 2011; Omoto, 2012), and generally, students taking a personality psychology course do not have many opportunities to consider how their deepened understanding of human behavior might be applied to social issues, or to see themselves as agents of change in communities and more broadly. Students in personality psychology courses consider various levels of analysis: ways in which they are like everyone else, ways in which they are like some other people, and ways in which they are unique. Service learning provides opportunities for students to interact with others who may be dissimilar to themselves in significant ways. Students' academic, civic, and personal knowledge and understanding are expanded as they consider different levels of analysis for their interactions with diverse others in community service activities and as they reflect on micro- and macrosystemic influences on behavior. Understanding various levels of analysis through service learning targets a variety of APA (2013) learning outcomes, such as, "Examine the sociocultural and international contexts that influence individual differences and address applicability of research findings across societal and cultural groups" (Indicator 1.1D, Knowledge Base in Psychology, p. 18), "Predict and explore how interaction across racial, ethnic, gender, and class divides can challenge conventional understanding of psychological processes and behavior" (Indicator 3.2C, Ethical and Social Responsibility in a Diverse World, p. 26), and "Work effectively with diverse populations" (Indicator 5.4F, Professional Development, p. 35). When themes such as levels of analysis are enhanced in a personality psychology course with service learning, students have the opportunity to understand better the causes of behavior in themselves and others and to see how personality concepts, theories, and research findings are relevant to service contexts, social and civic issues, and civic engagement. This reveals how different perspectives in personality psychology can be applied to furthering the public good, thus raising students' sense of social responsibility. Because a personality psychology course covers a broad range of theoretical models of personality rather than focusing on any particular population or behavior, a variety of service learning sites and activities might be appropriate (see Table 6.1 for examples).

SOCIAL PSYCHOLOGY AND SERVICE LEARNING

Similar to personality psychology, contemporary social psychology is dominated by basic research rather than applied or engaged research and theories. Omoto (2012) suggested, "In their respective chases to be recognized as legitimate and rigorous sciences, the fields of personality and social psychology may have opted to emphasize the theoretical over the practical" (p. 807). Likewise, Esses and Dovidio (2011) noted, "The current emphasis on precision and purity has produced a largely decontextualized science of behavior" (p. 4). Service learning is a promising tool for enriching social psychology courses because students have the opportunity to (a) experience many real-world applications, (b) see disciplinary concepts in connection with social issues and social systems in their communities, (c) engage with community partners toward common goals, and (d) reflect on ways they might be actively engaged with peers and community partners in social change, thus becoming psychologically literate citizens who remain active in their communities. Research on service learning within social psychology courses shows a variety of benefits, including increased student concern for their communities, desire for civic participation, endorsement of social justice ideals, self-efficacy about service, social and civic responsibility, academic self-efficacy, higher course satisfaction, and higher grades (Brown, 2011a, 2011b; Cipolle, 2010; Crone, 2013; Harnish & Bridges, 2012).

Instructors implementing service learning in social psychology courses should consider engaging students in community service activities that allow them to maximize direct contact with community residents and/or an organization's clients because this can increase the endorsement of social justice–related attitudes (Brown & Riddle, 2013). Instructors should also consider having students collaborate with diverse persons (e.g., diversity in age, racial

Table 6.1
Examples of Service Learning in Personality, Social, and Cultural Psychology Courses

Course theme in Personality Psychology	Type of service learning	Example project	Examples of activities
Individual differences in human behavior	Direct	Provide direct client services at a shelter for domestic violence.	Assist victims of domestic violence with basic transition needs (e.g., obtaining food, clothing, transportation), provide childcare during group counseling sessions.
	Indirect	Assist domestic violence shelter staff in creating resources to support clients.	Work with staff to consider needs of clients and what information would be most helpful to include in web resources and handouts for clients. Assist in creating the materials.
	Research	Conduct research on resilience in domestic violence survivors.	In collaboration with shelter staff, survey victims of domestic violence to identify individual differences, situational factors, and sociocultural variables that predict resilience. Summarize results and share findings with community partners and other audiences.
	Advocacy	Promote awareness of domestic violence in the local community.	Conduct research for grants to support program(s) to train police officers, legislators, and judges to improve the response of the judicial system toward certain crimes.

Course theme in Social Psychology	Type of service learning	Example project	Examples of activities
Work towards social justice	Direct	Provide social justice services.	Support the implementation or maintenance of services for victims of injustice.
	Indirect	Assist organizations in identifying need for social justice action and support implementation of programs.	Work with agency staff to identify, create, and implement services for children, women, or other victims of violent crimes.
	Research	Program evaluation of service(s) focused on social justice.	Work with agency staff to create a survey to evaluate the impact of a service offered to rescue victims of a particular type of crime and support their efforts toward justice.
	Advocacy	Assist organizations to identify resources to promote social justice programs.	Create educational materials that promote awareness of psychological and social factors in domestic violence; disseminate on college campuses, at community centers, police stations, and clinics and hospitals.

(*continues*)

Table 6.1
Examples of Service Learning in Personality, Social, and Cultural Psychology Courses (*Continued*)

Course theme in Cultural Psychology	Type of service learning	Example project	Examples of activities
Awareness of diverse cultures and stereotyping, prejudice, and discrimination	Direct	Provide direct services for an organization that supports refugees or other recent immigrants.	Work with clients to become acclimated to the new culture (e.g., language skills, moving into housing, accessing social services).
	Indirect	Assist with annual fundraising campaigns at organizations that support refugees or other recent immigrants.	Use psychological research on diverse cultures to create effective fundraising materials.
	Research	Study community attitudes toward refugees or other recent immigrants.	In collaboration with program staff, create and conduct a study of stereotyping and prejudice in the local community toward refugees or other recent immigrants. Summarize and share findings with community partner and other audiences.
	Advocacy	Promote awareness and advocate on behalf of immigration reform.	Work with a community partner who supports immigrants; create an awareness program about local immigrants and immigration reform efforts. Lobby to improve current immigration policies.

and ethnic background, socioeconomic status) to expand students' awareness of and appreciation for diversity, as well as to create opportunities to reduce stereotyping and prejudice (Keen & Hall, 2009). Finally, when possible, instructors may wish to incorporate service activities in which students encounter the complexities of social injustice. See Table 6.1 for sample service learning projects that could be conducted in social psychology courses; later in the chapter a specific example is featured in greater depth.

CULTURAL PSYCHOLOGY AND SERVICE LEARNING

Service learning can also enrich courses in cultural psychology in which diversity and culture are salient. Cultural psychology courses enhanced with service learning address multiple APA (2013) goals and the intersections of the three learning domains: academic, personal, and civic (see Figure 3.1). For instance, the academic content of the course may include theories of prejudice and discrimination. Such topics can be extended to the personal domain, with the goal of increasing student self-awareness through self-assessments and reflections prior to and during the service. The content may also overlap with the civic domain when the social, economic, and historic contexts of particular social issues and the cultural context are examined. Finally, the three domains intersect when the students demonstrate understanding of course content and their own attitudes, and they can assess the impact of their behaviors and attitudes as they advocate for and attempt to produce social change. The integration of the three domains can be supported by regular reflection activities structured with prompts guided by learning objectives (see Chapter 3 and Appendix C).

There are several recommendations to plan and execute service learning using ethical, reciprocal, and democratic relationships when working with diverse groups (see Chapter 3, this volume; Chapdelaine, Ruiz, Warchal, & Wells, 2005). Service learning courses with cultural, multicultural, cross-cultural, and international experiences have the potential to cross the borders of categories of race, ethnicity, age, religion, sexual orientation, language, and socioeconomic status. Even though there is the potential to reinforce stereotypes (Cipolle, 2010), extant research has demonstrated that well-designed service learning typically reduces stereotyping and facilitates cultural and racial understanding (Eyler, 2011; Eyler, Giles, Stenson, & Gray, 2001). The Teaching Tolerance Project (n.d.) recommended four steps to ensure that service learning is implemented to reduce stereotypes: incorporate reflection about student attitudes; work with, not for, communities; address real community issues; and study social policies and problems that contribute to community issues. Gurecka and Gent (2001) proposed that service learning projects "that emphasize political and/or social reconstruction or change rather than charity or giving are the most beneficial" (p. 41).

The APA is a rich resource for information related to cultural psychology. There are several divisions attending to ethnic minority issues, and the Public Interest Directorate sponsors initiatives that promote minority issues (see Exhibit 1.1 for objectives and issues that could be addressed in cultural psychology courses enhanced with service learning). These provide resources that students and faculty can integrate into the course and reflection activities. Table 6.1 provides a sample of different types of service learning projects and activities that might be implemented in cultural psychology courses. Other examples can be found in the literature (Fitch, 2005; Harmon-Vukic & Schanz, 2012; Naudé, 2012; O'Grady, 2000; Shupe, 2013; Simons et al., 2011; Stewart & Webster, 2011).

ILLUSTRATIVE SERVICE LEARNING EXAMPLE: SOCIAL PSYCHOLOGY

This example focuses on students in a social psychology course working with persons with HIV/AIDS (Finkelstein, 2002). Social psychology students could serve in a variety of capacities, according to the preferences of the community partner. They might help administer basic services, such as in a food pantry, or assist with outreach and prevention education activities that the organization provides. Direct contact with clients and opportunities to build relationships is desirable because students will have richer personal, academic, and civic learning opportunities in the context of these relationships. Instructors must provide students with regular opportunities to connect the weekly course material with their service experiences.

Normally, this occurs through a variety of reflection activities, which could be structured in-class discussions, weekly journals, or other written assignments before, during, and after service (see Appendix C; Chapter 3).

Chapter 3 provides a detailed discussion of reflection and suggestions for creating comprehensive, structured, developmentally progressive, and assessable reflection assignments on the basis of Bloom's (1956) taxonomy, APA (2013) learning goals, and the DEAL (describe, examine, and articulate learning) model of reflection (Ash & Clayton, 2004, 2009a, 2009b; see also Appendix C, this volume). Table 6.2 illustrates DEAL-based reflection prompts. The reflection activities afford social psychology students the opportunity for in-depth learning on multiple topics in the course in a civic context. For example, when students first encounter community partners in service learning at an HIV/AIDS support organization, they may commit the fundamental attribution error; that is, they assume that clients of the organization are afflicted with HIV or AIDS because of some sort of character flaw. Subsequent experiences and reflection on one's experiences can facilitate a shift away from these presumptions (Bringle & Velo, 1998) and can help them progress toward meeting APA learning outcome "Interact sensitively with people of diverse abilities, backgrounds, and cultural perspectives" (Indicator 4.3C, Communication, p. 31). Service learning can also greatly enrich the traditional in-class methods of teaching about prejudice and intergroup relations. Social psychological research has repeatedly demonstrated the merits of intergroup contact for reducing prejudice (White, 2011). Service learning at an HIV/AIDS support organization can provide college students with opportunities for intergroup contact with diverse others and opportunities to reflect on that contact.

Brandenberger (2013) described the transformation of perspective that occurs in service learning through intergroup contact as stereotypes are challenged and views on diversity are changed. White (2011) stated,

> If the concept of a psychologically literate citizen refers to students respecting diversity and using their knowledge in ethically and socially responsible ways to directly benefit their communities, then students who respond in non-prejudiced or socially inclusive ways can be considered highly literate global citizens. (p. 56)

Table 6.2
Sample DEAL Model Reflection Prompt

Learning domain	Civic learning and personal growth (Section 6 of Venn diagram in Figure 3.1)
APA learning outcome	Indicator 4.3: "Interact effectively with others" (APA, 2013, p. 31).
Course-specific learning objective	Students will become more skilled in direct forms of service as they increase their ability to communicate with diverse others.
DEAL/describe (objectively)	• When did this experience of interacting with others take place? • Where did it take place? • Who else was there? Who was not there? • What did you do? What did others do? What actions did you or others take? What did you or others communicate? • Who did not speak or act? Did you or others laugh, cry, make a face, complain, criticize, argue, and so forth?
DEAL/examine (Six levels are based on Bloom's [1956] taxonomy)	Knowledge: Identify and describe one effective (e.g., positive, helpful) interaction with a client at the HIV/AIDS support organization, and one interaction that you felt was ineffective (e.g., unpleasant, confusing, unhelpful). Who talked the most? What kinds of statements were made? What were you talking about? Who ended the interaction and why? Identify factors that influenced each of the participants in the interactions. Comprehension: For both examples, elaborate on the factors that you think made them effective or ineffective. Label social, cultural, and organizational factors on your list. In your own words, define in detail the factors that you identified. Application: Which factor seemed to be the most important in contributing to the effective interaction? To the ineffective interaction? Why? Predict how social, cultural, or organizational factors have influenced and will influence the effectiveness of your interactions with the clients. Interpret the knowledge you have gained from your service experiences, including how you could develop more effective future interactions. What were you trying to accomplish during the interaction? What about the other person(s)? Did you have the same goals, different goals, or conflicting goals? Analysis: Examine your current interaction style. What are some of your strengths and areas that could be improved? How have your interactions and communications changed during your community activities? Outline specific strategies for improvement (e.g., listening more carefully, recognizing the impact

Table 6.2
Sample DEAL Model Reflection Prompt (*Continued*)

	of social and cultural effects on communication style, asking questions to capture more detail, closely attending to nonverbal cues). How did this interaction help or interfere with you reaching your goals? What about the goals of the other person(s)? How did these interactions contribute to the common good of others and to the mission of the organization? How do you think the setting influenced the interaction? How might it have been a different interaction in a different setting?
	Synthesis: Using your list of specific strategies and the organization's standards of conduct, create an action plan for effective interactions with clients at the organization that could be generalized for use by future service learning students at the site. What advice would you give them? What warnings? Summarize social, cultural, and organizational factors that seem to have the greatest impact on frequently encountered interpersonal situations at the site. Consult with the organization's staff for input and feedback on your action plan. How will you approach future interactions with the same person or similar persons? What would you do that might help you reach your goals? The goals of the other person? The organization's goals?
	Evaluation: Assess your ability to interact effectively with people of diverse backgrounds in a community context, providing evidence in the form of your experiences with staff and clients at the HIV/AIDS support organization. Do you think that your communication skills have been strengthened through this experience? Why or why not? Do you think that your skills will generalize to other community settings? To work settings? Why or why not? Do you think that your interactions at the site have helped? Why or why not? Have they helped individuals? Have they helped the organization reach its mission? How might you help in similar situations in the future?
DEAL/articulate learning	As a result of completing this reflection, - I learned that . . . - I learned this when . . . - This learning matters because . . . - In light of this learning, in the future I will . . .

Note. APA = American Psychological Association; DEAL = describe, examine, and articulate learning model for critical reflection (Ash & Clayton, 2004, 2009a, 2009b; Jameson, Clayton, & Bringle, 2008).

Brown (2011a, 2011b) found that service learning reduced social dominance orientation, one of the strongest predictors of a variety of prejudices. These outcomes are consistent with APA (2013) Goal 3 (e.g., Indicator 3.3A, "Exhibit respect for members of diverse groups with sensitivity to issues of power, privilege, and discrimination," p. 27). However, instructors must use best practices in service learning as described in Chapter 3, or it could inadvertently end up reinforcing stereotypes and increasing prejudice (see Bowman & Brandenberger, 2012, on negative diversity experiences; Erickson & O'Connor, 2000).

Community partners must have a collaborative role in educating students in any high-quality service learning experience. For example, Finkelstein (2002) reported that Tampa AIDS Network (TAN) employees worked with the instructor to craft the service learning course, taught an HIV/AIDS training class to all students, provided orientations to students, and worked with the students during service activities. Students wrote papers in the course that were shared with department directors at TAN. The papers contained reflections on their service, linkages with social psychological theory, and suggestions for organizational improvement. In return, TAN directors provided written feedback on the usefulness of papers and the likelihood of adopting the suggestions. Finkelstein found that the staff praised the work, reported intentions to adopt some suggestions, and appreciated the assistance of service learners.

CONCLUSION

Working with community partners, service learning can be effectively implemented by instructors of social, personality, and cultural psychology courses to facilitate students' academic, civic, and personal growth and to benefit communities. Service learning can be applied to all APA (2013) learning goals to develop well-rounded, psychologically literate citizens. Especially in the case of personality and social psychology courses, which have the reputation of being overly focused on theory rather than practice, service learning can provide students with real-world applications and opportunities for civic engagement that promote the public good.

7

Integrating Service Learning Into the Curriculum: Developmental Psychology

Developmental psychology is one of the specific domains recommended for the psychology curriculum core (Dunn et al., 2010). Developmental psychology uses empirical methods to examine changes from conception to end of life, including biological, cognitive, and socioemotional perspectives. Although the theories and research typically presented in developmental courses describe general principles of human development, the courses also incorporate the understanding of diversity and the uniqueness of individuals. Furthermore, these courses have relevance for interventions and policies. This chapter presents several suggestions for integrating different types of service learning activities in developmental psychology courses and provides illustrations of how the activities meet the American Psychological Association's *APA Guidelines for the Undergraduate Psychology Major* (Version 2.0; APA, 2013) by enhancing

---

http://dx.doi.org/10.1037/14803-008
Service Learning in Psychology: Enhancing Undergraduate Education for the Public Good, by R. G. Bringle, R. N. Reeb, M. A. Brown, and A. I. Ruiz
Copyright © 2016 by the American Psychological Association. All rights reserved.

academic and civic learning and personal growth (see Appendix A and Table 3.1, this volume).

SERVICE LEARNING AND DEVELOPMENTAL PSYCHOLOGY COURSES

Service learning provides opportunities for students to examine theories and research findings through action, analyze community service activities related to course material, explore the civic aspects of their academic work, and develop a deeper appreciation of their own development. Brandenberger's (1998) theoretical framework for developmental psychology and service learning illustrated theoretical constructs relevant to the development of students. Brandenberger suggested that through service learning students can become informed and active citizens who are able to identify root causes of problems and propose feasible solutions. Furthermore, students can become more knowledgeable about course content and demonstrate intrapersonal development (Zucchero, 2011), achieve higher exam and empathy scores when compared with other course assignments (Lundy, 2007), and demonstrate positive relationships with community organizations (Whitbourne, Collins, & Skultety, 2001). In addition, community members reported satisfaction with services provided (Anstee, Harris, Pruitt, & Sugar, 2008). Bringle and Kremer (1993) reported that in a service learning course in which students accompanied a participant in an elderly companion program, the companions provided overwhelmingly positive reactions to the experience. Other service learning courses involving adults or the elderly also resulted in positive outcomes (Anstee et al., 2008; Whitbourne et al., 2001). Although some issues identified in research on community outcomes (e.g., time commitment, student training, sustainability) have to be addressed in service learning, research has shown that "community respondents are satisfied with service learning courses, view benefits of projects as outweighing costs, and believe that service learning facilitates campus–community partnerships" (Reeb & Folger, 2013, p. 412).

Service learning can be integrated into all developmental courses (Lifespan, Child Development, Adult Development, Psychology of Aging, or Death and Dying), at introductory or advanced levels, for majors only and for nonmajors. A few examples are available for service learning courses for Lifespan Development (Lundy, 2007), Aging (Bringle & Kremer, 1993; Whitbourne et al., 2001), Gerontology (Anstee et al., 2008), and Intergenerational courses (Kalisch, Coughlin, Ballard, & Lamson, 2013; Knapp, & Stubblefield, 2000; Penick, Fallshore, & Spencer, 2014; see also Roodin, Brown, & Shedlock, 2013, for a recent review beyond psychology; Zucchero, 2011). Table 7.1 illustrates how three developmental themes (multidimensional characteristics of development, diversity awareness, and impact of developmental psychology role in social policy) can be enriched through different types of service learning activities. One of the examples (companion to a relative of person receiving hospice care) is described in detail.

ILLUSTRATIVE SERVICE LEARNING EXAMPLE: DEATH AND DYING

In death and dying courses, students explore the final stages of development from various perspectives to understand the nature and process of the experience. With their community partners, instructors should clearly articulate the purposes and goals of service learning in the course (Perring, 2008), define both the instructors' and students' roles, establish classroom protocols, develop orientations and preparation for the community service activities, and work with students and community partners on how to deal with topics that have the potential to elicit emotionally charged feelings (Balk, 2008). An example of a service learning activity in this course consists of students providing direct service to a hospice facility by becoming a companion to a family member of a person receiving hospice care. Hospice care organizations usually welcome individuals interested in providing emotional support and companionship to the family members during this difficult time.

Prior to the beginning of the course, the hospice organization(s) that can benefit from the support of companions can be identified. To support reciprocity and articulate the roles and responsibilities of all involved, the

Table 7.1
Examples of Service Learning in Developmental Courses

Course theme in Developmental Psychology	Type of service learning	Example project	Examples of activities
Multidimensional characteristics of development	Direct	Provide support for hospice care services.	Become a companion to a relative of a person receiving hospice care.
	Indirect	Fundraise for a hospice care facility.	Organize events, prepare flyers, and collect funds for programs that support different dimensions of development.
	Research	Assist with a research project for a hospice care facility.	Identify research questions and methods with community partners at a hospice care organization, collect data, and analyze and present results.
	Advocacy	Support hospice care organization's mission.	Write letters to state representatives to support hospice services for the elderly or veterans.
Diversity awareness	Direct	Provide direct support to an elderly care center.	Assist at an elderly care center that caters to a minority or immigrant population.
	Indirect	Assist a community agency to disseminate information about different types of care.	Organize a panel of speakers to provide information to the community about aging and related issues as identified by the agency staff.
	Research	Support grant writing for an elderly care center.	Identify funding sources, review guidelines, collect relevant information, and prepare proposal for extending services to minority populations.

Table 7.1
Examples of Service Learning in Developmental Courses (*Continued*)

Course theme in Developmental Psychology	Type of service learning	Example project	Examples of activities
	Advocacy	Support community agency's mission.	Prepare and provide seminars or workshops (e.g., on Alzheimer's) for local community partners (e.g., police, funders).
Impact of developmental psychology on social policy	Direct	Participate in day care programs.	Interact with children and staff in day care settings; reflect on the impact of public policy on child development and parenting.
	Indirect	Create a resource for parents to identify quality day care.	Create webpage or flyer with guidelines on how to evaluate day care programs; reflect on the impact of public policy on child care.
	Research	Assist day care centers to determine quality of program.	Work with day care program staff to identify research questions, methods, collect and analyze data, and prepare reports; reflect on the impact of research on child care policy.
	Advocacy	Support leaders to identify quality day care services.	Provide local representatives with guidelines of good day care programs, identify resources to improve or create needed services.

instructor and organizational staff identify the specific nature of the activities that will meet the course and the organization's goal(s) (see Chapter 3). Together they prepare students, monitor their progress, and provide feedback to all partners regarding the progress or need for adjustments throughout the experience. In addition, the organization's staff matches students with families, identifies the individual who will be paired with the students, and collects feedback from the community participants. The instructor makes sure that goals, outcomes, assignments, and assessment are clearly presented in the syllabus, and conducts a final assessment of the project by all partners.

Student preparation before the service is critical for the ethical implementation of the project (Chapdelaine, Ruiz, Warchal, & Wells, 2005). Students must understand the nature of the community service activities, their expected role and its limitations, applicable legal guidelines, rules and policies of the participating organizations, and the importance of alerting the instructor (or supervisor) to any emerging issues. Part of the preparation is to inform students that participation in this course and service learning may alter their values and belief systems. In addition, most hospice organizations provide their own training on companions' roles and responsibilities (e.g., philosophy of hospice care, characteristics of the organization, policies and procedures, service performed, issues related to death and dying in a multidimensional context—biological and medical, psychological, social, spiritual, and contextual). This preparation and training meets APA (2013) Goal 3 (Ethical and Social Responsibility in a Diverse World) and can be implemented through workshops, readings, structured reflection, and discussion.

Students' meetings with relatives of hospice patients to listen and offer companionship may occur as the family member assists the patient or during other times at a variety of places agreed on by the agency. This service learning activity meets several other APA (2013) goals and the three learning domains (academic, personal, civic; see Chapter 3 and Table 3.1, this volume). Theories, principles, and research findings on death and dying can all be enhanced through critical reflection, thus contributing to Goal 1 (Knowledge Base in Psychology). Reflection activities can also address personal growth as students are asked to think about the course content from their perspectives and to put themselves in the place of the individuals they accompany. The students experience a unique opportunity to develop civic learning when they compare and contrast social policies with the experiences they have with the individual and then identify the consequences of such policies. Students may also face a variety of circumstances that require them to interact effectively with others (Goal 4, Communication), demonstrate professional skills (Goal 5, Professional Development), and use critical thinking (Goal 2, Scientific Inquiry and Critical Thinking).

Reflection is central to enhancing the service learning experience by generating and capturing learning; it should occur regularly and focus on each of the selected learning domains and goals for the course. Chapter 3 provides a detailed discussion of reflection and suggestions for creating comprehensive, structured, developmentally progressive reflection, and assessable assignments based on Bloom's (1956) taxonomy, APA (2013) learning goals, and the DEAL (describe, examine, and articulate learning) model of reflection (Ash & Clayton, 2004, 2009a, 2009b). Reflection should be done before, during, and after the service experience; it can be done individually, with the class, and ideally with the community staff and family members, and it may take many forms (see Appendix C). Regardless of how it is done, reflection should occur often and receive feedback.

Prior to beginning the community service activities, students can be asked to reflect on their existing knowledge, previous personal experiences, attitudes and values, expectations, and stereotypes (e.g., group discussions, written products). After they receive their orientation to the hospice organization, they can reflect on the civic learning domain (e.g., mission of the organization, community need, ability to contribute). Table 7.2 provides an example of prompts for reflection during the course, which can be adapted to other stages of the experience (i.e., before service, after service) and to other domains and goals. At the end of the service experience, the students can present their learning in a way that may take many formats, such as a written report, a journal based on reflections prepared during the semester, a mural, a video, a poster, or oral presentations (see Appendix C).

Table 7.2
Sample DEAL Model Reflection Prompt

Learning domain	Academic learning and civic learning (Section 4 of Venn diagram in Figure 3.1)
APA learning outcome	Indicator 3.3c: "Explain how psychology can promote civic, social, and global outcomes that benefit others" (APA, 2013, p. 27).
Course-specific learning objective	Using psychological content, students will identify policies and evaluate their role on human services and community resources for those dying, as well as for their families or companions.
DEAL/describe (objectively)	Describe the training provided by the hospice. • Who provided the training? Who attended? What information was covered? • When did the training take place? Where did it take place? • Who else was there? Who was not there? • What did you do? What did others do? What did you or others communicate? Who did not speak or act? Did you or others laugh, cry, make a face, complain, criticize, argue, and so forth?
DEAL/examine (Six levels are based on Bloom's [1956] taxonomy)	Knowledge: Identify policies that directly affect the care of those who are dying and their relatives. Identify the types of services provided by the hospice and other services available in the community. When someone learns they are dying, where can they go for different services? When someone learns that a relative is dying, what support is available for him or her? What course content is relevant to these policies and issues? Comprehension: Express the policies and the psychology content in your own words. Application: Who is responsible for what services? Who qualifies for the services? What policies are relevant for the services identified? What is your role as a resource? What theories and research in the course are consistent with the policies? Inconsistent? Analysis: Can you distinguish between the different services available? What are some of the advantages and some of the problems with the existing policies? What are consequences of the policies on existing services? Compare and contrast different policies and their consequences. What course theories and research findings are relevant to your analysis of the policies? Whose interests are being served by each policy? Whose interests are not being served? Who has and does not have access to hospice services?

Table 7.2
Sample DEAL Model Reflection Prompt (*Continued*)

	Synthesis: Based on course theories and research, what new recommendations do you have for operations and policies for hospices? What factors would you change if you were the person who needed care? If you knew someone close to you who needed care? What changes could benefit the policies relevant for the care of those dying? For their relatives? What kind of services do you suggest for people who are dying and their companions? How are your suggestions similar and different from existing services? What different policies would you like to see in place? Why would they be an improvement? What new research should be conducted to better inform policies?
	Evaluation: What are strengths of current services? Weaknesses? How does research support your evaluations? What evidence could be collected to support your evaluations? How would you feel if you were the person receiving the services? What would you suggest to solve the issues identified with existing services? What do you suggest be done to improve the policies available? How could policies and services be fairer? What might you do in the future to support hospice care or improve hospice care?
DEAL/articulate learning	As a result of completing this reflection, • I learned that . . . • I learned this when . . . • This learning matters because . . . • In light of this learning, in the future I will . . .

Note. APA = American Psychological Association; DEAL = describe, examine, and articulate learning model for critical reflection (Ash & Clayton, 2004, 2009a, 2009b; Jameson, Clayton, & Bringle, 2008).

Assessment can contribute to student learning through feedback given to students. Assessment can also document and evaluate how well students have met goals and outcomes (see Chapters 3 and 13). The assessment plan may include completion of companion hours, examinations, standard forms used by university centers to collect feedback from students and the agency (including client's response), or other measures. The assessment plan should also address particular goals selected for the service learning experience on the basis of the course learning objectives.

A formative assessment may use progressively more complex reflection prompts prepared during the semester.

A summative assessment can also be done at the end of the course to establish student and community outcomes. Because of the collaborative nature of service learning, the instructor and the community partners must clearly identify the outcomes of the service activities and communicate those to all members of the partnership. Through students' reflections and communications with the agency, the activities can be subsequently adjusted, and an evaluation of community outcomes should determine future commitment to the service learning activities.

CONCLUSION

Many key figures in the field of developmental psychology agree with the role of experience on development (Dewey, Erikson, Gilligan, James, Kohlberg, Piaget, Vygotsky, among others). An important benefit of service learning in developmental psychology courses is the opportunity students have to develop a deeper appreciation of their own development (personal growth) and to become psychologically literate citizens able to identify root causes of community problems and propose feasible solutions.

8

Integrating Service Learning Into the Curriculum: Cognition, Learning, and Behavioral Neuroscience

The American Psychological Association (APA) has proposed a core for the undergraduate psychology program (Dunn et al., 2010) and the introduction to psychology course (Gurung et al., 2014) with four content domains, two of which are cognitive and biological psychology. Because courses in these areas are not required of all majors, they are taken by 40% of undergraduate psychology majors (Stoloff et al., 2010). A characteristic of these courses is that they typically use laboratories (Dunn, 2006; Stoloff et al., 2010). Although participation in laboratory experiences increases student success (Stoloff, Curtis, Rodgers, Brewster, & McCarthy, 2012), service learning is one of the quality benchmarks for the undergraduate psychology curriculum (Dunn, McCarthy, Baker, & Halonen, 2011; Stoloff et al., 2012).

Service learning is a high-impact best practice (Association of American Colleges & Universities, 2011) that enhances practical skills and is "good preparation for citizenship, work and life" (para. 8). It can contribute

---
http://dx.doi.org/10.1037/14803-009
Service Learning in Psychology: Enhancing Undergraduate Education for the Public Good, by R. G. Bringle, R. N. Reeb, M. A. Brown, and A. I. Ruiz
Copyright © 2016 by the American Psychological Association. All rights reserved.

to all APA (2013) goals (Appendix A) and enhance academic learning, civic learning, and personal growth (see Table 3.1, Introduction, Chapter 1). However, suggestions for teaching activities in cognition, learning, and behavioral neuroscience courses (Conner, 1996; Copeland, Scott, & Houska, 2010; Crone & Portillo, 2013; Gronlund & Lewandowsky, 1992; Hager, 2011; Machado & Silva, 1998; Millis, 2001; Sternberg & Pardo, 1998; Vanags, George, Grace, & Brown, 2012) do not include service learning. This chapter describes service learning activities for cognition, learning, and behavioral neuroscience courses and illustrates in detail one of the projects that may be incorporated into these or other courses, with or without a laboratory.

SERVICE LEARNING IN COGNITION, LEARNING, AND BEHAVIORAL NEUROSCIENCE COURSES

Service learning in cognition courses may address the importance of context in cognitive development. For example, with increasing pressures to meet standards, service learning activities may be developed in conjunction with primary and secondary school teachers to enrich and augment the educational process of children beyond the standard curriculum. Children learn a concept in a particular context, and college students can introduce activities to assist children to transfer knowledge across domains. Also, workshops may be created to support after-school programs to enhance children's memory, reading and writing skills, or metacognition.

Community service activities in a learning course can enrich the application of psychology and provide students with practical experiences using learning principles for the public good. Instructors and students can work with organizations (i.e., health care clinics, behavior modification programs) to create and implement programs focused on a particular issue (e.g., to quit smoking). Behavioral principles could be presented in workshops (e.g., to parents who would like to change their children's behavior so that they would have fewer tantrums) or applied as intervention for individuals (e.g., students who need instructional accommodations or behavioral support).

Service learning in behavioral neuroscience courses can enrich a theme such as awareness of mental and physical health through community service activities. The students have an opportunity to connect the information they learn about the nervous system to social issues in the community and augment their learning with real-life situations beyond the classroom and laboratory. For instance, students may be assigned to be a companion to visit and interact with individuals with different brain disorders (e.g., Alzheimer's disease, dementia, schizophrenia) at organizations that provide a variety of services (e.g., rehabilitation centers, psychiatric centers or hospitals, specialized educational institutions, residential settings, behavioral programs, adult centers). Students may have the opportunity to integrate scientific information in a social setting while learning how stress, dietary habits, and other psychosocial factors influence the body and brain. For instance, the service learning project may involve supporting an awareness campaign of a particular subject of interest for the community.

In sum, many projects may be created to involve students in activities that support a diverse group of individuals (healthy or not), as well as staff working in organizations that provide mental health or health services. These activities are also a great opportunity for interdisciplinary projects. Several projects and activities to implement service learning in cognition, learning, and behavioral neuroscience courses are presented in Table 8.1.

ILLUSTRATIVE SERVICE LEARNING EXAMPLE: EDUCATIONAL FAIR

This section provides an in-depth example of an indirect service learning project: an educational fair that can be implemented in cognition, learning, or behavioral neuroscience courses with or without a laboratory. In this service learning project students explore a topic from the course and present information in a concise, understandable way to the public in the form of a display at an educational fair. The topic selection should be based on interests of community partners. The instructor and students could contact local organizations, their clients, government officials, residents, or practitioners to identify topics that would benefit local communities while also meeting the goals of the course. Students can learn more about their communities as they work with local agency staff to address identified issues. Many campus health centers are interested in working with

Table 8.1
Examples of Service Learning in Cognition, Learning, and Behavioral Neuroscience Courses

Course theme for Cognition	Type of service learning	Example project	Examples of activities
Importance of context in cognitive development	Direct	Enhance cognitive development.	Tutor children on cognitive skills using a variety of tasks.
	Indirect	Support acquisition of materials to enhance children's cognitive development.	Identify materials that are age appropriate and fundraise to support teachers' acquisition of materials on a variety of cognitive tasks.
	Research	Evaluate cognitive development of school-age children.	Assess cognitive development milestones of students in a classroom and discuss the implications of the findings with teachers.
	Advocacy	Advocate to maintain or increase recreational time for children in school settings.	Attend school board meetings to provide information about the importance of play and recess for children's cognitive development.

Course theme for Learning	Type of service learning	Example project	Examples of activities
Application of learning principles	Direct	Support educational learning.	Tutor children using a variety of learning principles.
	Indirect	Assist nonprofit agency activities director whose mission is to promote mental health.	Create educational games for diverse types of learning disorders and different ages; assess the impact of the games.

	Type of service learning	Example project	Examples of activities
	Research	Develop research on benefits of recess in elementary and secondary education.	Design a study to identify the impact behavior interventions (or lack thereof) have on learning and cognitive development.
	Advocacy	Provide educational information to community members.	Create displays with educational information for communities on the basis of topics of local interest; for instance, an educational fair at a school, where parents receive information that illustrates structured educational activities and their value.

Course theme for Behavioral Neuroscience	Type of service learning	Example project	Examples of activities
Awareness of mental and physical health issues	Direct	Interact with patients in a rehabilitation hospital or nursing home.	Help individuals at a rehabilitation hospital or nursing home to attend and participate in activities; design and carry out entertaining activities appropriate for the age and impairment.
	Indirect	Support community outreach.	Distribute educational materials for community agencies (e.g., drug and alcohol education and rehabilitation).
	Research	Assist a community agency to identify updated information for educational materials.	Conduct literature research to update educational or marketing materials to support awareness of mental health and services available.
	Advocacy	Promote and support educational outreach services.	Provide educational information to local government representatives about a topic (e.g., the impact of drugs and alcohol on communities) by organizing a panel of experts, workshops, or an educational fair.

students to promote health awareness on issues such as drug use, eating habits, stress, or dating behaviors.

A variety of course content is available for public education programs. For cognition courses, topics could include demonstrating ways to enhance children's education with games, improving memory, providing cognitive stimulation to elderly persons, and using problem-solving heuristics in everyday life. For learning courses, the topics could cover contingencies and many of the misunderstandings that lead to misapplications (e.g., types of reinforcements, schedules, differences between reinforcement and punishment). For a behavioral neuroscience course, the displays could focus on teratogens, stress, sleep (or lack of it), concussions, influence of environment on brain development and functioning, plasticity, and age-related neurocognitive processing's impact on everyday functioning (e.g., driving, memory).

On the basis of community partners' input, students select a topic or may have a topic assigned by the instructor, research it, and then use the information collected to educate the public. The activities necessary to complete this project meet several APA (2013) goals and learning domains (see Table 3.1). As students research their topic, they further develop understanding of concepts and principles relevant to the topic and identify applications of the material to everyday life situations, consistent with APA Goal 1 (Knowledge Base in Psychology). An advantage of this service learning activity is that students enhance their academic learning not only by conducting research on the topic but also by critically evaluating evidence and adapting it to applications that are appropriate to the audience (e.g., parents, teachers, principals, policymakers, other students).

Next, as the students prepare the display for the fair, on the basis of APA (2013) Goal 4 (Communication) they can explore different presentation formats that are appropriate for the topic and the audience. This activity may be done in groups, which will enhance teamwork capacity consistent with Goal 5 (Professional Development) and heighten personal growth. The fair may be organized to coincide with an awareness day, week, or month (e.g., May is Mental Health Month, November is Alzheimer's Awareness Month) or the promotion of an issue by different community organizations (e.g., neighborhood events, churches, schools, local government).

The service learning does not have to replace a laboratory component, but may be added to the course to provide students with opportunities to apply the content to everyday life beyond the laboratory. The fair meets APA (2013) Goal 3 (Ethical and Social Responsibility in a Diverse World) requirements when the students have the opportunity to "explain how psychology can promote civic, social, and global outcomes that benefit others" (Indicator 3.3c, p. 27). The fair can be displayed in a local school (Kern-Manwaring & Wickline, 2013), community center, or on campus.

An essential aspect of service learning is regular, structured reflection based on course learning goals and objectives (see Chapter 3). Using the DEAL (describe, examine, and articulate learning) model for critical reflection (Ash & Clayton, 2009a, 2009b), reflection starts with a description of the activity, followed by examination of the learning (guided by Bloom's, 1956, taxonomy, as appropriate for the course and the students' level), and then articulating learning. For the educational fair, students can reflect after each stage of the project: before, during, and after the fair and alone, with classmates, and potentially with the community group working with the class to determine the theme of the fair (Appendix C).

When students select the topic and complete the research, the reflection prompts may focus on the academic learning by highlighting APA (2013) Goal 1. If students work in groups, the prompts may include personal growth and address Goal 4 and teamwork capacity in Goal 5. As they prepare for the fair, reflections may emphasize civic learning, with prompts that focus on the ways students determined the appropriate communication format for the audience (Goal 4), and they can evaluate the expected benefits of psychology and the educational fair to all participants (Goal 3).

After the fair, reflection can focus on the connections across academic, civic, and personal domains. Students could be asked how the knowledge used in the fair (academic learning) applies to civic initiatives (e.g., policies, social issues) and benefits the audience and community (civic learning) and their sense of responsibility regarding the issue (personal growth). The reflection activities can have many formats, such as a blog, formal paper, class discussions, or a digital story about the service activities. Table 8.2

Table 8.2
Sample DEAL Model Reflection Prompt

Learning domain	Academic learning and civic learning (Section 4 of Venn diagram, Figure 3.1)
APA learning outcome	Indicator 3.3c: "Explain how psychology can promote civic, social, and global outcomes that benefit others" (APA, 2013, p. 27).
Course-specific learning objective	Students will prepare an educational fair display that demonstrates psychological understanding and appropriate use of concepts, principles, and applications of selected topics, and demonstrate understanding of civic and social benefits of the fair.
DEAL/describe (objectively)	<ul><li>Describe the preparation of materials for the educational fair display.</li><li>What were the tasks needed to prepare the display?</li><li>What steps were taken to prepare the display?</li><li>Describe the display and the information provided.</li><li>What were the tasks needed to prepare the fair?</li><li>Where will the fair take place? Who is invited to attend the fair?</li></ul>
DEAL/examine (Six levels are based on Bloom's [1956] taxonomy)	Knowledge: What are the goals of the display and the fair? What content was selected for the display? How was the community involved in the selection of the topic? What topics were discarded? When and how were the tasks accomplished? What are the social and civic benefits of the fair? What course content was included?
	Comprehension: Elaborate on the goals of the display and fair. What was the main idea of your display? How was the topic refined and focused? Describe the audience expected to attend the fair. Predict their reaction(s). Will they perceive the benefits you listed? Describe the course content in your own words.
	Application: Do you know of other examples of educational fairs in the area? On the topics of your fair? Do you know of other education campaigns that reached out to the audience of your fair? Would the content of the fair be as beneficial if presented in a different format? How did you adapt the course content to the audience?

Table 8.2
Sample DEAL Model Reflection Prompt (*Continued*)

	Analysis: What were the consequences of the fair and your display? Explain how the topic of your display and the fair were beneficial to the audience? What were the strengths and weaknesses of the displays and fair? What would happen if there were no fair or display? Indicate the potential effect of the application of the information prepared for the displays. How do you think individuals were influenced by the content?
	Synthesis: How different would the display be if you had unlimited resources? What advice would you have for students to do similar projects in the future? Do you think they should change it? Why or why not? How would you modify it? What questions would you ask if you had to recreate your display? What factors would you change if you had to do it again? Would any of those changes make it a better display for the audience? Are there different kinds of audiences that you think would benefit more from the fair? How could you reach a different audience? A broader audience? Were there questions that the psychology content did not answer?
	Evaluation: In what ways do you think this fair contributes to the public good? Is the purpose of the fair something that you care about? Why or why not? What evidence would you propose collecting to evaluate the effectiveness of the display and the fair? Would the evidence be convincing to you? Is the issue something you care about? Is influencing the public on this issue something that you care about? How do you think the audience would agree or disagree with your perspective? Which perspective is more valid? Why? What are the advantages and disadvantages of different methods for communicating the same information to the same and different audiences? How would you feel if you were the audience attending the fair? What were the strengths and weaknesses of the psychology content that you presented?
DEAL/articulate learning	As a result of completing this reflection, ▪ I learned that . . . ▪ I learned this when . . . ▪ This learning matters because . . . ▪ In light of this learning, in the future I will . . .

Note. APA = American Psychological Association; DEAL = describe, examine, and articulate learning model for critical reflection (Ash & Clayton, 2004, 2009a, 2009b; Jameson, Clayton, & Bringle, 2008).

presents an example of a set of reflection prompts that might be used for one of the reflection assignments and that can be adapted for other learning objectives.

An assessment plan should match the learning goals established for the educational fair (see Chapter 3 and 13 for more details) and include the target audience and community partners. Because the project was co-created with the community (e.g., organization, neighborhood), staff members (and maybe their clients) should be involved in assessing the goals of the activity from their perspective, and this should be shared with the students. Assessing students' learning and community impact can provide opportunities for research projects (see Chapter 13).

Finally, feedback from the audience who attended the educational fair can inform instructors and students of follow-up activities and other projects (Stewart, 2008). Participants' feedback to the students regarding the impact of their projects could be collected in several ways: through a survey collected at the display, through an audience pre- and posttest (Fox, 2007), and through individuals outside the fair asking attendees for opinions on content and format of the displays.

CONCLUSION

Although APA (2013) learning goals can be met in the classroom, implementing service learning in cognition, learning, and behavioral neuroscience courses offers many advantages to the students, instructor, and communities over traditional pedagogies. Service learning promotes students' active learning, but it further delivers firsthand knowledge of community issues and connects themes addressed by the course and the service activity. Students will appreciate that courses, usually taught with laboratories, can meet APA's mission to benefit society.

9

Integrating Service Learning Into the Curriculum: Statistics, Research Methods, and Research Capstone

Instructors of statistics and research methods courses aspire to teach psychology majors and intended majors to think like psychological scientists, develop skills in scientific inquiry, and improve critical thinking. Service learning is a potent way to connect the curricula of statistics and research methods courses with the social issues in communities to promote the academic learning, civic learning, and personal growth of students. This chapter describes the benefits of integrating service learning in statistics and research methods courses as well as service learning in research capstone courses as the culmination of the major's methodology scaffolding. Examples are given for how core themes in each course can be enhanced using service learning.

ENGAGING STUDENTS WITH SERVICE LEARNING IN STATISTICS AND RESEARCH COURSES

Although there is strong agreement on the importance of scientific methods in the undergraduate psychology curriculum, students are less drawn to these courses than to others in the major (Rajecki, Appleby, Williams, Johnson, & Jeschke, 2005). Presumably, instructors of statistics and research methods courses want to increase student engagement and effectively promote student learning of course content. Service learning is a high-impact practice (Kuh, 2008) that enhances student interest, stimulates civic engagement, facilitates comprehension of course content, and fulfills the learning goals outlined in the American Psychological Association's *APA Guidelines for the Undergraduate Psychology Major* (Version 2.0; APA, 2013).

Research on service learning in scientific methods courses reveals numerous benefits. For example: (a) students analyze real data; (b) service learning is active, inquiry-based learning in which students formulate research questions and learn to test them; (c) students experience the role of statistician and member of a research team; (d) students realize that statistical skills are useful in the real world; (e) projects provide rich, interesting classroom examples; (f) service learning directly benefits community partners; (g) service learning creates positive exposure for the university in communities; and (h) service learning can lead to ongoing collaboration and partnerships with groups outside the university (J. E. Anderson & Sungur, 1999; Harnish & Bridges, 2012; Keyton, 2001; Machtmes et al., 2009; Root & Thorme, 2001; Rosenthal, 2006).

SELECTING SERVICE LEARNING SITES AND ACTIVITIES FOR STATISTICS AND RESEARCH COURSES

There are four main types of service learning that instructors have to choose from: direct, indirect, research, and advocacy (see Chapter 3 for a description of each type). Table 9.1 provides illustrations of activities associated with each type in methodology courses. However, *research*

Table 9.1
Examples of Service Learning in Scientific Methods Courses

Course themes for Statistics, Research Methods, and Research Capstone	Types of service learning	Example projects	Examples of activities
Understand and use the scientific method as psychology's way of knowing. Select and conduct appropriate statistical analyses for specific research questions.	Direct	Tutor youth to strengthen math and literacy skills. Conduct a supplemental literature review on principles of learning.	Work directly with youth to explore the efficacy of different teaching and learning techniques. Review the scientific literature in psychology on learning in children. Tutoring program organizers receive the strongest student literature reviews to inform future tutor training.
	Indirect	Prepare booklets for community agencies that use statistical data and graphs to describe funding. Students assist agencies to prepare presentations to boards on fund allocations.	Perform statistical analyses with a focus on graphical displays based on databases at a community organization or from the psychological literature. Create written and oral presentation materials for organizations that include easily understood visual representations of statistical information and that link the analyses to the organization's mission, programs, and questions.
	Research	Design and conduct an assessment of the intrapersonal outcomes for a community center's self-defense training program for rape, domestic violence, and stalking victims.	Search the scientific literature to identify constructs and measures of those constructs that are relevant to participation in the program (e.g., self-efficacy, self-esteem) and their reliability and validity. In collaboration with the community partner, design and conduct a program assessment and present reports to community center staff to be used to inform the public about programmatic outcomes.
	Advocacy	Assist an organization that aids survivors of human trafficking to gather information and promote awareness of local human trafficking issues.	In collaboration with the community partner, gather data on local survivors of human trafficking. Critically evaluate the extant literature on human trafficking. Work with community partners to develop presentations, panel events, workshops, or written materials to increase awareness of human trafficking in the community.

service learning is likely to be the most natural fit in scientific methods courses. In research service learning, instructors and students collaboratively engage with community partners in research with the purpose of addressing a community issue, enhancing resources, or evaluating organizational effectiveness. Though the primary emphasis in research service learning is research, it can still provide direct contact with service populations (e.g., interviewing clients), indirect benefits to the organization, and information that can be used for advocacy by the organization, thus overlapping with the other types of service learning.

A key factor to consider in service learning site selection for scientific methods courses is the identification of community partners who will benefit from an analysis of the functioning or efficacy of some aspect of their organization (i.e., a program evaluation) or an analysis of issues that are of interest to a neighborhood, community members, clients, or advocacy group. Instructors of these courses should become familiar with the fundamentals of *participatory community action research* (PCAR). PCAR is a partnership of students, faculty, and community members who collaboratively engage in research with the purpose of investigating a pressing community issue to gather information that will be useful to the community and meet academic goals (Strand, Cutforth, Stoecker, Marullo, & Donohue, 2003; see Chapter 2, this volume, for more information). One of the risks of incorporating service learning into scientific methods courses is that instructors and students might interpret the service learning activities as doing something "for" communities rather than "with" communities. Also, students who are analyzing organizational data can do that without any civic perspective (i.e., civic learning) on what they are doing. PCAR, thoughtful course design, democratic partnerships and processes (i.e., inclusive, participatory, fair), and structured critical reflection can all contribute to the democratic (vs. technocratic) nature of civic engagement (Saltmarsh, Hartley, & Clayton, 2009).

A more detailed example follows of how service learning could be integrated into a research capstone course with a PCAR project. The research capstone course contains elements from the previous statistics and methodology courses on which it is based. Thus, portions of this example can be applied to any of those courses. The example includes a project, course theme, activities, relevant APA learning goals, and illustrative reflection prompts. Prior to the onset of any service learning activities, matters such as course registration, syllabus planning, community partnerships, and orientations must be organized by the instructor (see Chapter 3).

For service learning activities to be fully effective, they must involve regular, structured reflection by students on their service and on their academic, civic, and personal learning (Ash & Clayton, 2004, 2009a, 2009b; Bringle & Hatcher, 1999; Jameson, Clayton, & Bringle, 2008). A detailed discussion of reflection with a variety of examples can be found in Chapter 3. Table 9.2 provides sample DEAL (describe, examine, and articulate learning) model (Ash & Clayton, 2009a, 2009b) reflection prompts in a research methods course with a service learning project at a refugee resettlement agency. This example is focused on the intersection of civic and academic learning, but reflection prompts can address academic, civic, and personal learning domains and any combination of these domains (see Figure 3.1).

ILLUSTRATIVE SERVICE LEARNING COURSE EXAMPLE: RESEARCH CAPSTONE

A local refugee resettlement organization wants to evaluate how well its program facilitates successful adaptation to the host city by refugee populations that it serves. A partnership with the instructor and student service learners in a research capstone course could be of mutual benefit.

Formulating Research Questions

Instructors and students work with program staff and program clients, as appropriate, to gather background information and formulate specific research questions. This addresses APA (2013) Goal 2 (Scientific Inquiry and Critical Thinking), because students demonstrate psychology information literacy and engage in integrative thinking. This contributes to student attributes such as being well-informed, creative, and curious. The content of APA learning goals and outcomes should be tied to the reflection activities for students. Depending on time constraints and other

Table 9.2
Sample DEAL Model Reflection Prompt

Learning domain	Civic learning and academic learning (Section 4 of Venn diagram in Figure 3.1)
APA learning outcome	Indicator 3.1: "Apply ethical standards to evaluate psychological science and practice" (APA, 2013, p. 26).
Course-specific learning objective	Students will demonstrate understanding of and adherence to APA ethical standards and organizational codes of conduct or policies in their research activities at the refugee site.
DEAL/describe (objectively)	<ul><li>When did these experiences related to ethics take place? Where did it take place?</li><li>Who else was there? Who was not there?</li><li>What did you do? What did others do? What actions did you or others take? What did you or others communicate?</li><li>Who did not speak or act? Did you or others laugh, cry, make a face, complain, criticize, argue, and so forth?</li></ul>
DEAL/examine (Six levels are based on Bloom's [1956] taxonomy)	Knowledge: Identify principles from the APA code of ethics and the agency's code of conduct that are most relevant to your research project at the refugee agency. Comprehension: Summarize each of these principles in your own words, so that someone outside this course will understand them. How do they relate to your current understanding of the agency and its clients? Application: Which elements of ethics are most relevant to your community-based activities? Which are not? What are the implications of ethics to decisions that you made about the work? Analysis: Describe a problematic scenario in your research project that could violate or compromise APA ethical principles and/or the agency's code of conduct. How likely are those risks? How damaging might the consequences be? If this scenario occurred, what would an appropriate response be? Examine each aspect of your study's proposed methodology for its cultural congruence to the participants at the refugee agency. What aspects of the study could be considered unethical if they were not conducted in a culturally sensitive manner? Do you think your study's design would be equally ethical with an entirely different population of participants? Why or why not? Analyze any conflicting values or ethical considerations (e.g., from the perspective of clients, agency, community, research team). Whose self-interest is served by this research? Whose is not? Is this fair? Why? Why not?

Table 9.2
Sample DEAL Model Reflection Prompt (*Continued*)

	Synthesis: Carefully consider the ways that the community partner should or could be involved in effectively working through the scenario in concert with the research team and course instructor, so that all voices and perspectives are included. How could the process be most inclusive? More participatory? More just? Create an "ethics rubric" to assist future research teams in developing high-quality and ethical research projects at the agency. The rubric should integrate APA guidelines, other pertinent information contained in the agency's code of conduct, and general principles involved in working ethically and sensitively with the clients represented at the site. Provide a summary for future students of the ethical, cultural, and civic issues that have surfaced as a result of your work on this project, or that might occur in the future.
	Evaluation: Now that the data collection is concluded, assess how well your research team, the course instructor, and the community partners worked together to ensure that the APA and refugee agency's ethical standards were upheld. Were there any aspects of the study's design, methodology, or execution that you would change to improve its standards if you were to repeat the study? Why or why not? Where your methods culturally sensitive? Why or why not? How is each of these an ethical issue? To whom was the research beneficial? Evaluate the costs and benefits for each party in the research, including you. Was the research conducted in an inclusive manner? How could it have been improved by including others who were not included? How has your work on this project influenced how you might approach future projects that are similar? In what ways do you care about the research results and their implications for the organization, clients, policy, cultural issues, and community issues?
DEAL/articulate learning	As a result of completing this reflection, - I learned that . . . - I learned this when . . . - This learning matters because . . . - In light of this learning, in the future I will . . .

Note. APA = American Psychological Association; DEAL = describe, examine, and articulate learning model for critical reflection (Ash & Clayton, 2004, 2009a, 2009b; Jameson, Clayton, & Bringle, 2008).

factors (e.g., consideration of projects that fit the skills of the students; time frame; understanding of respective roles, expectations, and responsibilities), instructors may need to lay some of this groundwork with their community partners prior to the beginning of the semester. Service learning activities could be addressed sequentially across semesters that a course is offered (e.g., the first semester includes interviews to develop the research questions, the next semester the assessment procedures are developed and piloted, then full scale data collection and follow-up research are undertaken). If there are multiple research questions or if the research question is complex and multifaceted, it may be helpful for students to work in teams to make the project more efficient and manageable. Teamwork in a capstone research project connects with Goal 5 (Professional Development). As students work together in teams, they develop collaborative abilities and learn to more effectively self-regulate, becoming persons with the attributes of adaptableness, responsibility, sensitivity, and conscientiousness.

Reviewing the Literature

Next, students review the scientific literature in psychology and related fields to locate, critically evaluate, and summarize the extant research. This stage is aligned with APA (2013) Goal 1 (Knowledge Base in Psychology). Students must consider and evaluate relevant theoretical frameworks and determine which psychological principles apply to real-world social issues (critical thinking, social responsibility, different levels of analysis, application, sociocultural issues). They could also conduct asset-based community assessment (Kretzmann & McKnight, 1993) of the resources that are available to immigrant groups and what unmet needs there are in the community.

Designing the Study

In collaboration with the community partner, students select an appropriate quantitative or qualitative research design and high quality (e.g., reliable, valid) measures. Instructor guidance is particularly critical at this stage to ensure that the design is suitable to address the research questions and that ethical considerations such as autonomy, beneficence, and justice are taken into account. Qualitative methods may be used to shape the research project, and standardized assessments may have to be adapted or developed to fit the community partner's research questions and contextual elements (e.g., language skills).

As with the identification of research questions, the design stage relates most clearly to APA (2013) Goal 2. To succeed, students must have the attributes of being systematic, precise, and careful. Ongoing collaboration with program staff is critical, including obtaining their approval of the final study design, which should be conducted in accordance with APA's (2010) ethical guidelines for research. Depending on the situation, consulting with an organization's clients can also be a useful component of the study's design phase and can make the research more participatory and inclusive (see Chapter 2). For an introductory research methods course, the first three steps of this process may be the focus of the service learning project. The instructor's research team or other researchers could follow up with the remainder of the steps. Conversely, in situations in which the instructor and community partner have completed these initial steps prior to the beginning of the semester, students may begin participation at later stages.

Gaining Institutional Review Board Approval

Next, instructor and students must obtain institutional review board (IRB) approval. At many colleges and universities, IRB review can be done swiftly (i.e., 1–2 weeks) for projects that qualify as "exempt" from review or that are in the "expedited" review category. If rapid review is not possible or if a project requires full IRB review, the project may have to be submitted and approved prior to the start of the course. In this instance, capstone students would not participate in designing the study, but they could still review the literature (Step 2) and evaluate and document the reliability and validity of the selected or developed measurement instruments (Step 3). Students and community partners who will engage in data collection should complete the Collaborative Institutional Training Initiative modules (Collaborative Institutional Training Initiative Program, 2014) or an equivalent. This portion of the research project is most clearly aligned with APA (2013) Goal 3 (Ethical and Social Responsibility in a Diverse World). Student attributes developed by participation in IRB-related activities include being ethical, beneficent, moral, and rigorous.

Conducting the Study

Students (and possibly staff and clients) conduct the proposed study and collect data, working respectfully with the organization's staff and clients under instructor and program staff supervision. APA (2013) Goal 5 is central because students must comport themselves with a high level of competence and professionalism to execute a research project in the community. Students achieving this goal demonstrate the attributes of dependability, efficiency, responsibility, time-management capability, and preparedness. Their interactions with participants and community partners should display tolerance, respect, and trustworthiness, characteristics closely linked to Goal 3. Effective communication skills are also critical, which align with Goal 4 (Communication). While gathering data, students practice interacting sensitively with diverse persons, which requires careful listening and sometimes involves decoding covert messages. Communication is influenced by culture and subculture, so students have to be flexible and attentive as they consider multiple perspectives.

Analyzing Data and Summarizing Findings

If quantitative data are collected, students will select appropriate statistical analyses and analyze the data under the instructor's mentorship. In the case of qualitative data, the community partner may have greater involvement in the analysis, given the interpretive nature of the analysis and the importance of cross checking interpretations. Students will then create a presentation of the results in a professional, accessible, and usable format to the community partner and possibly others. This might be in the form of oral and/or written products. The comprehensible and precise presentation of results to different audiences is central to APA (2013) Goal 4 (Communication). Results can also be reported in an APA-style manuscript and poster or oral presentation for purposes of the course. Being able to craft effective communications that are tailored to different audiences is a valuable skill (see APA learning outcomes 4.1 and 4.2).

As in earlier stages, the community partners are important for furthering student learning, because program staff and clients can provide feedback to students on the study's process, outcomes, meaningfulness, and usefulness from their point of view. The community partner can communicate how the results might be used to implement organizational changes or for other purposes that benefit the organization and its clients (e.g., grant applications advocacy). Receiving constructively critical feedback from community partners and reflection structured by the DEAL model (see Chapter 3) can contribute to students' academic, civic, and personal growth. Healthy communication lines between instructor, students, and community partners allow for continued relationships and the potential for future collaborations beyond the research with students. When a project is structured with a deeper level of commitment to community partners and well-structured reflection on academic, civic, and personal objectives, it will develop greater levels of civic understanding and civic mindedness among students as well as other constituencies (Steinberg, Hatcher, & Bringle, 2011; see also Chapter 1, this volume).

CONCLUSION

Many psychology students approach scientific methods courses reluctantly, with disinterest, apprehension, or even anxiety. Service learning is recommended as an effective way to overcome these barriers and to motivate them to learn core methodological content within the major. Service learning integrates community involvement with scientific methods in a way that increases interest and stimulates student engagement with course concepts. Also, student anxiety about statistics and methods is reduced because material that can otherwise seem technical and foreign is familiarized by applying it to real-world social situations. In addition to being a high-impact pedagogy, service learning is an essential tool for instructors seeking to develop psychologically literate citizens who continue to contribute to their communities as curious, rigorous, ethical, and civic-minded graduates.

10

Future Directions: Incorporating Service Learning in Learning Communities, Interdisciplinary Courses, Online Courses, Civic Internships, and Study Abroad

Earlier chapters in Part II illustrated how service learning pedagogy can enhance academic learning, civic learning, and personal growth in specific courses throughout the psychology curriculum. This chapter discusses how service learning can enhance learning communities, interdisciplinary courses, online courses, civic internships, and study abroad. Like other psychology courses, service learning can contribute to all five learning goals and associated personal attributes from the American Psychological Association's *APA Guidelines for the Undergraduate Psychology Major* (Version 2.0; APA, 2013; see Appendixes A and B, this volume) in these courses, which are likely to become increasingly common in the undergraduate curriculum.

http://dx.doi.org/10.1037/14803-011
Service Learning in Psychology: Enhancing Undergraduate Education for the Public Good, by R. G. Bringle, R. N. Reeb, M. A. Brown, and A. I. Ruiz
Copyright © 2016 by the American Psychological Association. All rights reserved.

LEARNING COMMUNITIES AND SERVICE LEARNING

Learning communities date back to the 1920s with the advent of the Experimental College Program at the University of Wisconsin (B. L. Smith, 2001, 2003). A variation surfaced in the 1960s, and the contemporary version emerged in the 1980s. A goal of learning communities is to "strengthen the social and intellectual connections between students [to] build a *sense of community* among participants" (Zhao & Kuh, 2004, p. 116; see also Gabelnick, MacGregor, Matthews, & Smith, 1990). A *sense of community* is defined as "a feeling that members have of belonging, a feeling that members matter to one another and to the group, and a shared faith that members' needs will be met through their commitment to be together" (McMillan & Chavis, 1986, p. 9).

There are four types of learning communities (Lenning & Ebbers, 1999; Zhao & Kuh, 2004). First, *curricular learning communities* are "made up of students co-enrolled in two or more courses (often from different disciplines) ... linked by a common theme" (Zhao & Kuh, 2004, p. 116). This type is ideal for interdisciplinary service learning projects in which students from various disciplines address different aspects of a community issue in complementary ways and learn from one another through interdisciplinary reflection exercises.

Second, *classroom learning communities* "treat the classroom as the locus of community-building by featuring cooperative learning techniques and group process learning activities as integrating pedagogical approaches" (Zhao & Kuh, 2004, p. 116). Service learning can enhance this type of learning community because it emphasizes collaboration among students, instructors, and community partners, while also using structured reflection to connect course content with community-building activities (Eyler & Giles, 1999).

Third, *residential learning communities* "organize on-campus living arrangements so that students taking two or more common courses live in close physical proximity, which increases the opportunities for out-of-classroom interactions and ... learning opportunities" (Zhao & Kuh, 2004, p. 116). Service learning can provide a residential learning community with out-of-classroom (community) activities and opportunities to reflect on connections between course content and experiential work within the student cohort.

Fourth, *student-type learning communities* are "designed for targeted groups, such as academically unprepared students, historically underrepresented students, honors students, students with disabilities, or students with similar academic interests, such as women in ... engineering" (Zhao & Kuh, 2004, p. 116). Service learning can provide students with community activities that reflect shared interests (e.g., students in a psychology honors course develop a project on eating disorders for campus publications and events).

Little research has examined the benefits of incorporating service learning in learning communities. For residential learning communities, which have received the most attention, research has suggested that "students residing in living-learning communities, in contrast to students living in traditional university housing, were less likely to leave the university, had better academic skills, broader social networks, and higher rates of campus involvement" (Petracchi, Weaver, Engel, Kolivoski, & Das, 2010, p. 254; see also Lichtenstein, 2005). Petracchi et al. (2010) also found that a residential learning community that included service learning enhanced students' understanding and appreciation of the urban community, though results are viewed with caution because of a lack of control or comparison group. Future research is needed to determine (a) the effects of using service learning in learning communities on students' academic learning, civic learning, and personal growth and (b) whether certain variables (e.g., sense of community) mediate outcomes (see Chapter 13, this volume).

INTERDISCIPLINARY COURSES AND SERVICE LEARNING: TOWARD TRANSDISCIPLINARITY

According to Tress, Tress, and Fry (2006), *interdisciplinary* involves "several academic disciplines in a way that forces them to cross subject boundaries to ... solve a common ... goal" (p. 17) and *transdisciplinary* involves projects that "integrate ... different disciplines and *non-academic participants* [emphasis added] ... to [address] a common goal" (p. 17). The incorporation of service learning into an interdisciplinary course makes it transdisciplinary, which yields benefits (e.g., multiple perspectives beyond academic ones, improved social accountability, quality control).

Reviews of conceptual models to inform and guide interdisciplinary service learning courses (and engaged scholarship; Reeb, Snow, et al., 2014; Stoecker, Beckman, & Min, 2010) have concluded that a model should (a) conceptualize service learning activities from multiple disciplines at different levels of analysis (e.g., individual, family, sociocultural, community), (b) explain how multiple systems operate and interact, (c) guide project coordination so that work in multiple systems is complementary in addressing a community issue, (d) include multiple perspectives in reflection activities, and (e) conceptualize project modifications (e.g., because of economic changes) and expanding outcomes over time (see model in Reeb & Folger, 2013).

Reeb, Glendening, Farmer, Snow, and Elvers (2014) described a transdisciplinary service learning course, Engaged Scholarship for Homelessness, in which students across disciplines assist faculty, graduate students, and community partners with an ongoing research project that implements behavioral activation (Hopko, Lejuez, Ruggiero, & Eifert, 2003) in a homeless shelter. Activities are designed to enhance (a) self-sufficiency, (b) coping, and (c) shelter climate (previously a prison). Psychology majors may assist with stress management, premed majors may assist in health risk prevention, education majors may assist with general equivalency diploma training, sociology majors may assist in addressing social stigma, and social work students may assist in connecting the shelter to resources. Shelter activities are integrated into a comprehensive approach designed to improve the likelihood that guests will obtain (and retain) employment and housing. Students engage in structured reflection on the complementarity of activities across disciplines. In this ongoing participatory community action research project (Reeb et al., 2014; Reeb, Farmer, Glendening, & Kinsey, 2014; Reeb, Glendening, Farmer, & Kinsey, 2014), other service learning strategies, such as a one-credit service learning option for students (across disciplines) and continuous involvement of some students (across semesters and courses), support sustainability. Using a mix of research designs (see Chapter 13), student outcomes (e.g., community service self-efficacy, myths about homelessness) and community outcomes (e.g., housing and employment of guests, shelter social climate) have been studied.

ONLINE COURSES

Online service learning is growing, but there is a "scarcity of literature" on the topic (Waldner, McGorry, & Widener, 2012, p. 132). Waldner et al. (2012) provided the following rationale for online service learning initiatives: "Students are increasingly pursuing their education online, yet few are exposed to service learning in their online coursework. To remain relevant, service learning must also go online" (p. 123). Furthermore, service learning has the potential of contributing to online education, such as assisting in overcoming a sense of isolation that students may encounter in online education. In an online service learning course, at least some aspect of the instruction, reflection, or service takes place online (Guthrie & McCracken, 2010; Jacoby, 2014; Strait & Sauer, 2004; Waldner et al., 2012). Most existing online service learning courses are hybrids, representing some blend of online, campus, and/or community components.

Waldner et al. (2012) identified four types of online service learning and illustrated them with numerous examples. In *Type I (hybrid) online service learning*, "the class is conducted fully online and the service is conducted on site [e.g., community agency]" (p. 134), with the reflection online (e.g., interactive blogs). Students may (a) work at the same agency or similar agencies in different communities (domestic or international), (b) select a site from a list of approved agencies, or (c) arrange a service site according to criteria. In *Type II (hybrid) online service learning*, "the course is conducted on site [i.e., on campus] and the service is conducted fully online, usually with building online resources as the service component" (p. 135), such as compiling a collection of online resources for an agency. As opposed to direct service, a Type II online service component could be indirect service, advocacy, or research (Chapter 3 defines the different types of service learning). According to this definition of Type II, reflection would be on campus. In *Type III (hybrid) online service learning,* "instruction may be both on site [i.e., on campus] and online, as may the service component" (p. 135). In these hybrid types, reflection may involve some combination of online, campus, and/or community exercises. Finally, in *Type IV (extreme e-service learning),* "both the course and service are conducted online" (p. 137).

Though extreme e-service learning is viewed as an "unstudied practice" (Jacoby, 2014, p. 277), there is preliminary evidence of its efficacy. In a study comparing regular service learning classes with extreme e-service learning courses, McGorry (2014) found no significant differences on a postsemester survey assessing students' perception of practical skills, interpersonal skills, citizenship, and personal responsibility. The relative efficacy of the other types of online service learning is unknown. Chapter 13 reviews research designs that are helpful in examining the nature and outcomes of online service learning courses.

Potential benefits of online service learning include liberating service learning from geographical constraints, enhancing opportunities for service collaborations across locations and institutions, and allowing busy students to pursue service opportunities on their own schedule. Potential limitations include the need for technological training, the gap in technology between campus and service site, the difficulty for a faculty member to directly monitor the service, the difficulty for a faculty member to maintain direct relationships with community partners, the loss of service learning benefits that depend on face-to-face interactions, and the loss of sense of place or belonging, which may be "a precursor to engaging in action to care for localities and their inhabitants" (M. G. Sandy & Franco, 2014, p. 201; see also Jacoby, 2014; Waldner et al., 2012). Regarding the potential loss of sense of place, M. G. Sandy and Franco (2014) recommended collaborative mapping technologies (e.g., Google My Maps, WikiMapia, Ushahidi, or Crowdmap) to "cultivate a virtual sense of geographic place" (p. 201), which may facilitate perceptions of connectivity to a distant community or enhance asset-based community development initiatives (see Introduction, this volume). As noted by Jacoby (2014; see also Briggs, 2013), other examples of technologies with strong potential for online service learning include electronic portfolios, digital badges, gaming, learning analytics, open content, blogging, and Skype. As with all service learning, civic learning outcomes should be included in the course design and assessment.

CIVIC INTERNSHIPS

The purpose of an undergraduate internship is to "engage students in planned, educationally-related work and learning experiences that integrate knowledge and theory with practical application and skill development in a professional setting" (Council for the Advancement of Standards in Higher Education, 2006, p. 230). Academic credit is for the demonstrated learning, not for completing the activity. There should be clearly articulated learning objectives and regular reflection exercises (e.g., written assignments, group discussions, discussions with supervisors, peer-led discussions) that connect community activities to psychological theories and research in ways that enhance learning and skills. Students should examine critical incidents, issues, or challenges at the site and determine what the psychological literature has to offer to analysis, perspective, or resolution. Through structured assessment, students should demonstrate learning from the internship.

A well-designed internship can enhance metacognitive skills such as seeking information from resources (e.g., psychological literature), answering questions, seeking advice, obtaining guidance for circumstances encountered at the site, thinking critically, and developing "soft skills" (e.g., interpersonal skills). Unfortunately, not all internships are designed and implemented to incorporate all qualities of good experiential education: community activities, course material, regular structured reflection to generate and capture learning, and assessment of learning.

A *civic internship* involves all the attributes of a good internship and adds a civic learning component. The civic component can be enhanced through the nature of the community setting (e.g., nonprofit sector), the activities (e.g., work related to a social issue), the course materials connected to experiential work (e.g., readings from the psychological literature related to a social issue or special population), the nature of reflection prompts (e.g., civic problem solving), and assessment (i.e., civic learning goals that provide a basis for assessing learning).

INTERNATIONAL SERVICE LEARNING

Bringle, Hatcher, and Jones (2011) viewed *international service learning* (ISL) as the triple intersection of (a) service learning, (b) study abroad, and (c) international education. There is overlap between international education and study abroad, but the terms are not synonymous. Often, international education occurs in American classrooms (e.g., study of culture, language, history, politics) with no study abroad. Furthermore, study abroad does not necessarily include international education. Hovey and Weinberg (2009) distinguished "low-road" from "high-road" study abroad programs. *Low-road programs* provide superficial exposure to a host region—students "get the American college experience in a different time zone" (p. 36). In contrast, *high-road programs* emphasize international education—the experience is designed to "ensure deep cultural and linguistic immersion" and to "understand and respect local customs" (p. 37).

Service learning brings structured reflection to study abroad and a civic component to students' learning experiences and outcomes (Bringle, Hatcher, & Jones, 2011). ISL immerses students in local communities in ways that may not occur in traditional study abroad. Structured reflection (often absent in study abroad) can enhance critical thinking, personal growth, global civic development, and motivation or self-efficacy for service. ISL provides an experiential component that enables students to "practice, apply, test, evaluate, and criticize course content in ways that cannot occur in the classroom" (Bringle, Hatcher, & Jones, 2011, p. 12), whereas study abroad and international education "broadens the perspective of a service learning course and provides opportunities to compare and contrast American and international perspectives on course content and civic education issues" (pp. 12–13). Ruiz, Warchal, Chapdelaine, and Wells (2011) reviewed ethical issues, safety procedures, and risks and benefits for ISL. Wells, Warchal, Ruiz, and Chapdelaine (2011) also provided "Ethical Issues for Research on International Service Learning."

Any service learning course in Part II could be developed with international partners to augment learning objectives and develop global citizenship. International documents could be consulted as domestic and international partners plan, design, implement, and assess ISL courses. The International Bill of Human Rights includes the Universal Declaration of Human Rights (United Nations General Assembly, 1948); the International Covenant on Civil and Political Rights (United Nations Human Rights, 2014a); and the International Covenant on Economic, Social, and Cultural Rights (United Nations Human Rights, 2014b). The Millennium Development Goals (MDGs; United Nations General Assembly, 2000) include eight goals that United Nations member states are committed to pursuing: (a) eradicating extreme poverty and hunger; (b) achieving universal primary education; (c) promoting gender equality and empowering women; (d) reducing child mortality; (e) improving maternal health; (f) combating HIV/AIDS, malaria, and other diseases; (g) ensuring environmental sustainability; and (h) developing a global partnership for development. MDGs are connected to the APA Public Interest Directorate (e.g., violence against women; see Exhibit 1.1, this volume). Structured reflection could (a) identify themes across documents, (b) relate course content and service to themes, (c) consider implications of international documents for the APA Public Interest Directorate, or (d) relate documents to readings on advocacy service learning (Mitchell, 2008), which explores social justice issues, systemic analysis of public policy, and social change initiatives (Chapters 1 and 2, this volume).

ISL is a powerful way to increase student immersion, consider multiple perspectives (e.g., national, ethnic, economic, sociocultural), develop personal skills, and engage students with diverse populations. "We expect that . . . research will demonstrate an intensification effect—that ISL will have the capacity to intensify any previously documented outcome from study abroad, service learning, or international education in isolation" (Bringle & Hatcher, 2011, p. 22). Kiely (2004) found transformational changes in ISL students on six dimensions: political (e.g., demonstrating social responsibility at local and global levels), moral (e.g., showing mutual respect), intellectual (e.g., questioning assumptions), cultural (e.g., reconsidering dominant U.S. culture), personal (e.g., reconsidering career plans), and spiritual (e.g., examining purpose in life). Niehaus and Crain (2013) found that, relative to students in domestic service learning, ISL students participated more in orientations and reflection, engaged more with community members, reported learning more from community members (and host staff), and reported a higher intensity of experiences.

CONCLUSION

The pedagogical approaches discussed in this chapter encourage the development of innovative courses and facilitate collaboration within psychology, across disciplines, and between campus and community partners (domestic and/or international). When service learning is integrated into these pedagogical approaches, it will enhance the pursuit of APA's (2013; see Appendixes A and B, this volume) Goal 1, Knowledge Base in Psychology (e.g., "Describe applications of psychology," p. 19), and associated personal attributes (e.g., open mindedness); Goal 2, Scientific Inquiry and Critical Thinking (e.g., "Incorporate sociocultural factors in scientific inquiry," p. 22), and related personal traits (e.g., creativity); Goal 3, Ethical and Social Responsibility in a Diverse World (e.g., "Adopt values that build community," p. 27) and related personal attributes (e.g., community involvement); Goal 4, Communication (e.g., "Interact effectively with others," p. 31) and related personal attributes (e.g., respectfulness); and Goal 5, Professional Development (e.g., "Enhance teamwork," p. 35) and related attributes (e.g., being collaborative).

THREE

FACULTY ENGAGEMENT

11

Faculty Development for Service Learning

Many faculty members are unfamiliar with service learning as a pedagogy (e.g., Abes, Jackson, & Jones, 2002). This chapter focuses on faculty development activities and programs to support the development, implementation, and improvement of service learning courses. In addition, it describes what attracts instructors to design and implement service learning and the characteristics of service learning practitioners. Concrete strategies for faculty recruitment and development are presented with suggestions for tailoring activities to different stages of professional careers. Finally, the role that service learning as engaged scholarship can assume in tenure and promotion documentation is discussed.

Instructors can follow several pathways to integrate service learning into their courses (Bringle, 2011). Some are drawn to service learning because they understand how community service can enrich students' learning. Sometimes this is motivated by a passion the faculty member has

http://dx.doi.org/10.1037/14803-012
Service Learning in Psychology: Enhancing Undergraduate Education for the Public Good, by R. G. Bringle, R. N. Reeb, M. A. Brown, and A. I. Ruiz
Copyright © 2016 by the American Psychological Association. All rights reserved.

for a particular social issue. Other instructors engage in professional service with community partners and then develop service learning courses because they understand how students and community can contribute to and benefit from the community service. Still other instructors become engaged in community-based research, and this serves as the precipitator for engaging students and enriching courses with community service activities. When Welch (2006) asked instructors to reflect on their practice, many were unable to isolate their political and moral reasons for using service learning from their professional and personal sense of self, and they reported factors similar to those that motivate students' civic engagement: political, moral, spiritual, and personal factors.

Related to the reasons that motivate instructors to implement service learning, instructors reported that "they derive satisfaction from service learning's effectiveness as a way to present disciplinary content material, enhancement of critical thinking, and relevance to course material" (Hesser, 1995, p. 34). Service learning can instill the value of community service, citizenship, and diversity; connect theory and practice; clarify connections between learning goals and assessment; and improve teaching outcomes (McKay & Rozee, 2004). Other benefits include developing or strengthening relationships with communities, other instructors, campus staff, and administrators; getting recognition from peers; receiving support from campus staff and community partners; and integrating engaged teaching, research, and service (McKay & Rozee, 2004; Rice & Stacey, 1997).

Engaged instructors understand the benefits of service learning and are aware that service learning is a counternormative pedagogy to many traditional approaches used in higher education (Checkoway, 2013; Clayton & Ash, 2004; Howard, 1998; Jameson, Clayton, Jaeger, & Bringle, 2012). This counternormative nature includes the teaching and learning process (e.g., collaborative, focus on process and outcomes), faculty roles (e.g., facilitator rather than expert), student roles (e.g., active rather than passive, reflection generates and captures learning), the roles of others as educators (e.g., community partners, residents), how learning takes place (e.g., on and off campus, through reflection rather than from the instructor), and criteria of learning (e.g., broadly defined in the academic, civic, and personal domains; Clayton & Ash, 2004). Each of these attributes is presumed to create a tension not only for students but also for faculty because of the entrenched nature of teaching traditions within higher education. Understanding what motivates and deters instructors who implement service learning will assist department chairs, faculty leaders, and directors and staff of development programs to create or further develop faculty programs that will be most beneficial for their particular institutional context (Chism, Palmer, & Price, 2013).

FACULTY CHARACTERISTICS

Instructors who implement service learning courses have demonstrated some unique characteristics, distinct from those who do not adopt this pedagogy. Since 1995, the annual Higher Education Research Institute Faculty Survey has consistently found that most instructors teaching service learning courses were women (Astin et al., 2006; DeAngelo et al., 2009; Demb & Wade, 2012; Hurtado, Eagan, Pryor, Whang, & Tran, 2012), who were non-White (Demb & Wade, 2012), with a humanistic focus and constructivist epistemology (Checkoway, 2013), and who were involved in community-centered disciplines (e.g., social sciences, education, the health professions, social work). The rate for each discipline varied widely (Abes et al., 2002), with over 20% of instructors in social sciences reporting that they teach a service learning course (Astin et al., 2006). Concerning faculty rank and tenure, Demb and Wade (2012) noted,

> Some research suggests strongly that commitment to service is highest in faculty members with less status, or junior faculty (Antonio, Astin, & Cress, 2000; Baez, 2000; O'Meara, 2002) ... other studies ... [suggest] that if not already currently involved in service learning, junior faculty and non-tenured faculty were the least likely to begin participation (Abes et al., 2002). Yet others argue that the faculty members who personally value service focus on it after receiving tenure ... (Holland, 1999; Jaeger & Thornton, 2006). (p. 341)

Estimates of the number of instructors teaching service learning courses varies from 7% of instructors (Campus Compact, 2013) to 18% of instructors in the Higher Education Research Institute survey 2010–2011. Because of the low number of instructors teaching service learning courses, faculty development programs are important means for increasing participation.

RECRUITMENT STRATEGIES

To encourage instructors to adopt service learning, department chairs and faculty development directors and staff should consider different factors that motivate instructors, what they perceive are the benefits or obstacles of service learning, and then use this information to create a recruitment plan. Instructors have been described in different ways on the basis of how they engage with innovative pedagogy (innovators, early adopters, early majority, late majority, and laggards; McKay & Rozee, 2004), their attitude toward service learning ("already doing it, curious, indifferent, or hostile," Bringle, as cited in Conley, 2000, para. 13), or where they fall on a continuum from commitment to resistance (Clayton & O'Steen, 2010). Recruitment strategies within a psychology department can begin with determining the topography of interest across faculty and then tailoring strategies to improve attitudes toward service learning, even if everyone does not participate.

One strategy is to demonstrate the value of service learning and its benefits, which should enhance the chances of influencing some of those innovators or curious faculty, particularly those who are student-oriented and teaching-oriented in their professional interests. Faculty members have been found to be motivated to participate in service learning because of their interest in student learning outcomes (Abes et al., 2002). Other instructors may be motivated by a scientist–practitioner model that integrates research, teaching, and community work. On the basis of a review of 2 decades of research on service learning faculty, O'Meara and Niehaus (2009) identified the following factors as being related to faculty interest: demographics, identity and life experiences, epistemology and personal goals, institutional contexts, disciplinary and department contexts, and instructors' relationships with community partners.

Another recruitment strategy is to address the concerns that keep instructors from implementing service learning. Hou (2010) found that instructors who adopt service learning perceive higher benefits at the classroom and community level, and instructors who do not use service learning expect barriers at the classroom level. By providing concrete solutions to the specific concerns, the chairs and staff are able to demonstrate the commitment of the department (or institution) to support service learning. For instructors who identify barriers, three issues seem most salient: time constraints, negative course evaluations, and logistical issues (McKay & Rozee, 2004; see also Chapter 12, this volume). Other instructors have reported that what keeps them from using service learning is lack of knowledge of the pedagogy (Abes et al., 2002; Banerjee & Hausafus, 2007; Harwood et al., 2005).

It takes time and commitment to design a service learning course and offer it the first time (Conley, 2000). Faculty can benefit from assistance with course development from experienced service learning instructors and campus staff. Partnerships with community organizations are essential to good course design. These have to be established during course design to ensure that students' service activities are aligned not only with the course's learning objectives but also with community goals. Selecting goals that meet the academic standards of the course and that benefit community constituencies requires informed decisions, collaboration with community partners, and use of principles of good practice for service learning (Heffernan, 2001; Howard, 1998; Jacoby, 2014). Appropriate attention has to be given to students' preparation (Chapdelaine, Ruiz, Warchal, & Wells, 2005) and support for the community service activities.

When a service learning course is designed, classroom activities must be coordinated with out-of-class experiences (see Chapter 3). Decisions have to be made on reflection and assessment that connect the community service activities to the course content, and choices have to be made about different course formats (e.g., option in a course, required of all students, fourth credit option). Faculty may become more familiar with service learning as a pedagogy through workshops, speaker series, team teaching with an experienced instructor, and participating in communities of practice, which also can lead to research and publications on service learning (Abes et al., 2002; Bringle, Hatcher, & Clayton, 2006; Chism et al.,

2013). Seed grants, faculty release time, teaching assistants, and campus resources to help with logistics can also mitigate some of challenges to implementing service learning courses (Jacoby, 2014).

Additional strategies should be considered for new instructors who are looking for connections on a new campus, those who may be facing review and are interested in exploring engaged scholarship, or faculty members who have a few years to build their dossier (Clayton & O'Steen, 2010). For these groups, experienced service learning instructors can serve as examples, communicate their practice with these colleagues, give realistic accounts of conducting service learning courses, and serve as mentors to educate and support them (Abes et al., 2002; McKay & Rozee, 2004). Another recruitment strategy that also works to further develop and support faculty is to form a community of practice, a core group of instructors who learn about and implement the pedagogy at the same time (McKay & Rozee, 2004; Rice & Stacey, 1997). They can provide each other with support and they can benefit from a range of departmental and campus resources to enhance a course with community service activities (see Chapter 12, this volume, for other departmental strategies).

FACULTY DEVELOPMENT PROGRAMS

After recruiting instructors, there should be support in place to maintain and improve service learning courses. The recommendations for faculty development for service learning are based on faculty development models that focus on individual instructors' characteristics and motivations, and teaching and learning theories. The recommendations for faculty development also incorporate a developmental approach that starts at the doctoral level and differentiates the tasks for various stages of faculty careers.

Graduate Training

Support for faculty development should start at the doctoral level by preparing future faculty for work on civically engaged teaching, research, and professional service (Bringle, Hatcher, Jones, & Plater, 2006; Chism et al.,

2013; P. D. Nelson, 2004; Reich & Nelson, 2010; Sandmann, Saltmarsh, & O'Meara, 2008). Graduate programs in psychology typically emphasize science and professional roles (Buskist & Irons, 2006; P. D. Nelson, 2004), without attention to the civic aspects of education and its goals (see Chapter 1, this volume). The American Psychological Association (APA) Board of Educational Affairs created awards to stimulate innovative practices in graduate departments and small grants for workshops and conferences to address challenges faced by those departments. P. D. Nelson (2004) promoted these initiatives with the expectation that they would incorporate the scholarship of engagement. The "Next Generation Engagement Project" is directed at developing engaged scholars among undergraduate students, graduate students, and early career faculty (Saltmarsh, Zlotkowski, & Horowitz, 2010).

Faculty Programs

Faculty development program goals should be tailored to the characteristics of the individuals they plan to support. Understanding typical characteristics of service learning instructors, as described earlier, can refine the goals and strategies of faculty development programs (e.g., improving quality, expanding engaged work). For instance, support programs for novices may include opportunities for teaching service learning courses under the guidance of an experienced service learning instructor (or instructors) or providing community service to develop skills and become familiar with local organizations (Blanchard, Strauss, & Webb, 2012).

Faculty members become focused on different tasks at different stages of their professional careers. Although there is overlap between the activities accomplished at each professional development stage, O'Meara (2003) suggested different tasks for novice to late career faculty. Novice faculty should pay attention to the mission of the institution and the expectations of the department (see Chapter 12, this volume). These faculty are generally concerned about workload, support, and rewards, which should be discussed with the department chair. Beginning career faculty members can consider integrating teaching, research, and service; documenting outcomes; and publishing engaged scholarship. They might also identify a senior faculty mentor or join a faculty community of practice focused on service learning. Mid-career faculty may be more focused on service learning scholarship, grants applications, and becoming mentors to others. Late-career faculty members are in a position to promote institutional changes to support service learning as they continue other professional activities (e.g., writing, mentorship, publishing, engaged research). Recognizing all engaged faculty at any rank with an academic title (e.g., "public scholar," "engaged scholar") would establish the legitimacy of their work.

The format of faculty development programs should also incorporate a conceptual basis from teaching and learning theory. For instance, activities can be based on (a) identifying a need, (b) creating a plan to change practice, (c) implementing the plan, (d) assessing the outcome, and (e) reflecting on implications for future teaching (Chism et al., 2013). Bringle, Hatcher, Jones, et al. (2006), on the basis of Kolb's (1984) theory of experiential learning, suggested strategies that can be based on (a) abstract conceptualizations (e.g., workshops, speaker series), (b) active experimentation (e.g., redesigning a syllabus, writing grants, team teaching), (c) concrete experiences (e.g., providing instructors with community service experiences), and (d) reflective observation (e.g., supporting instructors in professional presentations, scholarship). Faculty development programs can also provide workshops on external funding, highlight instructors who have successfully received funding, and identify faculty to build a community of engaged scholars. And just as important, campus and departmental activities should include a goal for developing an appreciation and understanding of the role of service learning and engaged scholarship among those who will be involved in the evaluation of those who implement service learning; those faculty should understand the characteristics, impact, and value of it, even if they do not use service learning.

Communities of practice support instructors' interactions throughout different stages of faculty development beyond recruitment (Blanchard et al., 2012; Bringle, Games, Ludlum, Osgood, & Osborne, 2000; Harwood et al., 2005; Rice & Stacey, 1997). An evaluation of communities used to assist instructors in implementing innovative pedagogies demonstrated that the

> communities created the conditions for faculty participants to develop their competency with service-learning, gain a better understanding of the extent to which the institution supported the practice, and explore the value of the pedagogy for student growth and their own professional development. (Furco & Moely, 2012, p. 146)

For communities of practice or experienced service learning faculty who want to mentor or conduct workshops, the "Faculty Toolkit for Service Learning in Higher Education" (Seifer & Connors, 2007) is a helpful resource. It contains 10 units, including the definition of service learning, the pursuit of community partnerships, the planning and implementation of a service learning course, and service learning scholarship. Another helpful resource is the book *Service-Learning Essentials: Questions, Answers, and Lessons Learned* (Jacoby, 2014). Key issues regarding the pedagogy should be emphasized (see Introduction and Chapter 3, this volume); for example, service learning is academically grounded, is integrated, and not an add-on; civic learning is an important goal; reflection is a learning strategy; all participants are learners and teachers; and students have to be prepared for such a transformational learning experience (Clayton & O'Steen, 2010). Jameson et al. (2012) found that faculty participation in a 12-month learning community focused on developing civic engagement scholarship programs (i.e., service learning, engaged research) and resulted in evidence of faculty learning of new discoveries regarding community-engaged scholarship competencies.

Institutional and Discipline Support

Institutional resources can also contribute to faculty development (see Chapter 12). Administrative support for service and engagement results in a greater likelihood of instructors' participation in engagement initiatives (Abes et al., 2002; Banerjee & Hausafus, 2007; Bringle & Hatcher, 1996; Demb & Wade, 2012; Driscoll, 2000). For instance, administrators can address obstacles such as time issues by providing faculty with service learning assistants, staff support, merit incentives, and release time to maintain and support service learning. Chapter 12 further addresses how psychology departments can support civically engaged teaching, service, and scholarship.

APA has supported service learning initiatives (see Chapter 12, this volume; APA, 2013; Bringle & Duffy, 1998; Cranney & Dunn, 2011; Halpern, 2010; P. D. Nelson, 2004; Reich & Nelson, 2010); however, there are still some challenges to the place, salience, use, and perceived importance of service learning, both in the curriculum and in faculty roles and rewards. Boyer's (1990, 1996) proposed redefinition of scholarship has been applied to psychology (Buskist, Carlson, Christopher, Prieto, & Smith, 2008; Gurung, Ansburg, Alexander, Lawrence, & Johnson, 2008; Halpern et al., 1998; Halpern & Reich, 1999; Irons & Buskist, 2008). Concerning service, the emphases are on professional service and administration (Mathie et al., 2004), not on civic engagement. Furthermore, the role and position of service learning still warrants elevation within the discipline as a high-impact pedagogy (Kuh, 2008).

TENURE AND PROMOTION

"The future growth and sustainability of service-learning depends to a large extent on the faculty, and the success with which universities are able to support and reward their efforts" (Driscoll, 2000, p. 39). There have been calls for instructors to increase engaged scholarship in general and service learning in particular and for departments and campuses to implement standards and processes to include such scholarship in the promotion and tenure process (Franz, 2011). "Many faculty still resist the rhetoric of civic responsibility in their scholarship because of a concern for 'how it counts' or how community-engaged scholarship aligns with promotion and tenure guidelines within the context of the research imperative" (Moore & Ward, 2008, p. 5).

Many institutions base faculty evaluations and decisions about tenure and promotion on research, teaching, and service. At many institutions and in psychology departments, these three domains receive different weights. Some institutions and psychology departments fail to encompass engaged scholarship in tenure and promotion policies (Boyer, 1990, 1996; Bringle et al., 2000; Bringle, Hatcher, & Clayton, 2006; Checkoway, 2013; Demb & Wade, 2012; Mathie et al., 2004; Moore & Ward, 2008, 2010; O'Meara, 2003, 2005). Those faculty who adopt service learning must be intentional in demonstrating its value in their dossiers (Bringle, Hatcher, & Clayton, 2006; Moore & Ward, 2008). Rice (1996) put forth the goal of the complete and connected scholar, based in part on Boyer's (1990) foundational reexamination of the professoriate. By *complete*, Rice meant balance and integration of faculty work across teaching, research, and service. *Connected* refers to faculty work being connected to others, including those in communities. Helping faculty become complete and connected scholars should be an aspiration that faculty members have for themselves and institutions have for their faculty.

Dossiers can demonstrate the impact of service learning as engaged scholarship through different strategies when emphasizing teaching, service, and research (Bringle, Hatcher, & Clayton, 2006). Typically, dossiers that include service learning should demonstrate how the integration of service learning enhanced student learning and led to positive student outcomes (Chapter 13). Dossiers with an emphasis on professional service should demonstrate how service learning courses benefited the community partners and created, strengthened, and sustained community partnerships and how professional service led to community change. Dossiers concentrating on service learning research should demonstrate products that followed guidelines for scholarship (Diamond & Adams, 1995; Glassick, Huber, & Maeroff, 1997; see also Chapters 2 and 13, this volume).

Part of the picture of institutional and departmental capacity to honor engaged academic work is the ability to evaluate it. Several scholarship criteria have been proposed for engaged scholarship in general and service learning in particular. Glassick et al. (1997) proposed that instructors' work could be evaluated as scholarship on the basis of six criteria: clear goals, adequate preparation, appropriate methods, significant results, effective communication and dissemination, and reflective critique. Diamond and

Adams (1995) identified six criteria for evaluating scholarship, including discipline-related expertise, innovation, replicability, documentation, peer review, and significant impact. Both sets of scholarship criteria offer guidance for psychology departments and their institutions to refine assessment of the scholarship of engagement and service learning. In addition, chairs may consult the National Review Board for the Scholarship of Engagement (Wade & Demb, 2012), which provides a pool of peer reviewers for external review of dossiers containing scholarship of engagement, including service learning.

Several resources are available for planning, creating, and organizing a dossier for tenure and promotion review that support service learning as engaged scholarship. Franz (2011) described recommendations for assembling engaged scholarship dossiers. The *Community-Engaged Scholarship Review, Promotion & Tenure Package* (Jordan, 2007), the *Community-Engaged Scholarship Toolkit* (Calleson, Kauper-Brown, & Seifer, 2005), and the *Research University Engaged Scholarship Toolkit* (Stanton, Connolly, Howard, & Litvak, 2013) can serve as guides for both engaged faculty and review committees.

CONCLUSION

Service learning is a pedagogy that benefits students, individual faculty, departments, and institutions of higher education while promoting the public good. The characteristics of the faculty, the context of the college or university as well as the community will determine the success of the implementation and development of service learning programs. Many programs started with one champion or a group of champions as the facilitators for institutionalizing of service learning (Young, Shinnar, Ackerman, Carruthers, & Young, 2007). "Without the faculty, nothing lasting is likely to happen" (Checkoway, 2013, p. 79). Intentional approaches to faculty recruitment and development are warranted if service learning is to become an expected and pervasive component of the undergraduate psychology curriculum.

12

The Engaged Psychology Department

In his watershed treatise on the professoriate and scholarship, Ernest Boyer (1990) asserted that the aim of education

> is not only to prepare students for productive careers, but also to enable them to live lives of dignity and purpose; not only to generate new knowledge, but to channel that knowledge toward humane ends; not merely to study government, but to help shape a citizenry that can promote the public good. (p. 160)

Educating democratically engaged citizens has a long history (e.g., Dewey, 1899, 1916) and has regained prominence in the broader literature on higher education (Ehrlich, 2000; Fitzgerald & Primavera, 2013; Jacoby et al., 2009; Kezar, Chambers, & Burkhardt, 2005; Peters, 2010; Saltmarsh & Hartley, 2011; Saltmarsh & Zlotkowski, 2011; see also Chapter 1, this volume). Yet without the active commitment of the disciplines and faculty

http://dx.doi.org/10.1037/14803-013
Service Learning in Psychology: Enhancing Undergraduate Education for the Public Good, by R. G. Bringle, R. N. Reeb, M. A. Brown, and A. I. Ruiz
Copyright © 2016 by the American Psychological Association. All rights reserved.

within them, it is difficult to realize the goal of democratic civic engagement in education (Zlotkowski, 1997–2006, 2000).

Within the discipline of psychology, the recommendations of the American Psychological Association's (APA) National Conference on Undergraduate Education included a call for psychology departments to commit themselves to the development of the psychologically literate citizen (Halpern, 2010). McGovern et al. (2010) described the *psychologically literate citizen* as "someone who responds to the call for ethical commitment and social responsibility as a hallmark of his or her lifelong liberal learning" (p. 10). Educating psychologically literate citizens has also gained international recognition as a guiding principle for the discipline (Cranney & Dunn, 2011). This chapter describes the role that psychology departments can play in developing psychologically literate citizens by working on a coherent, systematic, discipline-based approach to civic learning within the undergraduate curriculum. The nature of engaged departments is explored, and suggestions are provided for building departments with engagement integrated into teaching, research, and service (see Introduction). Departments are encouraged to consider how democratic partnerships (i.e., inclusive, participatory, fair; Saltmarsh, Hartley, & Clayton, 2009) with the community can provide the basis for service learning courses as well as engaged research and scholarship and engaged professional service. Finally, a review for how to assess engaged departments is provided.

WHAT IS THE ENGAGED DEPARTMENT, AND WHY IS IT IMPORTANT?

The term *engagement* within higher education is frequently used to refer to active and collaborative teaching and learning. This chapter, however, focuses on planning, implementing, and assessing activities, infrastructure, reward systems, and a culture of norms that enhance civic engagement (i.e., teaching, research, and service in and with communities), with particular emphasis on civically engaged pedagogies (i.e., service learning). Bringle, Hatcher, and Clayton (2006) described *civic engagement* in the following way:

> Civic engagement is a subset of community involvement and is defined by both location as well as process (it occurs not only in

but also with the community). According to this distinction, civic engagement develops partnerships that possess integrity and that emphasize participatory, collaborative, and democratic processes (e.g., design, implementation, assessment) that provide benefits to all constituencies. (p. 258)

This definition emphasizes community assets, democratic processes, collaboration, respect for diverse ways of knowing (see Part I, this volume), and the collective capacity of multiple constituencies as coeducators, cogenerators of knowledge, and coresearchers (Dostilio et al., 2013). *Democratic civic engagement* "seeks the public good *with* the public and not merely *for* the public as a means to facilitating a more active and engaged democracy" (Saltmarsh et al., 2009, p. 9).

Although much good work has been done to encourage civic engagement in higher education at the macrolevel of the institution (e.g., activities to organize university presidents; see Campus Compact, 1999) and at the microlevel (e.g., individual faculty members and courses), the emphasis on engagement is also critical at the mesolevel of departments. Departments are the core academic units that have significant potential to effect change and wield transformative power to help institutions reconnect to their public purposes (Kecskes, 2006; Kecskes, Gelmon, & Spring, 2006). To address the need for greater departmental engagement, Campus Compact published *The Engaged Department Toolkit* (Battistoni, Gelmon, Saltmarsh, Wergin, & Zlotkowski, 2003), and sponsored Engaged Department Institutes, bringing department members together to conduct strategic planning and enhance engagement at the departmental level. Battistoni et al. (2003) described this process as one in which "the emphasis shifts from individual faculty, courses, and curricular redesign to collective faculty culture—changing the culture from one of 'my work' to one of 'our work'" (p. 13). The engaged department shares a common commitment to civic engagement and public scholarship. This includes a shared set of values (e.g., a mission or vision statement, common language, the presence of these values in publications and public messages, presence in the reward structure), a common commitment to community partners (who work with different members of the department across time on a variety of activities and projects), and a comprehensive and strategically planned engaged curriculum.

BUILDING ENGAGED PSYCHOLOGY DEPARTMENTS

Kecskes's (2006) *Engaging Departments* provided case studies of 11 departments that underwent the process toward greater civic engagement. Although none of the featured departments was a psychology department, their accounts demonstrate in each case that change is a multiphase, complex process that requires common components for success, regardless of discipline. Zlotkowski and Saltmarsh (2006) asserted that the success of collective work that aspires to having an engaged department rests on five key factors, to be discussed in turn:

- *Leadership*: Advocacy for faculty initiatives and creation of a supportive environment.
- *Collaboration*: A collaborative faculty culture that emphasizes shared work.
- *Rewards*: Incentives for community-based teaching and scholarship.
- *Infrastructure*: Institutional mechanisms to support faculty in community-based academic work.
- *Curricula*: Civic engagement accepted as core academic work.

Leadership

As Wood (1990) pointed out, "Educational programs . . . need champions. Those champions must be found in the faculty if an innovation is to be profound and long-lasting" (p. 53). Department leaders are important champions who can create a climate in which civic engagement can thrive. Leadership includes department chairs, senior faculty, respected faculty, and faculty in key roles. Recent benchmarking guidelines for program leadership in psychology suggested that "distinguished" (i.e., excellent) department leaders implement community service commitments that broadly engage other faculty and students (Halonen, 2013). Kecskes (2008) provided a series of recommendations for leaders interested in furthering department engagement: (a) take stock of extant civic engagement activities in the department, (b) make time during department meetings to discuss civic engagement, (c) notice and appreciate success by spotlighting excellence in departmental civic engagement activities, (d) recognize and include students as full participants and assets, (e) allocate department resources strategically to support civic engagement, (f) envision and invite expanded roles for community partners, (g) evaluate and document civic engagement activities, and (h) ask the right questions to encourage ongoing conversation about the department's public purposes.

Departmental Collaboration

Wergin (2003) asked, humorously,

> Why is it that when you talk about departmental collaboration people treat it as an oxymoron? Why is it that, even though I wrote "The Collaborative Department" (1994) nearly ten years ago, I continue to be kidded by colleagues who say that it was the only book of pure fantasy ever published by the AAHE? (p. 42)

Wergin identified multiple barriers to departmental collaboration. Faculty individualism is one barrier: Faculty members too often prefer self-guided scholarly pursuits to collective activities. The culture of the profession tends to draw individualists who are attracted to the freedom and flexibility of academic work (Bennett, 1998). Also, since World War II, the lure of federal grant dollars and the basic research that is essential to attain them is not as compatible with engaged scholarship and teaching (Alpert, 1985). Basic research is often conducted in relatively siloed labs, and principal investigators need not necessarily collaborate with other department members or with community members and other constituents to achieve their scholarly aims. A third barrier to collaboration is *mission creep*: "the unending desire to improve the status of the institution by moving up the Carnegie ladder" (Wergin, 2003, p. 43). As departmental and institutional prestige is largely indexed by the ability to garner federal grant dollars and produce publications in top-tier journals, faculty members are rewarded for being ambitious and competitive, more than for being collaborative team players.

These and other barriers to collaboration vary significantly across institutions, and it may be easier to achieve a collaborative departmental culture in smaller departments at teaching-focused institutions and within institutions that value applied and action research in addition to basic research. To encourage more collaborative departments across institutional types, a first step is developing an atmosphere of inquiry, such that faculty members engage in regular reflection on their department's identity and its work and connect their reflection to actions to make changes (Wergin, 2003). Department leaders must emphasize a shared understanding of faculty work (i.e., teaching, service, scholarship), with the premise that faculty work is community property, open to peer collaboration, and reviewed for its public meaning (Walshok, 1999). Collaborative departments also create a shared sense of mission and collective responsibility, starting with identifying the ways in which individual faculty expertise and interests add value to the department and the ways in which the department adds value to the institution. Together, these suggestions focus departments on how their individual members can work effectively toward mutually defined and agreed on goals.

Rewards

An incentive structure is essential to encouraging and supporting department-wide civic engagement in teaching and scholarship. Although a variety of personal factors (e.g., demographics, identity, life experiences, personal goals, politics, values) and social factors (e.g., relationships with community partners; institutional, disciplinary, and departmental contexts) may motivate individual faculty members to pursue engagement activities (O'Meara & Niehaus, 2009; Welch, 2006), without a supportive reward structure, departments will have difficulty stimulating and sustaining programmatic engagement. Incentives include faculty load accommodations for civic engagement activities (e.g., community partnership development) and teaching service learning courses. The time required for these should not be considered "service," but rather should be valued and compensated as part of a faculty member's core professional academic tasks (Bringle, Hatcher, & Clayton, 2006). The legitimacy and value of civically engaged teaching and research must be acknowledged in the promotion and tenure evaluation of faculty members (Boyer, 1990). Rewards also include internal grants for engaged scholarship and internal and external awards for exemplary civic engagement (Chapter 11 has additional ideas on faculty development).

Infrastructure

Infrastructure is another important factor in the success of engaged department initiatives (Zlotkowski & Saltmarsh, 2006). Departmental infrastructure includes staff who aid in partnership development and the logistics of service learning activities and other civic engagement activities. Departments can provide teaching and research assistantships to assist faculty with engaged teaching and research, and seed grants for professional development activities. At many institutions, vital infrastructure is located in a central, campus-wide community engagement and service learning office that serves as a clearinghouse for assistance with community–campus collaboration (e.g., transportation, orientation, reflection, faculty development, partnership development). Academic and Student Affairs may help to support and sustain the work of this central office, and they may also directly assist departments (Kecskes, 2006). Other resources may be available such as chaplains, career centers, sustainability offices, and public relations offices (Jacoby, 2014).

Curricula

There are many excellent resources to support psychology departments in developing psychologically literate students throughout the curriculum. Chapters in Halpern (2010) (a) included recommendations for departments to require a common core in their undergraduate curricula (Dunn et al., 2010), (b) suggested principles for quality undergraduate education in psychology that mandate the creation of a coherent curriculum (Halpern et al., 2010), and (c) reviewed desired outcomes of undergraduate education that have direct curricular implications (Landrum et al., 2010). Furthermore, there are well-articulated benchmarks for assessing the quality of undergraduate psychology programs and their curricula (Dunn, McCarthy, Baker, & Halonen, 2011; Halonen, Dunn, Baker, & McCarthy, 2011). Most recently, the *APA Guidelines for the Undergraduate Psychology Major* (Version 2.0; 2013) described the learning goals to be achieved during a student's undergraduate education.

However, these resources are generally focused on the concept of psychological literacy, with only occasional attention to psychologically literate citizenship (McGovern et al., 2010) or how to achieve it. Departments seeking to develop coherent curricula that incorporate civic engagement can consult Chapter 1 of this volume, which examines the importance of civic learning and its connections to the APA's learning goals for undergraduates. Making service learning pervasive and expected in the psychology curriculum is the most efficacious pathway to developing greater civic engagement within departments (Altman, 1996; Bringle & Duffy, 1998; Chenneville, Toler, & Gaskin-Butler, 2012; Conway, Amel, & Gerwien, 2009; Reich & Nelson, 2010) and helping undergraduate students attain greater breadth and depth in the APA goals. First, enhancing the undergraduate curriculum with service learning is desirable because the curriculum is enduring. Departments of psychology are not static; there is turnover in faculty, staff, students, and community partners. Integrating service learning in the entire undergraduate curriculum is a way of intentionally building engagement into student experiences beyond the interest and commitment of individual faculty members. Second, if a department is not providing high quality, regular service learning courses to students, it is not demonstrating high quality civic engagement, a position supported by the framework of the Carnegie Foundation's Community Engagement Elective Classification (Zuiches, 2008). Third, service learning can spawn additional activities (e.g., service, engaged research, grants). Fourth, service learning across the curriculum provides a basis for a sequenced, developmental approach to learning goals, particularly civic learning goals (e.g., introductory, service courses, major courses, capstone; see Halonen et al., 2011, for more on developmental benchmarking strategies).

ASSESSING ENGAGED DEPARTMENTS

Kecskes (2008, 2009) developed a self-assessment rubric to assist departments in examining their current capacity for community engagement and to help departments identify further opportunities for enhanced engagement. The rubric has six dimensions and several components that make up each dimension (see Table 12.1). In addition, each dimension is divided into four phases of development: awareness building, critical mass building, quality building, and the institutionalization phase. These phases aid departments in locating themselves along a continuum from beginning to advanced on each dimension's components.

Table 12.1
Dimensions and Components of the Creating Community Engaged Departments Rubric

Dimension	Components
I. Mission and culture supporting community engagement	- Mission - Definition of community engaged teaching - Definition of community engaged research - Definition of community engaged service - Climate and culture - Collective self-awareness
II. Faculty support and community engagement	- Faculty knowledge and awareness - Faculty involvement and support - Curricular integration of community engagement - Faculty incentives - Review, promotion, and tenure process integration - Tenure track faculty
III. Community partner and partnership support and community engagement	- Placement and partnership awareness - Mutual understanding and commitment - Community partner voice - Community partner leadership - Community partner access to resources - Community partner incentives and recognition
IV. Student support and community engagement	- Student opportunities - Student awareness - Student incentives and recognition - Student voice, leadership, and departmental governance

(*continues*)

Table 12.1
Dimensions and Components of the Creating Community Engaged Departments Rubric (*Continued*)

Dimension	Components
V. Organizational support for community engagement	• Administrative support • Facilitating entity • Evaluation and assessment • Departmental planning • Faculty recruitment and orientation • Marketing • Dissemination of community engagement results • Budgetary allocation
VI. Leadership support for community engagement	• Department-level leadership • Campus-level leadership from departmental faculty • National-level leadership from departmental faculty

Note. From *Creating Community-Engaged Departments: Self-Assessment Rubric for the Institutionalization of Community Engagement in Academic Departments* (pp. 2–3), by K. Kecskes, 2009. Retrieved from http://www.pdx.edu/sites/www.pdx.edu.cae/files/Engaged%20Department%20RUBRIC%20-%20Kecskes%202009-paginated.pdf. Copyright 2009 by Kevin Kecskes. Reprinted with permission.

CONCLUSION

Psychology departments play a pivotal role in advancing an agenda of civic engagement in undergraduate education. Engaged leadership, improved collaboration, built-in rewards, sound infrastructure, and a coherent curriculum rich in service learning opportunities are key factors that must be attended to for departments to be effective in this role. Working together on a shared civic agenda, departments and community partners serve the public good as they educate current and future generations of democratically engaged, psychologically literate citizens.

13

Assessment, Research, and Scholarship on Service Learning

Innovative pedagogies such as service learning provide opportunities to document the efficacy of their specific attributes and evaluate the generalizability of broad principles of teaching and learning beyond traditional pedagogies. Because service learning expands the domains of learning objectives to include not only academic learning but also civic learning and personal growth, there are many opportunities to conduct assessment and research on the breadth and depth of its impact. In addition, as a hub science (Cacioppo, 2007), enriching the curriculum with community service activities can have an impact on integrative courses (e.g., learning communities composed of multiple courses that are taken by a cohort of students, interdisciplinary courses [Chapter 11], and capstone courses [Chapter 10]). Furthermore, the transdisciplinary nature of the psychology curriculum (McGovern et al., 2010) and research on service learning (Clayton, Bringle, & Hatcher, 2013a, 2013b) suggest that service learning

http://dx.doi.org/10.1037/14803-014
Service Learning in Psychology: Enhancing Undergraduate Education for the Public Good, by R. G. Bringle, R. N. Reeb, M. A. Brown, and A. I. Ruiz
Copyright © 2016 by the American Psychological Association. All rights reserved.

can contribute to the outcomes of postsecondary education that are most significant and that transcend content knowledge: epistemological sophistication, reflective judgment, liberal arts competencies, declines in authoritarianism and dogmatism, principled moral reasoning, and critical thinking (Pascarella & Terenzini, 2005).

Presumably, all instructors gather some formative information (e.g., the types of questions students ask in class, students' confusion over a point in a lecture) and summative information (e.g., exam performance, end-of-semester course evaluations). If this information is not used to modify and improve instruction, they are merely "going through the motions" (Gurung & Schwartz, 2009, pp. 12–13). The motivation of these instructors may be to provide only "good-enough teaching," which is analogous to good-enough mothering (Winnicott, 1953) in that they are motivated just enough to obtain reasonable teaching evaluations and avoid students' complaints to others (e.g., the department chair, other students). Some effort to be responsive to feedback, to be informed about good practice, and to modify and improve instruction is indicative of "sincere teaching" (Gurung & Schwartz, 2009, pp. 13–14). *Scholarly teaching* is a reflective practice that aligns with qualities of good reflection: It connects theory (e.g., of learning) to practice (i.e., design and implementation of instruction), occurs regularly, is structured, results in feedback from others (e.g., students, peers, experts), and provides opportunities for exploring and developing values as part of the teaching process (Bringle & Hatcher, 1999). Scholarly teaching (Huber & Hutchings, 2005) includes effectively incorporating evidence-based best practices and systematically gathering and using evidence about reaching the desired learning outcomes to improve a course. A higher standard is the *scholarship of teaching and learning* (SoTL), which includes empirical research as well as other forms of scholarship. Not only will scientist–educators who engage in SoTL research have the attributes of scholarly teaching but they will also gather evidence that can inform other educators and that can contribute to the generalizable knowledge and understanding of teaching and learning (Bringle, Hatcher, & Clayton, 2006; Huber & Hutchings, 2005). This chapter explores how assessment can provide a basis for scholarly teaching and SoTL research on service learning.

STUDENT ASSESSMENT

Service learning, at its best, should be scholarly teaching both in implementation and assessment. Good assessment of learning depends on aligning learning goals and objectives with course design, implementing the course according to course design, and using appropriate and meaningful measures of learning. Unpredictable circumstances may confound implementation, and service learning courses can be more unpredictable than traditional pedagogies. Formative assessment (e.g., during a course) can be directed toward determining the degree to which implementation is aligned with course design and monitoring mediating variables that are presumed to result in students achieving learning objectives. Summative assessment is focused on the degree to which the intended goals and objectives were met. For some purposes (e.g., providing feedback, giving grades, making changes to a course during the semester or prior to the next offering), this framework may be adequate. However, posttest only designs and pre-, posttest only designs are limited in their ability to make causal statements about why outcomes occurred.

As noted in Chapter 3, the American Psychological Association's *APA Guidelines for the Undergraduate Psychology Major* (Version 2.0; APA, 2013; hereafter referred to as APA Guidelines 2.0) provide goals and indicators that are too broad; instructors must write more specific learning objectives for a selected goal area and outcome that is to be assessed. In addition, having explicit criteria against which student performance will be evaluated will make assessment more meaningful. Chapters in Part II of the present volume provide examples of specific learning objectives, how reflection can be structured using the DEAL (describe, examine, and articulate learning) model for critical reflection (Ash & Clayton, 2004, 2009a, 2009b; Jameson, Clayton, & Bringle, 2008) and Bloom's (1956) taxonomy to generate and assess learning, and how students can then produce written products that generate learning and capture their learning in the academic, civic, and personal domains (Table 3.1, this volume). Furthermore, Bloom's taxonomy provides a basis for giving feedback to students about the level of learning that is represented in their work. The level of expected performance might depend on an instructor's decisions about the salience or depth of different learning objectives within a course or where a course occurs in the overall curriculum (i.e., analysis is expected in lower level courses, synthesis and evaluation in upper level courses).

Types of Evidence

Assessing student outcomes in a service learning course could use solely traditional methods to assess academic learning (e.g., multiple-choice examinations). This might seem defensible because if service learning enhances academic learning, it will do so on a multiple-choice examination. There are at least two problems with using this approach as the sole basis for assessing student outcomes in a service learning course. First, research that compared service learning courses with non–service learning courses (Mpofu, 2007; Strage, 2000; Wurr, 2002) found no differences on measures of factual knowledge, but service learning students were superior on assessments that measured higher order thinking tasks (e.g., analytical essays, case-based assignments). Second, traditional measures of student learning only measure academic learning, to the exclusion of civic learning and personal growth and their combinations (see Figure 3.1). Assessment procedures that measure learning objectives for civic learning and personal growth balance the assessment in a manner consistent with the rationale for having service learning and provide instructors with opportunities to give students feedback on each area of growth.

For some purposes, self-report measures (e.g., scales, rating forms, open response items, interviews, focus groups) can be useful for both formative and summative evaluation (Gelmon, Holland, Driscoll, Spring, & Kerrigan, 2001). Self-report measures assess students' attitudes, behavioral intentions, past behaviors, feelings, or beliefs. Although self-report instruments can be useful (Bringle, Phillips, & Hudson, 2004), they can also be influenced by social desirability response set, inaccuracies, not reflecting processes that determined outcomes, and being based on inaccurate or biased memories (Kolek, 2013; Steinberg, Bringle, & Williams, 2010). Self-assessments of skill, character, and learning may be particularly flawed (Bowman & Seifert, 2011; Dunning, Heath, & Suls, 2004).

Having assessment measures of student performance and evidence from authentic learning situations such as service learning may provide more meaningful data and complement other types of evidence. Performance measures might be written products (e.g., reflection papers written in response to structured prompts; see chapters in Part II), other types of products from the service activities (e.g., accuracy of information contained in products generated for the community organization and clients), and assessment of a student's performance by community partners or peers (Appendix C). These can have clear learning objectives and criteria for assessing them that provide feedback and can serve summative and formative purposes.

Is It Important to Assess Civic Growth?

Although academic learning is traditionally the primary or sole focus of assessment in psychology courses, civic learning is a defining characteristic of service learning and central to the goal of producing psychologically literate citizens. Chapter 1 discusses the varied nature that *civic* can have and posits that there can be civic aspects to learning associated with all five goals in the APA Guidelines 2.0 (Appendix A; Table 3.1). Delineating specific civic learning objectives for some or all of the goals is important to the capacity to assess civic learning. When these learning objectives are developed for reflection according to the DEAL model and Bloom's (1956) taxonomy (see Chapter 3, this volume), it is possible to document the degree to which students are demonstrating the desired level of civic learning (Ash & Clayton, 2009a, 2009b).

Is It Possible to Assess (and Grade) Personal Growth?

It is possible to assess (and grade) personal growth. There is a common misunderstanding that personal growth is "too personal" and is an inappropriate domain for assessment (e.g., grades). The availability of personal growth for assessment depends on the degree to which learning objectives are specified for this domain. Figure 3.1 illustrates that personal growth learning objectives can be distinct from academic learning and civic learning, or can be integrated with one or both. For example, students can learn about leadership as a result of their community-based experiences. If this is a personal learning objective for the service learning course, the DEAL model can structure prompts to generate learning about leadership from the community service activities and Bloom's (1956) taxonomy can be used to assess the degree to which students articulate their learning about themselves with regard to how they describe and define leadership, what assumptions and biases they may have about leadership, how they successfully or unsuccessfully used leadership skills at their service site, the degree to which they can critically analyze their leadership skills (e.g., strengths, weaknesses, consequences of various aspects of leadership), how they developed new views of themselves and others as leaders, and then evaluate various approaches to being leaders in different settings (i.e., personal growth). If leadership is a topic in the psychology course, the material from the course can be part of the basis on which students analyze their personal development as leaders during the service learning course (i.e., academic and personal). The reflection could also ask students to write about how their leadership, as analyzed using course content, is related to the leadership functions they have used or observed at the service site and the potential use of leadership in collaborative activities in future civic venues and civic activities (i.e., personal, academic, and civic). In all cases, Bloom's taxonomy can provide a basis for the degree to which students are demonstrating their understanding of themselves as leaders and how they have grown as a result of the community service experience and course content (Ash & Clayton, 2009a, 2009b).

Although personal growth can be associated with all five goals in the APA Guidelines 2.0 (see Table 3.1), Goal 5 (Professional Development) provides numerous areas for which learning objectives can be written for the personal growth of students in service learning courses. For example, students can provide documentation for what they have learned about themselves as a result of the community service activities concerning civic problem solving in an applied setting, self-management skills, their response to feedback from others, how they developed alternative strategies for conflict management, their strengths and weaknesses in collaborative or team work, their ability to work effectively with diverse groups, and clarification of career plans. The selection of one or more of these outcomes and the development of corresponding learning objectives and reflection prompts would be guided by the overall purpose that the instructor has for the service learning course and consideration for the types of community service activities in which students are involved.

However, personal growth is not limited to Goal 5 in the APA Guidelines 2.0. Students can grow personally with regard to academic work (e.g., their view of themselves as a student, their academic skills, how they personally use academic material in their lives), research and critical thinking (e.g., their view of themselves as researchers, their use of critical thinking in reading media, how psychology has influenced their views of sociocultural determinants of behavior), ethical and social responsibility (e.g., how they are more sensitive to ethical issues, their empathy for others, dealing with ethical dilemmas at the service site, their sense of social responsibility toward others now and in the future), and their communication skills (e.g., how they have changed as a result of interacting with diverse others, how they have grown as a communicator, interpersonal issues that they have faced when communicating, how they tailor interpersonal communications to different audiences; see Table 3.1). Each of these domains can generate learning objectives that lead to reflection prompts based on Bloom's (1956) taxonomy, and products can be evaluated for the degree to which the student products demonstrate a level or levels of Bloom's taxonomy (Ash & Clayton, 2009a, 2009b).

Curricular Assessment

The APA Guidelines 2.0 provide a basis for assessing the psychology curriculum at a metacourse level and for evaluating the achievements of graduating students. Again, learning objectives and criteria for evaluating performance have to be developed, appropriate evidence gathered, and a basis for interpreting the results has to be established. One approach is to use standardized examinations to evaluate student achievement across courses (e.g., Dolinsky & Kelley, 2010; Stoloff & Feeney, 2002). Some institutions have student e-portfolios that provide a basis for documenting curricular outcomes across time and across educational experiences. Student e-portfolios also provide a framework in which authentic evidence can be gathered for performance on different levels of outcomes (e.g., foundational, baccalaureate) for formative and summative purposes (Banta, Griffin, Flateby, & Kahn, 2009). Jameson et al. (2008) used the DEAL model to evaluate different levels of student learning across sequenced service learning courses in a multicourse curriculum on the nonprofit sector. Curricular assessment can stimulate conversations among faculty concerning priorities for learning outcomes, coherence across courses, and faculty development activities to support achieving outcomes (see Chapters 11 and 12, this volume; Chen & Penny Light, 2010; Gelmon et al., 2001).

ASSESSMENT, SERVICE LEARNING, AND SCHOLARSHIP OF TEACHING AND LEARNING RESEARCH

The vast majority of the focus of assessment and SoTL research has been on student outcomes (Gurung & Schwartz, 2009), which are understandably important. This is also the case for assessment and SoTL research on service learning (Eyler, Giles, Stenson, & Gray, 2001). Generally, it is understandable that instructors are most interested in assessing student performance for purposes of giving feedback to students, giving grades, obtaining feedback to improve a course, documenting teaching to others (e.g., annual reviews, promotion dossiers), and as a basis for SoTL. Using evidence gathered through assessment provides input into SoTL research that explores how characteristics of the course design, moderator variables, and mediating variables contribute to learning outcomes (Steinberg, Bringle, & McGuire, 2013). In addition, there are opportunities to compare and contrast traditional pedagogies with high-impact pedagogies such as service learning (Chism, Palmer, & Price, 2013).

When comparing and contrasting service learning with traditional pedagogies, there are two unique and interesting attributes that provide opportunities to explore their contributions to student learning through research. First, the democratic nature of service learning (i.e., being fair, inclusive, participatory; Saltmarsh, Hartley, & Clayton, 2009) provides a basis for exploring how the processes of service learning contribute to academic learning, civic learning, and personal growth in unique ways. Bringle, Clayton, and Bringle (2015), using social psychological theory and research, suggested that democratic processes (e.g., democratic relationships, critical reflection) are necessary for developing democratic outcomes (i.e., democratic skills, civic identity). The democratic nature of service learning has implications not only for what is studied about the pedagogy (e.g., the process of the pedagogy, the outcomes of the pedagogy) but also how the research is structured and conducted. Chapter 2 presents a rationale for expanded research methods and epistemologies that include participatory community action research.

Second, service learning is counternormative compared with traditional pedagogies (Clayton & Ash, 2004; Howard, 1998). For example, its counternormative nature includes the teaching and learning process (e.g., collaboration, focus on process as well as outcomes), faculty roles (e.g., facilitator rather than expert), student roles (e.g., being responsible for learning rather than being passive, using reflection to generate and capture learning), the roles of others as educators (e.g., community partners, residents), how learning takes place (e.g., off campus in addition to on campus, through reflection rather than from the instructor), and criteria of learning (e.g., broadly defined in academic, civic, and personal growth; Clayton & Ash, 2004). How these factors operate in the learning environment and contribute to or detract from learning outcomes can be studied through SoTL research.

Populations

Because service learning is collaborative and democratic in vision, it expands the constituencies who are involved and the potential focus for the outcomes that occur. Democratic engagement that is the basis for service learning considers all partners as coeducators, colearners, and cogenerators of knowledge (Dostilio et al., 2013). Nevertheless, students have received the most attention (Eyler et al., 2001). Among the most important constituencies, in addition to students, are faculty, administrators (e.g., chair, dean), staff at community organizations, and residents or clients (Bringle, Clayton, & Price, 2009; Clayton, Bringle, Senor, Huq, & Morrison, 2010). Clayton et al. (2013a, 2013b) presented analyses of the extant research; theoretical perspectives, including many from psychology and cognate areas; measurement approaches; implications for practice; and future research agendas for students, faculty, communities, institutions of higher education, and partnerships. These provide excellent resources for SoTL research on service learning. Service learning research can be focused on students' academic outcomes from service learning (Jameson, Clayton, & Ash, 2013), cognitive growth (Fitch, Steinke, & Hudson, 2013), civic learning (Battistoni, 2013), personal development (Brandenberger, 2013), and intercultural competence (Deardorff & Edwards, 2013).

Faculty

Faculty members make changes to integrate a community service component into a course, and they may change in terms of their orientation to not only community engaged teaching but also engaged professional service and engaged research that possesses the same attributes and values as service learning (e.g., collaboration, democratic processes, an asset-based orientation, reciprocity). Just as the counternormative nature of service learning creates dissonance in students for the traditional norms of instruction, it can also occur for faculty who initiate service learning and successfully continue to offer service learning courses and improve their courses. Most research on faculty has focused on their motives for implementing (or not implementing) service learning (e.g., Abes, Jackson, & Jones, 2002), although there have been several research studies that have targeted additional questions (e.g., Jameson, Clayton, Jaeger, & Bringle, 2012; O'Meara, 2005; O'Meara & Niehaus, 2009: Pribbenow, 2005; see also Chapter 11, this volume). Reviews of literature, theories, and measurement strategies as well as research agendas have been developed for factors related to faculty development associated with service learning (Chism et al., 2013), faculty motivations for service learning and civic engagement (O'Meara, 2013), and faculty as learners (Clayton, Hess, Jaeger, Jameson, & McGuire, 2013).

Administrators and Staff

Even more neglected than faculty are the campus administrators and staff who are in positions to advocate for the use of service learning and support it through the distribution of resources. These include executive leaders (e.g., presidents, chancellors, provosts), deans, chairs, and staff (e.g., in centers for teaching and learning, offices of service learning). Although presidents have provided critical support to service learning and civic engagement, they have not been the focus of much research. O'Meara (2005) found that two of three chief academic officers reported institutional changes (e.g., mission, promotion criteria, incentive grants) on the basis of a broader definition of scholarly work. However, only about one third reported increases in the scholarship of engagement. Deans' and chairs' understanding of service learning and SoTL research on service learning is important because they direct resources and review faculty work for merit increases and promotion and tenure (see Chapter 12). Sandmann and Plater (2013) provided an overview of theories and research on institutional leadership for service learning (see also O'Meara, Lounder, & Hodges, 2013).

Community Impact

There are opportunities to explore the outcomes of service learning on individuals (e.g., clients, residents), organizations, community issues, neighborhoods, and communities. This research can be program evaluation (i.e., what the outcomes are of a service learning project), theory-based research evaluating hypotheses about why change occurs, and different perspectives on proximal orientations to change (e.g., the impact on clients in the short term) or on distal outcomes (e.g., impact on quality of life in a neighborhood, decreased recidivism). Too often research on community impact has neglected the relationship between the process and the outcomes. Thus, research can examine hypotheses connecting process and outcomes regarding the extent to which particular variables mediate, moderate, or influence the effects of service learning on communities.

Reeb and Folger (2013) provided an overview of theory, research, and measurement issues associated with the community impact of service learning (see also Gelmon et al., 2001), and Reeb, Snow, et al. (2014) provided a comprehensive discussion of models and variables to consider in measuring community outcomes. Littlepage and Gazley (2013) examined issues associated with organizational capacity and service learning.

Partnerships

The presumption is that service learning must reflect democratic qualities to teach democratic habits and skills. Dewey (1916) noted that building democratic capacities is contingent on face-to-face interactions in the public sphere, and "society must have a type of education which gives individuals a personal interest in social relationships" (p. 99). Bringle et al. (2015), using psychological theory and research, explored how the democratic nature of partnerships can be related to the development of civic identity in students. Although largely unexplored, engaging in democratic partnerships can also enhance civic skills and civic identity of faculty, staff at community organizations, institutional staff and leaders on campus, community leaders, and residents. Bringle and Clayton (2013) presented an overview of research issues and a research agenda for studying partnerships between persons involved in service learning, and Janke (2013) examined research possibilities at the interorganizational level.

Research on Service Learning

R. A. Smith (2012) stated, "I do not believe that it is 'fair' to expect SoTL research to use the most stringent experimental designs such as random assignment to groups or controlling all extraneous variables" (p. 12). We disagree most strongly with this statement. The only way that SoTL research in general, or SoTL research on service learning, can contribute to theory and practice is to conform to the highest standards for evidence-based research on teaching and learning. The U.S. Department of Education's (2003) position also aligns with the position that scientifically based research is imperative for improving the knowledge base of teaching and learning. Poor research is unethical research, and SoTL research on service learning must adhere to standards for good research by encompassing theory, design, practice, and measurement (Bringle, Hatcher, & Clayton, 2013; Steinberg et al., 2013).

The bulk of research on service learning suffers from the following deficiencies: Service learning is variably defined and implemented, the evidence is heavily dependent on students' self-reports, it uses small samples (often students from one course), there is no control for self-selection of students into service learning courses, there is no comparison or control group, constructs are poorly measured, the research is not guided by testing theory, the research design lacks the capacity to make causal inferences, and the outcomes are typically measured only at the end of the semester (Bringle, 2008). Similar deficiencies exist in research on community outcomes (Reeb & Folger, 2013). Nevertheless, the quality of research on service learning is improving, and resources are available for guiding improvements in research (e.g., Bringle, 2003; Bringle & Hatcher, 2000, 2005; Clayton et al., 2013a, 2013b; Steinberg et al., 2010).

Theory

Too much research on service learning has been atheoretical. Theory is relevant to course design, a theory of change, and to the basis for measuring outcomes (Campbell-Patton & Patton, 2010). Bringle (2003, 2005) advocated for theory from cognate areas to inform research on service learning, highlighting examples from psychology (e.g., self-determination theory, intergroup contact hypothesis, attribution theory, functional theory of volunteering, equity theory). Wilkenfeld, Lauckhardt, and Torney-Purta (2010) identified additional psychological theories that are relevant to service learning: social cognitive theory, moral development, role taking, motivational change, and sociopolitical development. Peterson and Seligman (2004) identified theories and measures associated with numerous attributes relevant to civic engagement: primarily, citizenship, kindness, and teamwork; secondarily, all of the remaining character strengths. Chapters in Clayton et al. (2013a, 2013b) explored how theories can inform research agendas for SoTL research on students, faculty, institutions, communities, and partnerships. Psychology is rich with theories that are relevant to the processes and outcomes of service learning courses for all constituencies, and their use is an underdeveloped aspect of SoTL research on service learning. Furthermore, service learning provides an opportunity for in vivo evaluations and refinements of psychological theories (see Bringle, 2003; Clayton et al., 2013a, 2013b), including evaluating theory-based hypotheses for service learning in the laboratory (Brown, 2011b; Stukas, Snyder, & Clary, 1999).

Research Design

Although high-quality qualitative research, correlational research, and quasiexperimental designs can illuminate the nature of service learning, we have a preference for seeing more research conducted on service learning that reflects solid experimental designs and good measurement (see also Bringle & Hatcher, 2000). This may include research that incorporates qualitative methods or measures in an experimental study, or sequencing quantitative and qualitative research strategies in phases of research (Creswell & Plano Clark, 2011). Strategies from psychotherapy outcome research (Kazdin, 1998; Lambert, Bergin, & Garfield, 2004) can be used to identify the active ingredients of service learning courses. In the *package strategy*, outcomes for students (or other constituencies) engaged in a service learning course that has a package of multiple components (e.g., involving different types of service or reflection methods) could be compared with outcomes of students in a section of the course that does not have a service component. In the *constructive strategy*, outcomes of students in a service learning project with the full package of components could be compared with outcomes of students in the same service learning project plus some supplemental component (e.g., adding graduate students or community professionals working directly alongside undergraduate students). With the *dismantling strategy* (the opposite of constructive strategy), student outcomes of a service learning project having multiple components are compared with student outcomes of this package minus one or more components (e.g., a service learning project is modified to no longer include a certain type of service or reflection method). The *para-*

metric strategy involves comparing the effects of the total package with the effects of the package when some important component is altered (e.g., more time spent in service, more written reflection).

Random assignment seems to present an aspect of a good research design that is unattainable in research on service learning. However, self-selection of students into service learning courses, when it occurs, is a major problem for interpreting results. Brown (2011a, 2011b) used random assignment in service learning courses, and Brown (2011b) and Stukas et al. (1999) used random assignment in a laboratory setting to evaluate theory-based hypotheses related to service learning. Random assignment is also possible for different aspects of course design (e.g., type of reflection, amount of reflection). Alternative approaches to random assignment to control for self-selection of students include blind selection (i.e., students do not know when registering for multiple sections of a course which sections are service learning), delayed treatment (i.e., when limited capacity exists and there is a waiting group, randomly assigning students to service learning and waiting groups, where the waiting group is the control group), pre- and posttest quasiexperimental designs with comparison groups, and statistical controls for preexisting differences (Steinberg et al., 2013).

Measurement

Good measurement starts with clearly defined constructs, preferably within a theoretical context. Although self-report measures are prevalent in service learning research, Chapter 3 presents the basis for collecting authentic evidence of student outcomes based on demonstrated learning (vs. self-reported learning). Principles for good measurement also apply to SoTL research on other constituencies (faculty, university staff, administrators, agency staff, residents, clients). Measures that include both quantitative and qualitative indices of constructs can provide convergence, and the qualitative measures may contribute information about the "how" and "why" from the respondents' perspective (Creswell & Plano Clark, 2011). Considerations of good operationalization apply both to the intervention (independent variable—i.e., measuring qualities of the service learning course) and outcomes (dependent variable).

CONCLUSION

No part of this discussion precludes assessment and research incorporating the values of service learning and civic engagement into how assessment and research are conducted. Just as service learning is a collaborative and democratic activity (inclusive, participatory, fair), so too can assessment and research on service learning incorporate those values and processes. Chapter 2 provides a basis for how to design research in the community as a collaborative, democratic activity. This approach can be generalized to SoTL research on service learning.

Gurung and Schwartz (2009) noted that the benefits of SoTL research include energizing and enhancing classroom teaching, providing research opportunities, strengthening promotion and tenure documents, and enhancing satisfaction with teaching. SoTL research can also provide opportunities to collaborate with other instructors in the department, in other departments on campus, or with faculty at other institutions on multiple-section research studies that can increase the sample size and the generalizability of the research. Developmental approaches to evaluating and studying student outcomes over a longer length of time than one semester can occur when sequences of courses have been enhanced with service learning or studying alumni (Ruiz & Warchal, 2013). Although this discussion has largely focused on assessing student outcomes, we encourage good research on other constituencies associated with service learning and civic engagement (Clayton et al., 2013a, 2013b).

McGovern et al. (2010) noted that psychology "is at the juncture of the humanities and the sciences where students gain the human-focused values and the scientific tools necessary to see and to care about the human condition and to improve it" (p. 25). This assertion is provocative but, alas, warrants empirical investigation and support. How would the value of the undergraduate psychology curriculum be enhanced among psychologists, educators, administrators, and the public if evidence were gathered to support that assertion and its implications for the personal and civic lives of students, their interpersonal relationships, their careers, the quality of their lives, and their communities?

Appendix A: American Psychological Association Learning Goals and Outcomes Indicators

APPENDIX A

	Learning goals				
	1. Knowledge Base in Psychology	2. Scientific Inquiry and Critical Thinking	3. Ethical and Social Responsibility in a Diverse World	4. Communication	5. Professional Development
Outcomes	1.1 Describe key concepts, principles, and overarching themes in psychology.	2.1 Use scientific reasoning to interpret psychological phenomena.	3.1 Apply ethical standards to evaluate psychological science and practice.	4.1 Demonstrate effective writing for different purposes.	5.1 Apply psychological content and skills to career goals.
	1.2 Develop a working knowledge of psychology's content domains.	2.2 Demonstrate psychology information literacy.	3.2 Build and enhance interpersonal relationships.	4.2 Exhibit effective presentation skills for different purposes.	5.2 Exhibit self-efficacy and self-regulation.
	1.3 Describe applications of psychology.	2.3 Engage in innovative and integrative thinking and problem solving.	3.3 Adopt values that build community at local, national, and global levels.	4.3 Interact effectively with others.	5.3 Refine project-management skills.
		2.4 Interpret, design, and conduct basic psychological research.			5.4 Enhance teamwork capacity.
		2.5 Incorporate sociocultural factors in scientific inquiry.			5.5 Develop meaningful professional direction for life after graduation.

Note. Adapted from *APA Guidelines for the Undergraduate Psychology Major* (Version 2.0), by the American Psychological Association, 2013. Retrieved from http://www.apa.org/ed/precollege/undergrad/index.aspx. Copyright 2013 by the American Psychological Association.

Appendix B: American Psychological Association Learning Goals and Inferred Attributes

APPENDIX B

	Learning goals				
	1. Knowledge Base in Psychology	2. Scientific Inquiry and Critical Thinking	3. Ethical and Social Responsibility in a Diverse World	4. Communication	5. Professional Development
Attributes inferred from successful performance	Capable of coping with complexity and ambiguity	Amiably skeptical	Beneficent	Attentive	Adaptable
	Conversant about psychological phenomena	Careful	Civically engaged	Comprehensible	Collaborative
		Collaborative	Community involved	Flexible	Confident
		Constructively critical	Conventional	Investigative	Conscientious
	Curious	Creative	Courageous	Precise	Dependable
	Flexible in thinking	Curious	Ethical	Prepared	Directed
	Knowledgeable about psychology	Intentional	Fair-minded	Respectful	Efficient
	Motivated	Inventive	Generous		Industrious
	Open-minded	Logical	Moral		Intuitive
	Prepared	Open-minded	Reliable		Prepared
	Psychologically literate	Persistent	Respectful		Reflective
		Precise	Rigorous		Resilient
		Self-directed	Sensitive		Resourceful
		Self-starting	Tolerant		Responsible
		Systematic	Trustworthy		Sensitive
		Tolerant of ambiguity			

Note. Adapted from *APA Guidelines for the Undergraduate Psychology Major* (Version 2.0), by the American Psychological Association, 2013. Retrieved from http://www.apa.org/ed/precollege/undergrad/index.aspx. Copyright 2013 by the American Psychological Association.

Appendix C:
Reflection Map

APPENDIX C

	Before service	During service	After service
Reflect alone	• Written reflection on expectations, reservations, stereotypes, and goals • "Letter to self" to be opened at the end of the semester • Research on community issue or agency	• Written reflection based on DEAL model • Critical incident journal—Students analyze a particular event that occurred with regard to academic, civic, and personal antecedents and implications for future work • Ethical case study—Students identify and analyze a situation and practice ethical decision making as they choose a course of action and explore and clarify values	• Reflective essay using prior reflections • Digital story on learning outcomes • Portfolio of academic work and service • Present advocacy products to audiences (e.g., legislators) • Produce research report • Write a letter to students in next year's course about what to expect and give advice
Reflect with classmates	• Group discussion on expectations, hopes, reservations, stereotypes, and goals • Sharing information about prior community service experiences and service learning course	• Group discussion on drafts of written reflection • Planning group activities at site • Group discussion on ethical issues at service site	• Team presentation in class and at community site • Product delivered to community site (e.g., web page, brochure) • Research report • Present advocacy products to audiences (e.g., legislators)
Reflect with community partners	• Orientation • Determination of community service goals • Asset mapping	• Regular meetings with staff and residents • Mid-semester assessment of service activities with partners	• Obtain feedback on service activities, products, and results • Present research results • Evaluation of meeting service goals • Make presentations with community partners (e.g., government officials, funders) • Celebrate with partners

Note. DEAL = describe, examine, and articulate learning model for critical reflection (Ash & Clayton, 2004, 2009a, 2009b; Jameson, Clayton, & Bringle, 2008). From "Creating Your Reflection Map," by J. Eyler, 2001, *New Directions for Higher Education, 2001*, p. 37. Copyright 2002 by Wiley. Adapted with permission.

References

Abes, E. S., Jackson, G., & Jones, S. R. (2002). Factors that motivate and deter faculty use of service-learning. *Michigan Journal of Community Service Learning, 9*(1), 5–17.

Alpert, D. (1985). Performance and paralysis: The organizational context of the American research university. *The Journal of Higher Education, 56,* 241–281. http://dx.doi.org/10.2307/1981734

Altman, I. (1996). Higher education and psychology in the millennium. *American Psychologist, 51,* 371–378. http://dx.doi.org/10.1037/0003-066X.51.4.371

American Psychological Association. (2010). *Ethical principles of psychologists and code of conduct (2002, Amended June 1, 2010).* Retrieved from http://www.apa.org/ethics/code/index.aspx

American Psychological Association. (2013). *APA guidelines for the undergraduate psychology major* (Version 2.0). Washington, DC: Author.

American Psychological Association. (2014a). *About the public interest directorate.* Retrieved from http://www.apa.org/pi/about/index.aspx

American Psychological Association. (2014b). *Civic engagement and service learning.* Retrieved from http://apa.org/education/undergrad/slce.aspx

American Psychological Association. (2014c). *Public interest directorate.* Retrieved from http://www.apa.org/pi/

American Psychological Association (2015). *About the Public Interest Directorate.* Retrieved from http://www.apa.org/pi/about/index.aspx

Anderson, J. E., & Sungur, E. A. (1999). Community service statistics projects. *The American Statistician, 53,* 132–136.

Anderson, L. W., & Krathwohl, D. A. (2001). *A taxonomy for learning, teaching, and assessing: A revision of Bloom's taxonomy of educational objectives.* New York, NY: Academic Press.

REFERENCES

Anstee, J. K., Harris, S. G., Pruitt, K. D., & Sugar, J. A. (2008). Service-learning projects in an undergraduate gerontology course: A six-stage model and application. *Educational Gerontology, 34,* 595–609. http://dx.doi.org/10.1080/03601270801949419

Antonio, A. L., Astin, H. S., & Cress, C. M. (2000). Community service in higher education: A look at the nation's faculty. *Review of Higher Education, 23,* 373–398. http://dx.doi.org/10.1353/rhe.2000.0015

Ash, S. L., & Clayton, P. H. (2004). The articulated learning: An approach to guided reflection and assessment. *Innovative Higher Education, 29,* 137–154. http://dx.doi.org/10.1023/B:IHIE.0000048795.84634.4a

Ash, S. L., & Clayton, P. H. (2009a). Generating, deepening, and documenting learning: The power of critical reflection for applied learning. *Journal of Applied Learning in Higher Education, 1,* 25–48.

Ash, S. L., & Clayton, P. H. (2009b). *Learning through critical reflection: A tutorial for students in service-learning (Instructor version).* Raleigh, NC: Authors.

Association of American Colleges & Universities. (2011). *The LEAP vision for learning: Outcomes, practices, impact, and employers' views.* Retrieved from http://leap.aacu.org/toolkit/wp-content/uploads/2010/12/LEAP-Vision_Summary.pdf

Association of American Colleges and Universities' Liberal Education and America's Promise Initiative. (n.d.). *Higher education for democracy: A Report of the President's Commission on Higher Education.* Retrieved from http://www.aacu.org/sites/default/files/files/LEAP/he_for_democracy.pdf

Association of Public and Land Grant Universities. (2012). *The land grant tradition.* Washington, DC: Author.

Astin, A. W., & Sax, L. J. (1998). How undergraduates are affected by service participation. *Journal of College Student Development, 39,* 251–263.

Astin, A. W., Sax, L. J., & Avalos, J. (1999). The long-term effects of volunteerism during the undergraduate years. *The Review of Higher Education, 21,* 187–202.

Astin, A. W., Vogelgesang, L. J., Misa, K., Anderson, J., Denson, N., Jayakumar, J., . . . Yamamura, E. (2006). *Understanding the effects of service-learning: A study of students and faculty.* Los Angeles, CA: Higher Education Research Institute.

Baez, B. (2000). Race-related service and faculty of color: Conceptualizing critical agency in academe. *Higher Education, 39,* 363–391.

Baird, B. N. (2008). *The internship, practicum, and field placement handbook: A guide for the helping professions.* Saddle Brook, NJ: Prentice Hall.

Balk, D. E. (2008). Psychology, grief, and the student. In C. M. Moreman (Ed.), *Teaching death and dying* (pp. 97–116). Oxford, England: Oxford University Press. http://dx.doi.org/10.1093/acprof:oso/9780195335224.003.0009

REFERENCES

Banerjee, M., & Hausafus, C. O. (2007). Faculty use of service-learning: Perceptions, motivations, and impediments for the human sciences. *Michigan Journal of Community Service Learning, 14*(1), 32–45.

Banta, T. W., Griffin, M., Flateby, T. L., & Kahn, S. (2009, December). *Three promising alternatives for assessing college students' knowledge and skills* (NILOA Occasional Paper No. 2). Urbana, IL: University of Illinois and Indiana University, National Institute for Learning Outcomes Assessment.

Barr, R. B., & Tagg, J. (1995). From teaching to learning: A new paradigm for undergraduate education. *Change, 27*(6), 12–25. http://dx.doi.org/10.1080/00091383.1995.10544672

Battistoni, R. (2002). *Civic engagement across the curriculum: A resource book for faculty in all disciplines.* Providence, RI: Campus Compact.

Battistoni, R. M. (2013). Civic learning through service learning. In P. H. Clayton, R. G. Bringle, & J. A. Hatcher (Eds.), *Research on service learning: Conceptual frameworks and assessment. Vol. 2A: Students and faculty* (pp. 111–132). Sterling, VA: Stylus.

Battistoni, R. M., Gelmon, S. B., Saltmarsh, J., Wergin, J., & Zlotkowski, E. (2003). *The engaged department toolkit.* Providence, RI: Campus Compact.

Bennett, J. B. (1998). *Collegial professionalism: The academy, individualism, and the common good.* Phoenix, AZ: Oryx Press.

Benson, L., Harkavy, I., & Puckett, J. (2011). Democratic transformation through university-assisted community schools. In J. Saltmarsh & M. Hartley (Eds.), *To service a larger purpose: Engagement for democracy and the transformation of higher education* (pp. 48–81). Philadelphia, PA: Temple University Press.

Billig, S. H., & Eyler, J. S. (2003). The state of service-learning and service-learning research. In S. H. Billig & J. S. Eyler (Eds.), *Deconstructing service-learning: Research exploring context, participation, and impacts* (pp. 253–264). Charlotte, NC: Information Age.

Blanchard, L. W., Strauss, R. P., & Webb, L. (2012). Engaged scholarship at the University of North Carolina at Chapel Hill: Campus integration and faculty development. *Journal of Higher Education Outreach and Engagement, 16*, 97–128.

Bloom, B. S. (Ed.). (1956). *Taxonomy of educational objectives: Handbook I. Cognitive domain.* New York, NY: David McCay.

Bowman, N. A. (2011). Promoting participation in a diverse democracy: A meta-analysis of college diversity experiences and civic engagement. *Review of Educational Research, 81*, 29–68. http://dx.doi.org/10.3102/0034654310383047

Bowman, N. A., & Brandenberger, J. W. (2012). Experiencing the unexpected: Toward a model of college diversity experiences and attitude change. *The Review of Higher Education, 35*, 179–205. http://dx.doi.org/10.1353/rhe.2012.0016

REFERENCES

Bowman, N. A., & Seifert, T. A. (2011). Can college students accurately assess what affects their learning and development? *Journal of College Student Development*, 52, 270–290. http://dx.doi.org/10.1353/csd.2011.0042

Boyer, E. L. (1990). *Scholarship reconsidered: Priorities of the professoriate*. Princeton, NJ: Carnegie Foundation for the Advancement of Teaching.

Boyer, E. L. (1996). The scholarship of engagement. *Journal of Higher Education Outreach and Engagement*, 1, 11–20.

Brandenberger, J. W. (1998). Developmental psychology and service-learning: A theoretical framework. In R. G. Bringle & D. K. Duffy (Eds.), *With service in mind: Concepts and models for service-learning in psychology* (pp. 68–84). Washington, DC: American Association for Higher Education. http://dx.doi.org/10.1037/10505-004

Brandenberger, J. W. (2013). Investigating personal development outcomes in service learning. In P. H. Clayton, R. G. Bringle, & J. A. Hatcher (Eds.), *Research on service learning: Conceptual frameworks and assessment. Vol. 2A: Students and faculty* (pp. 133–156). Sterling, VA: Stylus.

Briggs, S. (2013, July 16). *10 emerging educational technologies and how they are being used across the globe*. Retrieved from http://www.opencolleges.edu.au/informed/features/the-ten-emerging-technologies-in-education-and-how-they-are-being-used-across-the-globe/

Bringle, R. G. (2003). Enhancing theory-based research on service-learning. In S. H. Billig & J. S. Eyler (Eds.), *Deconstructing service-learning: Research exploring context, participation, and impacts* (pp. 3–21). Charlotte, NC: Information Age.

Bringle, R. G. (2005). Designing interventions to promote civic engagement. In A. Omoto (Ed.), *Processes of community change and social action* (pp. 167–187). Mahwah, NJ: Erlbaum.

Bringle, R. G. (2008, October). *Civic engagement and student success: Making the impact we intend*. Invited keynote address at Minnesota Campus Compact, Minneapolis, MN.

Bringle, R. G. (2011, May). *Integrating community-based research and development into the curriculum and co-curriculum*. Plenary presentation at the 2nd ASEAN University Network Regional Forum on University Social Responsibility and Sustainability, Kuala Lumpur, Malaysia.

Bringle, R. G., & Clayton, P. H. (2012). Civic education through service-learning: What, how, and why? In L. McIlrath, A. Lyons, & R. Munck (Eds.), *Higher education and civic engagement: Comparative perspectives* (pp. 101–124). New York, NY: Palgrave. http://dx.doi.org/10.1057/9781137074829.0013

Bringle, R. G., & Clayton, P. H. (2013). Conceptual frameworks for partnerships in service learning. In P. H. Clayton, R. G. Bringle, & J. A. Hatcher (Eds.),

Research on service learning: Conceptual frameworks and assessment. Vol. 2B: Communities, institutions, and partnerships (pp. 539–571). Sterling, VA: Stylus.

Bringle, R. G., Clayton, P. H., & Bringle, K. E. (2015). Teaching democratic thinking is not enough: The case for democratic action. *Partnerships: A Journal of Service Learning & Civic Engagement, 6*, 1–26.

Bringle, R. G., Clayton, P. H., & Plater, W. M. (2013). Assessing diversity, global, and civic learning: A means to change in higher education. *Democracy and Diversity, 13*(3), 4–6.

Bringle, R. G., Clayton, P. H., & Price, M. F. (2009). Partnerships in service learning and civic engagement. *Partnerships: A Journal of Service Learning & Civic Engagement, 1*, 1–20.

Bringle, R. G., & Duffy, D. K. (Eds.). (1998). *With service in mind: Concepts and models for service learning in psychology.* Washington, DC: American Association for Higher Education. http://dx.doi.org/10.1037/10505-000

Bringle, R. G., Games, R., Ludlum, C., Osgood, R., & Osborne, R. (2000). Faculty Fellows Program: Enhancing integrated professional development through community service. *American Behavioral Scientist, 43*, 882–894.

Bringle, R. G., Games, R., & Malloy, E. A. (Eds.). (1999). *Colleges and universities as citizens.* Needham Heights, MA: Allyn & Bacon.

Bringle, R. G., & Hatcher, J. A. (1996). Implementing service learning in higher education. *The Journal of Higher Education, 67*, 221–239. http://dx.doi.org/10.2307/2943981

Bringle, R. G., & Hatcher, J. A. (1999). Reflection in service learning: Making meaning of experience. *Educational Horizons, 77*, 179–185.

Bringle, R. G., & Hatcher, J. A. (2000). Meaningful measurement of theory-based service-learning outcomes: Making the case with quantitative research. *Michigan Journal of Community Service Learning, 7*(1), 68–75.

Bringle, R. G., & Hatcher, J. A. (2005). Service learning as scholarship: Why theory-based research is critical to service learning. *Acta Academica, 3*(Supplementum), 24–44.

Bringle, R. G., & Hatcher, J. A. (2011). International service learning. In R. G. Bringle, J. A. Hatcher, & S. G. Jones (Eds.), *International service learning: Conceptual frameworks and research* (pp. 3–28). Sterling, VA: Stylus.

Bringle, R. G., Hatcher, J. A., & Clayton, P. H. (2006). The scholarship of civic engagement: Defining, documenting, and evaluating faculty work. *To Improve the Academy, 25*, 257–279.

Bringle, R. G., Hatcher, J. A., & Clayton, P. H. (2013). Research on service learning: An introduction. In P. H. Clayton, R. G. Bringle, & J. A. Hatcher (Eds.), *Research on service learning: Conceptual frameworks and assessment. Vol. 2A: Students and faculty* (pp. 3–25). Sterling, VA: Stylus.

REFERENCES

Bringle, R. G., Hatcher, J. A., & Jones, S. G. (Eds.). (2011). *International service learning: Conceptual frameworks and research.* Sterling, VA: Stylus.

Bringle, R. G., Hatcher, J. A., Jones, S. G., & Plater, W. M. (2006). Sustaining civic engagement: Faculty development, roles, and rewards. *Metropolitan Universities, 17,* 62–74.

Bringle, R. G., Hatcher, J. A., & Muthiah, R. (2010). The role of service-learning on retention of first-year students to second year. *Michigan Journal of Community Service Learning, 16*(2), 38–49.

Bringle, R. G., & Kremer, J. F. (1993). Evaluation of an intergenerational service-learning project for undergraduates. *Educational Gerontology, 19,* 407–416. http://dx.doi.org/10.1080/0360127930190504

Bringle, R. G., Phillips, M. A., & Hudson, M. (2004). *The measure of service learning: Research scales to assess student experiences.* Washington, DC: American Association for Higher Education. http://dx.doi.org/10.1037/10677-000

Bringle, R. G., & Steinberg, K. (2010). Educating for informed community involvement. *American Journal of Community Psychology, 46,* 428–441. http://dx.doi.org/10.1007/s10464-010-9340-y

Bringle, R. G., Studer, M. H., Wilson, J., Clayton, P. H., & Steinberg, K. (2011). Designing programs with a purpose: To promote civic engagement for life. *Journal of Academic Ethics, 9,* 149–164. http://dx.doi.org/10.1007/s10805-011-9135-2

Bringle, R. G., & Velo, P. M. (1998). Attributions about misery: A social psychological analysis. In R. G. Bringle & D. K. Duffy (Eds.), *With service in mind: Concepts and models for service-learning in psychology* (pp. 51–67). Washington, DC: American Psychological Association. http://dx.doi.org/10.1037/10505-003

Bronfenbrenner, U. (1979). *The ecology of human development: Experiments by nature and design.* Cambridge, MA: Harvard University Press.

Brown, M. A. (2011a). Learning from service: The effect of helping on helpers' social dominance orientation. *Journal of Applied Social Psychology, 41,* 850–871. http://dx.doi.org/10.1111/j.1559-1816.2011.00738.x

Brown, M. A. (2011b). The power of generosity to change views on social power. *Journal of Experimental Social Psychology, 47,* 1285–1290. http://dx.doi.org/10.1016/j.jesp.2011.05.021

Brown, M. A., & Riddle, A. (2013, November). *How service learning impacts the development of students' social justice attitudes: A closer look at moderating factors.* Paper presented at the International Association for Research on Service Learning and Community Engagement, Omaha, NE.

Buskist, W., Carlson, J. F., Christopher, A. N., Prieto, L., & Smith, R. A. (2008). Models and exemplars of scholarship in the teaching of psychology. *Teaching of Psychology, 35,* 267–277. http://dx.doi.org/10.1080/00986280802373908

REFERENCES

Buskist, W., & Irons, J. (2006). Teaching matters: The truth about the job market in academic psychology. *APS Observer, 19*(9), 14–17.

Butin, D. W. (2010). "Can I major in service-learning?" An empirical analysis of certificates, majors, and minors. *Journal of College and Character, 11*, 1–19. http://dx.doi.org/10.2202/1940-1639.1035

Cacioppo, J. T. (2007). The structure of psychology. *APS Observer, 20*(11), 3 & 50–51.

Calabrese, J. D., & Corrigan, P. W. (2005). Beyond dementia praecox: Findings from long-term follow-up studies of schizophrenia. In R. O. Ralph & P. W. Corrigan (Eds.), *Recovery in mental illness: Broadening our understanding of wellness* (pp. 63–84). Washington, DC: American Psychological Association. http://dx.doi.org/10.1037/10848-003

Calleson, D., Kauper-Brown, J., & Seifer, S. D. (2005). *Community-engaged scholarship toolkit.* Seattle, WA: Community-Campus Partnerships for Health. Retrieved from http://www.communityengagedscholarship.info

Campbell, D. T., & Fiske, D. W. (1959). Convergent and discriminant validation by the multitrait-multimethod matrix. *Psychological Bulletin, 56*, 81–105. http://dx.doi.org/10.1037/h0046016

Campbell-Patton, C., & Patton, M. Q. (2010). Conceptualizing and evaluating the complexities of youth civic engagement. In L. R. Sherrod, J. Torney-Purta, & C. A. Flanagan (Eds.), *Handbook of research on civic engagement in youth* (pp. 593–619). Hoboken, NJ: Wiley. http://dx.doi.org/10.1002/9780470767603.ch22

Campus Compact. (1999). *Presidents' declaration on the civic responsibility of higher education.* Retrieved from http://www.compact.org/wp-content/uploads/2009/02/Presidents-Declaration.pdf

Campus Compact. (2013). *Creating a culture of assessment: 2012 Campus Compact annual member survey.* Boston, MA: Author.

Celio, C. I., Durlak, J., & Dymnicki, A. (2011). A meta-analysis of the impact of service-learning on students. *Journal of Experiential Education, 34*, 164–181. http://dx.doi.org/10.5193/JEE34.2.164

Centre for Social Justice and Community Action, Durham University, & National Co-ordinating Centre for Public Engagement. (2012). *Community-based participatory research: A guide to ethical principles and practice.* Retrieved from https://www.dur.ac.uk/resources/beacon/CBPREthicsGuidewebNovember20121.pdf

Chalmers, A. F. (1999). *What is this thing called science?* (3rd ed.). Queensland, Australia: University of Queensland Press.

Chapdelaine, A., Ruiz, A., Warchal, J., & Wells, C. (2005). *Service-learning code of ethics.* Boston, MA: Anker.

REFERENCES

Charlton, S., & Lymburner, J. (2011). Fostering psychologically literate citizens: A Canadian perspective. In J. Cranney & D. S. Dunn (Eds.), *The psychologically literate citizen: Foundations and global perspectives* (pp. 234–248). New York, NY: Oxford University Press. http://dx.doi.org/10.1093/acprof:oso/9780199794942.003.0060

Checkoway, B. (2013). Strengthening the scholarship of engagement in higher education. *Journal of Higher Education Outreach and Engagement, 17,* 7–21.

Chen, H. L., & Penny Light, T. (2010). *Electronic portfolios and student success: Effectiveness, affordability, and efficiency.* Washington, DC: American Association of Colleges and Universities.

Chenneville, T., Toler, S., & Gaskin-Butler, V. T. (2012). Civic engagement in the field of psychology. *Journal of the Scholarship of Teaching and Learning, 12*(4), 58–75.

Chew, S. L., Bartlett, R. M., Dobbins, J. E., Hammer, E. Y., Kite, M. E., Loop, T. F., ... Rose, K. C. (2010). A contextual approach to teaching: Bridging methods, goals, and outcomes. In D. F. Halpern (Ed.), *Undergraduate education in psychology: A blueprint for the future of the discipline* (pp. 95–112). Washington, DC: American Psychological Association.

Chism, N. V. N., Palmer, M. M., & Price, M. F. (2013). Investigating faculty development for service learning. In P. H. Clayton, R. G. Bringle, & J. A. Hatcher (Eds.), *Research on service learning: Conceptual frameworks and assessment. Vol. 2A: Students and faculty* (pp. 187–214). Sterling, VA: Stylus.

Cipolle, S. B. (2010). *Service learning and social justice: Engaging students in social change.* Lanham, MD: Rowman & Littlefield.

Clayton, P. H., & Ash, S. L. (2004). Shifts in perspective: Capitalizing on the counter-normative nature of service-learning. *Michigan Journal of Community Service Learning, 11*(1), 59–70.

Clayton, P. H., Bringle, R. G., & Hatcher, J. A. (Eds.). (2013a). *Research on service learning: Conceptual frameworks and assessment. Vol. 2A: Students and faculty.* Sterling, VA: Stylus.

Clayton, P. H., Bringle, R. G., & Hatcher, J. A. (Eds.). (2013b). *Research on service learning: Conceptual frameworks and assessment. Vol. 2B: Communities, institutions, and partnerships.* Sterling, VA: Stylus.

Clayton, P. H., Bringle, R. G., Senor, B., Huq, J., & Morrison, M. (2010). Differentiating and assessing relationships in service-learning and civic engagement: Exploitive, transactional, and transformational. *Michigan Journal of Community Service Learning, 16*(2), 5–21.

Clayton, P. H., Hess, G. R., Jaeger, A. J., Jameson, J. K., & McGuire, L. E. (2013). Theoretical perspectives and research on faculty learning in service learning.

In P. H. Clayton, R. G. Bringle, & J. A. Hatcher (Eds.), *Research on service learning: Conceptual frameworks and assessment. Vol. 2A: Students and faculty* (pp. 245–278). Sterling, VA: Stylus.

Clayton, P. H., & O'Steen, B. (2010). Working with faculty: Designing customized developmental strategies. In B. Jacoby & P. Mustascio (Eds.), *Looking in, reaching out: A reflective guide for community service-learning professionals* (pp. 95–136). Boston, MA: Campus Compact.

Cobb, S. (1976). Social support as a moderator of life stress. *Psychosomatic Medicine, 38,* 300–314. http://dx.doi.org/10.1097/00006842-197609000-00003

Collaborative Institutional Training Initiative Program. (2014). *Collaborative Institutional Training Initiative at the University of Miami.* Retrieved from https://www.citiprogram.org/

Conley, A. (2000). Service learning: Enhancing the educational experience, improving communities, changing lives. *Research & Creative Activity, 22*(3). Retrieved from http://www.indiana.edu/~rcapub/v22n3/p32.html

Conner, D. B. (1996). From Monty Python to *Total Recall*: A feature film activity for the cognitive psychology course. *Teaching of Psychology, 23,* 33–35. http://dx.doi.org/10.1207/s15328023top2301_6

Conway, J. M., Amel, E. L., & Gerwien, D. P. (2009). Teaching and learning in the social context: A meta-analysis of service learning's effects on academic, personal, social, and citizenship outcomes. *Teaching of Psychology, 36,* 233–245. http://dx.doi.org/10.1080/00986280903172969

Copeland, D. E., Scott, J. R., & Houska, J. (2010). Computer-based demonstrations in cognitive psychology: Benefits and costs. *Teaching of Psychology, 37,* 141–145. http://dx.doi.org/10.1080/00986281003626680

Corrigan, P. W. (2000). Mental health stigma as social attribution: Implications for research methods and attitude change. *Clinical Psychology: Science and Practice, 7,* 48–67. http://dx.doi.org/10.1093/clipsy.7.1.48

Corrigan, P. W., & O'Shaughnessy, J. R. (2007). Changing mental illness stigma as it exists in the real world. *Australian Psychologist, 42,* 90–97. http://dx.doi.org/10.1080/00050060701280573

Corrigan, P. W., & Ralph, R. O. (2005). Introduction: Recovery as consumer vision and research paradigm. In R. O. Ralph & P. W. Corrigan (Eds.), *Recovery in mental illness: Broadening our understanding of wellness* (pp. 3–17). Washington, DC: American Psychological Association. http://dx.doi.org/10.1037/10848-001

Council for the Advancement of Standards in Higher Education. (2006). Internship programs: CAS standards and guidelines. In L. Dean (Ed.), *CAS professional standards for higher education* (6th ed., pp. 230–236). Washington, DC: Author.

REFERENCES

Cranney, J., & Dunn, D. (Eds.). (2011). *The psychologically literate citizen: Foundations and global perspectives.* New York, NY: Oxford University Press. http://dx.doi.org/10.1093/acprof:oso/9780199794942.001.0001

Creswell, J. W., & Plano Clark, V. L. (2011). *Designing and conducting mixed methods research* (2nd ed.). Thousand Oaks, CA: Sage.

Crone, T. S. (2013). The effects of service-learning in the social psychology classroom. *Journal of Service-Learning in Higher Education, 2,* 62–74.

Crone, T. S., & Portillo, M. C. (2013). Jigsaw variations and attitudes about learning and the self in cognitive psychology. *Teaching of Psychology, 40,* 246–251. http://dx.doi.org/10.1177/0098628313487451

Curwood, S., Munger, F., Mitchell, T., MacKeigan, M., & Farrar, A. (2011). Building effective community–university partnerships: Are universities truly ready? *Michigan Journal of Community Service Learning, 17*(2), 15–26.

Dalton, J., & Wolfe, S. (2012). Joint column: Education connection and the community practitioner. *The Community Psychologist, 45*(4), 7–13.

DeAngelo, L., Hurtado, S. H., Pryor, J. H., Kelly, K. R., Santos, J. L., & Korn, W. S. (2009). *The American college teacher: National norms for the 2007–2008 HERI Faculty Survey.* Los Angeles, CA: Higher Education Research Institute, UCLA.

Deardorff, D. K., & Edwards, K. E. (2013). Framing and assessing students' intercultural competence in service learning. In P. H. Clayton, R. G. Bringle, & J. A. Hatcher (Eds.), *Research on service learning: Conceptual frameworks and assessment. Vol. 2A: Students and faculty* (pp. 157–185). Sterling, VA: Stylus.

Demb, A., & Wade, A. (2012). Reality check: Faculty involvement in outreach & engagement. *The Journal of Higher Education, 83,* 337–366. http://dx.doi.org/10.1353/jhe.2012.0019

Dewey, J. (1899). *The school and society.* Chicago, IL: University of Chicago Press.

Dewey, J. (1916). *Democracy and education.* New York, NY: Macmillan.

Dewey, J. (1938). *Experience and education.* New York, NY: Touchstone.

Dewey, J. (1946). *Problems of men.* New York, NY: Philosophical Library.

Diamond, R., & Adams, B. (1995). *Recognizing faculty work: Reward systems for the year 2001.* San Francisco, CA: Jossey-Bass.

Dolinsky, B., & Kelley, J. M. (2010). For better or for worse: Using an objective program assessment measure to enhance an undergraduate psychology program. *Teaching of Psychology, 37,* 252–256. http://dx.doi.org/10.1080/00986283.2010.510978

Dostilio, L. D. (2012). *Democratically engaged community–university partnerships: Reciprocal determinants of democratically oriented roles and processes* (Unpublished doctoral dissertation). School of Education, Duquesne University, Pittsburgh, PA.

Dostilio, L. D., Brackmann, S. M., Edwards, K. E., Harrison, B., Kliewer, B. W., & Clayton, P. H. (2013). Reciprocity: Saying what we mean and meaning what we say. *Michigan Journal of Community Service Learning, 19*(1), 17–32.

Douglass, B. (1980). The common good and the public interest. *Political Theory, 8*, 103–117.

Driscoll, A. (2000). Studying faculty and service-learning: Directions for inquiry and development [special issue]. *Michigan Journal of Community Service Learning, 1*, 35–41.

Duffy, D. K. (2004). Service-learning, resilience, and community: The challenges of authentic assessment. In D. S. Dunn, C. M. Mehrotra, & J. S. Halonen (Eds.), *Measuring up: Educational assessment challenges and practices for psychology* (pp. 243–256). Washington, DC: American Psychological Association. http://dx.doi.org/10.1037/10807-013

Duffy, J., Barrington, L., West, C., Heredia, M., & Barry, C. (2011). Service-learning integrated throughout a college of engineering (SLICE). *Advances in Engineering Education, 2*(4). Retrieved from http://advances.asee.org/wp-content/uploads/vol02/issue04/papers/aee-vol02-issue04-p09.pdf

Dunn, D. S. (2006). Teaching courses with laboratories. In W. Buskist & S. F. Davis (Eds.), *Handbook of the teaching of psychology* (pp. 125–130). Malden, MA: Blackwell. http://dx.doi.org/10.1002/9780470754924.ch21

Dunn, D. S., Brewer, C. L., Cautin, R. L., Gurung, R. A. R., Keith, K. D., McGregor, L. N., . . . Voigt, M. J. (2010). The undergraduate psychology curriculum: Call for a core. In D. F. Halpern (Ed.), *Undergraduate education in psychology: A blueprint for the future of the discipline* (pp. 47–61). Washington, DC: American Psychological Association. http://dx.doi.org/10.1037/12063-003

Dunn, D. S., McCarthy, M. A., Baker, S. C., & Halonen, J. S. (2011). *Using quality benchmarks for assessing and developing undergraduate programs*. San Francisco, CA: Wiley.

Dunning, D., Heath, C., & Suls, J. M. (2004). Flawed self-assessment: Implications for health, education, and the workplace. *Psychological Science in the Public Interest, 5*, 69–106. http://dx.doi.org/10.1111/j.1529-1006.2004.00018.x

Ehrlich, T. (Ed.). (2000). *Civic responsibility and higher education*. Phoenix, AZ: Oryx Press.

Endler, N. S., & Parker, J. D. (1990). Multidimensional assessment of coping: A critical evaluation. *Journal of Personality and Social Psychology, 58*, 844–854. http://dx.doi.org/10.1037/0022-3514.58.5.844

Erickson, J. A., & O'Connor, S. E. (2000). Service-learning: Does it promote or reduce prejudice? In C. R. O'Grady (Ed.), *Integrating service-learning and multicultural education in colleges and universities* (pp. 59–70). Mahwah, NJ: Erlbaum.

Esses, V. M., & Dovidio, J. F. (2011). Social psychology, social issues, and social policy: What have we learned? *Social Issues and Policy Review, 5*, 1–7. http://dx.doi.org/10.1111/j.1751-2409.2011.01023.x

Eyler, J. (2001). Creating your reflection map. *New Directions for Higher Education, 2001*, 35–43. http://dx.doi.org/10.1002/he.11

Eyler, J. S. (2002). Reflection: Linking service and learning—Linking students and communities. *Journal of Social Issues, 58*, 517–534. http://dx.doi.org/10.1111/1540-4560.00274

Eyler, J. S. (2011). What international service learning research can learn from research on service learning. In R. G. Bringle, J. A. Hatcher, & S. G. Jones (Eds.), *International service learning: Conceptual frameworks and research* (pp. 225–241). Sterling, VA: Stylus.

Eyler, J. S., & Giles, D. E., Jr. (1999). *Where's the learning in service-learning?* San Francisco, CA: Jossey-Bass.

Eyler, J. S., Giles, D. E., Jr., Stenson, C. M., & Gray, C. J. (2001). *At a glance: What we know about the effects of service-learning on college students, faculty, institutions, and communities, 1993–2000* (3rd ed.). Nashville, TN: Vanderbilt University.

Felten, P., & Clayton, P. H. (2011). Service-learning. In W. Buskist & J. E. Groccia (Eds.), *Evidence-based teaching: New directions for teaching and learning, 128* (pp. 75–84). San Francisco, CA: Jossey-Bass.

Finkelstein, M. A. (2002). Engaged scholarship in the classroom: The social psychology of HIV/AIDS. *Journal of Higher Education Outreach and Engagement, 7*, 69–80.

Fitch, P. (2005). In their own voices: A mixed methods approach to studying outcomes of intercultural service learning with college students. In S. Root, J. Callahan, & S. H. Billig (Eds.), *Improving service-learning practice: Research on models to enhance impacts* (pp. 187–211). Greenwich, CT: Information Age.

Fitch, P., Steinke, P., & Hudson, T. D. (2013). Research and theoretical perspectives on cognitive outcomes of service learning. In P. H. Clayton, R. G. Bringle, & J. A. Hatcher (Eds.), *Research on service learning: Conceptual frameworks and assessment. Vol. 2A: Students and faculty* (pp. 57–84). Sterling, VA: Stylus.

Fitzgerald, H. E., & Primavera, J. (Eds.). (2013). *Going public: Civic and community engagement.* East Lansing: Michigan State University Press.

Florida Department of Education. (2009). *Standards for service-learning in Florida: A guide for creating and sustaining quality practice.* Tallahassee, FL: Florida Learn & Serve.

Fox, C. M. (2007). Brain awareness day. *Journal of College Science Teaching, 37*, 40–45.

Franco, R., Duffy, D., Baratian, M., Hendricks, A., & Renner, T. (2007). *Service-learning course design for community colleges.* Providence, RI: Campus Compact.

REFERENCES

Franz, N. K. (2011). Tips for constructing a promotion and tenure dossier that documents engaged scholarship endeavors. *Journal of Higher Education Outreach and Engagement, 15,* 15–29.

Fretz, E., & Longo, N. (2010). Students co-creating an engaged academy. In H. Fitzgerald, C. Burack, & S. Seifer (Eds.), *Handbook of engaged scholarship: Contemporary landscapes, future directions* (pp. 313–329). East Lansing: Michigan State University Press.

Friedman, T. L. (2000). *The Lexus and the olive tree: Understanding globalization.* New York, NY: Anchor Books, Random House.

Furco, A. (1996). Service-learning: A balanced approach to experiential education. In B. Taylor & Corporation for National Service (Eds.), *Expanding boundaries: Service and learning* (pp. 2–6). Washington, DC: Corporation for National Service.

Furco, A., & Moely, B. E. (2012). Using learning communities to build faculty support for pedagogical innovation: A multi-campus study. *The Journal of Higher Education, 83,* 128–153. http://dx.doi.org/10.1353/jhe.2012.0006

Gabelnick, F., MacGregor, J., Matthews, R. S., & Smith, B. L. (1990). *Learning communities: Creating connections among students, faculty, and disciplines.* San Francisco, CA: Jossey-Bass.

Gibbons, M., Limoges, C., Nowotny, H., Schwartzman, S., Scott, P., & Trow, M. (1994). *The new production of knowledge: The dynamics of science and research in contemporary societies.* Thousand Oaks, CA: Sage.

Gelmon, S. B., Holland, B. A., Driscoll, A., Spring, A., & Kerrigan, S. (2001). *Assessing service-learning and civic engagement: Principles and techniques.* Boston, MA: Campus Compact.

Glassick, C. E., Huber, M. T., & Maeroff, G. I. (1997). *Scholarship assessed: Evaluation of the professoriate.* San Francisco, CA: Jossey-Bass.

Gottlieb, K., & Robinson, G. (Eds.). (2002). *A practical guide for integrating civic responsibility into the curriculum.* Washington, DC: Community College Press.

Greenleaf, R. K. (2002). *Servant leadership: A journey into the nature of legitimate power and greatness* (25th anniversary ed.). New York, NY: Paulist Press.

Gronlund, S. D., & Lewandowsky, S. (1992). Making TV commercials as a teaching aid for cognitive psychology. *Teaching of Psychology, 19,* 158–160. http://dx.doi.org/10.1207/s15328023top1903_7

Gurecka, L. E., & Gent, P. J. (2001). Service-learning: A disservice to people with disabilities? *Michigan Journal of Community Service Learning, 8,* 36–43.

Gurung, R. A. R., Ansburg, P. I., Alexander, P. A., Lawrence, N., & Johnson, D. E. (2008). The state of the scholarship of teaching and learning in psychology. *Teaching of Psychology, 35,* 249–261. http://dx.doi.org/10.1080/00986280802374203

Gurung, R. A. R., Freeman, J., Cacioppo, J., Hackathorn, J., Enns, C., Loop, T., & Franz, S. (2014). *APA Board of Educational Affairs working group on strengthening the common core of the introductory psychology course*. Washington, DC: American Psychological Association.

Gurung, R. A. R., & Schwartz, B. M. (2009). *Optimizing teaching and learning*. Chichester, England: Wiley-Blackwell.

Guthrie, K. L., & McCracken, H. (2010). Teaching and learning social justice through online service-learning courses. *International Review of Research in Open and Distance Learning, 11*, 78–94.

Hager, L. D. (2011). Tools for teaching cognitive psychology: Using public service announcements for education on environmental sustainability. *Teaching of Psychology, 38*, 162–165. http://dx.doi.org/10.1177/0098628311411784

Halonen, J. S. (2013). Promoting effective program leadership in psychology: A benchmarking strategy. *Teaching of Psychology, 40*, 318–329. http://dx.doi.org/10.1177/0098628313501045

Halonen, J. S., Dunn, D. S., Baker, S., & McCarthy, M. A. (2011). Departmental approaches for educating psychologically literate citizens. In J. Cranney & D. Dunn (Eds.), *The psychologically literate citizen: Foundations and global perspectives* (pp. 131–145). New York, NY: Oxford University Press. http://dx.doi.org/10.1093/acprof:oso/9780199794942.003.0038

Halpern, D. F. (Ed.). (2010). *Undergraduate education in psychology: A blueprint for the future of the discipline*. Washington, DC: American Psychological Association. http://dx.doi.org/10.1037/12063-000

Halpern, D. F., Anton, B., Beins, B. C., Bernstein, D. J., Blair-Broeker, C. T., Brewer, C. L., . . . Rocheleau, C. A. (2010). Principles for quality undergraduate education in psychology. In D. F. Halpern (Ed.), *Undergraduate education in psychology: A blueprint for the future of the discipline* (pp. 161–173). Washington, DC: American Psychological Association. http://dx.doi.org/10.1037/12063-010

Halpern, D. F., & Hakel, M. D. (2003). Applying the science of learning to the university and beyond. *Change, 35*(4), 37–41.

Halpern, D. F., & Reich, J. N. (1999). Scholarship in psychology: Conversations about change and constancy. *American Psychologist, 54*, 347–349. http://dx.doi.org/10.1037/0003-066X.54.5.347

Halpern, D. F., Smothergill, D. W., Allen, M., Baker, S., Baum, C., Best, D., . . . Weaver, K. A. (1998). Scholarship in psychology: A paradigm for the twenty-first century. *American Psychologist, 53*, 1292–1297. http://dx.doi.org/10.1037/0003-066X.53.12.1292

REFERENCES

Harmon-Vukić, M. E., & Schanz, K. (2012). A cultural immersion course in psychology. *Teaching of Psychology, 39*, 142–145. http://dx.doi.org/10.1177/0098628312437703

Harnish, R., & Bridges, K. R. (2012). Promoting student engagement: Using community service-learning projects in undergraduate psychology. *PRISM, 1*, 82–92.

Hartman, E. (2013). No values, no democracy: The essential partisanship of a civic engagement movement. *Michigan Journal of Community Service Learning, 19*(2), 58–71.

Harwood, A. M., Ochs, L., Currier, D., Duke, S., Hammond, J., Moulds, L., . . . Werder, C. (2005). Communities for growth: Cultivating and sustaining service-learning teaching and scholarship in a fellow program. *Michigan Journal of Community Service Learning, 12*(1), 41–51.

Hatcher, J. A., & Bringle, R. G. (1997). Reflection: Bridging the gap between service and learning. *Journal of College Teaching, 45*, 153–158. http://dx.doi.org/10.1080/87567559709596221

Hatcher, J. A., Bringle, R. G., & Muthiah, R. (2004). Designing effective reflection: What matters to service learning? *Michigan Journal of Community Service Learning, 11*(1), 38–46.

Heffernan, K. (2001). *Fundamentals of service-learning course construction*. Providence, RI: Campus Compact.

Hessels, L. K., & Van Lente, H. (2008). Re-thinking new knowledge production: A literature review and a research agenda. *Research Policy, 37*, 740–760. http://dx.doi.org/10.1016/j.respol.2008.01.008

Hesser, G. (1995). Faculty assessment of student learning: Outcomes attributed to service-learning and evidence of changes in faculty attitudes about experiential education. *Michigan Journal of Community Service Learning, 2*(1), 33–42.

Holland, B. (1999). Factors and strategies that influence faculty involvement in public service. *Journal of Public Service and Outreach, 4*, 37–43.

Homa, N., Hackathorn, J., Brown, C. M., Garczynski, A., Solomon, E. D., Tennial, R., . . . Gurung, R. A. R. (2013). An analysis of learning objectives and content coverage in introductory psychology syllabi. *Teaching of Psychology, 40*, 169–174. http://dx.doi.org/10.1177/0098628313487456

Hopko, D. R., Lejuez, C. W., Ruggiero, K. J., & Eifert, G. H. (2003). Contemporary behavioral activation treatments for depression: Procedures, principles, and progress. *Clinical Psychology Review, 23*, 699–717. http://dx.doi.org/10.1016/S0272-7358(03)00070-9

REFERENCES

Hou, S. I. (2010). Developing a faculty inventory measuring perceived service-learning benefits and barriers. *Michigan Journal of Community Service Learning, 16*(2), 78–89.

Hovey, R., & Weinberg, A. (2009). Global learning and the making of citizen diplomats. In R. Lewin (Ed.), *Study abroad and the making of global citizens: Higher education and the quest for global citizenship* (pp. 33–48). New York, NY: Routledge.

Howard, J. P. F. (1998). Academic service learning: A counternormative pedagogy. *New Directions for Teaching and Learning, 73,* 21–29. http://dx.doi.org/10.1002/tl.7303

Howard, J. P. F. (2001). *Service-learning course design workbook.* Ann Arbor, MI: University of Michigan.

Huber, M. T., & Hutchings, P. (2005). *The advancement of learning: Building the teaching commons.* San Francisco, CA: Jossey-Bass.

Huber, M. T., & Hutchings, P. (2010). Foreword. In M. B. Smith, R. S. Nowacek, & J. L. Bernstein (Eds.), *Citizenship across the curriculum* (pp. ix–xiii). Bloomington: Indiana University Press.

Hurtado, S., Eagan, M. K., Pryor, J. H., Whang, H., & Tran, S. (2012). *Undergraduate teaching faculty: The 2010–2011 HERI Faculty Survey.* Los Angeles, CA: Higher Education Research Institute, UCLA.

Irons, J. G., & Buskist, W. (2008). The scholarships of teaching and pedagogy: Time to abandon the distinction? *Teaching of Psychology, 35,* 353–356. http://dx.doi.org/10.1080/00986280802373957

Jacoby, B. (2014). *Service-learning essentials: Questions, answers, and lessons learned.* New York, NY: Wiley.

Jacoby, B., & Associates. (2009). *Civic engagement in higher education: Concepts and practices.* San Francisco, CA: Jossey-Bass.

Jaeger, A., & Thornton, C. (2006, November). *Neither honor nor compensation: Faculty and public service.* Paper presented at the meeting of the Association for the Study of Higher Education, Philadelphia, PA.

James, W. (1996). *Pragmatism: A new name for some old ways of thinking.* New York, NY: Longmans, Green, and Company. (Original work published 1907)

Jameson, J. K., Clayton, P. H., & Ash, S. L. (2013). Conceptualizing, assessing, and investigating academic learning in service learning. In P. H. Clayton, R. G. Bringle, & J. A. Hatcher (Eds.), *Research on service learning: Conceptual frameworks and assessment. Vol. 2A: Students and faculty* (pp. 85–110). Sterling, VA: Stylus Publishing.

Jameson, J. K., Clayton, P. H., & Bringle, R. G. (2008). Investigating student learning within and across linked service-learning courses. In M. A. Bowdon, S. H. Billig, & B. A. Holland (Eds.), *Advances in service-learning research: Scholar-*

REFERENCES

ship for sustaining service-learning and civic engagement (pp. 3–27). Charlotte, NC: Information Age Publishing.

Jameson, J. K., Clayton, P. H., Jaeger, A. J., & Bringle, R. G. (2012). Investigating faculty learning in the context of community-engaged scholarship. *Michigan Journal of Community Service Learning, 18*(2), 40–55.

Janke, E. M. (2013). Organizational partnerships in service learning. In P. H. Clayton, R. G. Bringle, & J. A. Hatcher (Eds.), *Research on service learning: Conceptual frameworks and assessment. Vol. 2B: Communities, institutions, and partnerships* (pp. 573–598). Sterling, VA: Stylus.

Jordan, C. (Ed.). (2007). *Community-engaged scholarship review, promotion & tenure package.* Retrieved from http://depts.washington.edu/ccph/pdf_files/CES_RPT_Package.pdf

Kalisch, H. R., Coughlin, D. R., Ballard, S. M., & Lamson, A. (2013). Old age is a part of living: Student reflections on intergenerational service-learning. *Gerontology & Geriatrics Education, 34*, 99–113. http://dx.doi.org/10.1080/02701960.2012.753440

Kaugars, A. S. (2011). *Evaluating the impact of service learning on student outcomes in a health psychology course.* Retrieved from http://epublications.marquette.edu/cgi/viewcontent.cgi?article=1095&context=psych_fac

Kazdin, A. E. (1998). *Research design in clinical psychology* (3rd ed.). New York, NY: Allyn & Bacon.

Kecskes, K. (2006). *Engaging departments: Moving faculty culture from private to public, individual to collective focus for the common good.* San Francisco, CA: Jossey-Bass.

Kecskes, K. (2008). Engagement in the disciplines. *The Department Chair, 18*(3), 16–18.

Kecskes, K. (2009). *Creating community-engaged departments: Self-assessment rubric for the institutionalization of community engagement in academic departments.* Retrieved from http://www.pdx.edu/sites/www.pdx.edu.cae/files/Engaged%20Department%20RUBRIC%20-%20Kecskes%202009-paginated.pdf

Kecskes, K., Gelmon, S. B., & Spring, A. (2006). Creating engaged departments: A program for organizational and faculty development. *To Improve the Academy, 24*, 147–165.

Keen, C., & Hall, K. (2009). Engaging with difference matters: Longitudinal student outcomes of co-curricular service-learning programs. *The Journal of Higher Education, 80*, 59–79. http://dx.doi.org/10.1353/jhe.0.0037

Kern-Manwaring, N., & Wickline, V. B. (2013). Health matters: Service-learning interdisciplinary health fair in nursing and psychology provides student satisfaction and growth. *Association for University Regional Campuses of Ohio (AURCO) Journal, 19*, 113–125.

Keyton, J. (2001). Integrating service-learning in the research methods course. *Southern Journal of Communication, 66*, 201–210. http://dx.doi.org/10.1080/10417940109373199

Kezar, A. J., Chambers, T. C., & Burkhardt, J. C. (2005). *Higher education for the public good: Emerging voices from a national movement.* San Francisco, CA: Jossey-Bass.

Kiely, R. (2004). A chameleon with a complex: Searching for transformation in international service-learning. *Michigan Journal of Community Service Learning, 10*(2), 5–20.

Knapp, J. L., & Stubblefield, P. (2000). Changing students' perception of aging: The impact of an intergenerational service learning course. *Educational Gerontology, 26*, 611–621. http://dx.doi.org/10.1080/03601270050200617

Kolb, D. A. (1984). *Experiential learning: Experience as the source of learning and development.* Englewood Cliffs, NJ: Prentice-Hall.

Kolek, E. A. (2013). Can we count on counting? An analysis of the validity of community engagement survey measures. *International Journal of Research on Service-Learning and Community Engagement, 1*, 92–108.

Kretchmar, M. D. (2001). Service learning in a general psychology class: Description, preliminary evaluation, and recommendations. *Teaching of Psychology, 28*, 5–10. http://dx.doi.org/10.1207/S15328023TOP2801_02

Kretzmann, J. P., & McKnight, J. L. (1993). *Building communities from the inside out: A path toward finding and mobilizing a community's assets.* Evanston, IL: Center for Urban Affairs and Policy.

Kuh, G. D. (2008). *High-impact educational practices: What they are, who has access to them, and why they matter.* Washington, DC: Association of American Colleges and Universities.

Lagemann, E. C. (1989). The plural worlds of educational research. *History of Education, 29*, 185–214. http://dx.doi.org/10.2307/368309

Lambert, M. J., Bergin, A. E., & Garfield, S. L. (2004). *Bergin and Garfield's handbook of psychotherapy and behavior change* (5th ed.). New York, NY: Wiley.

Landrum, R. E., Beins, B. C., Bhalla, M., Brakke, K., Briihl, D. S., Curl-Langager, R. M., . . . Van Kirk, J. J. (2010). Desired outcomes of an undergraduate education in psychology from departmental, student, and societal perspectives. In D. F. Halpern (Ed.), *Undergraduate education in psychology: A blueprint for the future of the discipline* (pp. 145–160). Washington, DC: American Psychological Association. http://dx.doi.org/10.1037/12063-009

Lazarus, R., & Folkman, S. (1984). *Stress, appraisal, and coping.* New York, NY: Springer.

Lenning, O. T., & Ebbers, L. H. (1999). *The powerful potential of learning communities: Improving education for the future* (ASHE-ERIC Higher Education

Report, Vol. 26, No. 6). Washington, DC: ERIC Clearinghouse on Higher Education.

Levine, P. (2013). *We are the ones we have been waiting for: The promise of civic renewal in America.* New York, NY: Oxford University Press.

Lewin, K. (1952). *Field theory in social science: Selected theoretical papers.* London, England: Tavistock.

Lichtenstein, M. (2005). The importance of classroom environments in the assessment of learning community outcomes. *Journal of College Student Development, 46,* 341–356. http://dx.doi.org/10.1353/csd.2005.0038

Lightfoot, C. (2013, January). *Educating global citizens: The psychology classroom as seedbed for civil society.* Paper presented at the meeting of the National Institute for the Teaching of Psychology, Tampa, FL.

Lisman, C. D. (1997). The tension of theory and practice in service-learning. In T. Pickeral & K. Peters (Eds.), *Tensions inherent in service-learning: Achieving a balance* (pp. 77–89). Mesa, AZ: Campus Compact National Center for Community Colleges.

Littlepage, L., & Gazley, B. (2013). Examining service learning from the perspective of community organization capacity. In P. H. Clayton, R. G. Bringle, & J. A. Hatcher (Eds.), *Research on service learning: Conceptual frameworks and assessment. Vol. 2B: Communities, institutions, and partnerships* (pp. 419–437). Sterling, VA: Stylus.

Lockeman, K., & Pelco, L. (2013). The relationship between service learning and degree completion. *Michigan Journal of Community Service Learning, 20*(1), 18–30.

Lundy, B. L. (2007). Service learning in life-span developmental psychology: Higher exam scores and increased empathy. *Teaching of Psychology, 34,* 23–27. http://dx.doi.org/10.1080/00986280709336644

Machado, A., & Silva, F. (1998). Greatness and misery in the teaching of the psychology of learning. *Journal of the Experimental Analysis of Behavior, 70,* 215–234. http://dx.doi.org/10.1901/jeab.1998.70-215

Machtmes, K., Johnson, E., Fox, J., Burke, M. S., Harper, J., Arcemont, L., ... Aguirre, R. T. (2009). Teaching qualitative research methods through service-learning. *Qualitative Report, 14,* 155–164.

Marchese, T. J. (1997). The new conversation about learning: Insights from neuroscience and anthropology, cognitive studies and work-place studies. In American Association for Higher Education (Ed.), *Assessing impact: Evidence and action* (pp. 79–95). Washington, DC: American Association for Higher Education.

Masters, K. S., France, C. R., & Thorn, B. E. (2009). Enhancing preparation among entry-level clinical health psychologists: Recommendations for "best practices" from the first meeting of the Council of Clinical Health Psychology Training Programs (CCHPTP). *Training and Education in Professional Psychology, 3*(4), 193–201. http://dx.doi.org/10.1037/a0016049

Mathews, D. (1995). The politics of diversity and the politics of difference: Are academics and the public out of sync? *Higher Education Exchange,* 66–71.

Mathie, V. A., Buskist, W., Carlson, J. F., Davis, S. F., Johnson, D. E., & Smith, R. A. (2004). Expanding the boundaries of scholarship in psychology through teaching, research, service, and administration. *Teaching of Psychology, 31,* 233–241. http://dx.doi.org/10.1207/s15328023top3104_2

McGorry, S. Y. (2014). No significant difference in service learning online. *Journal of Asynchronous Learning Networks, 14*(4), 45–54.

McGovern, T. V., Corey, L., Cranney, J., Dixon, W. E., Jr., Holmes, J. D., Kuebli, J. E., . . . Walker, S. J. (2010). Psychologically literate citizens. In D. F. Halpern (Ed.), *Undergraduate education in psychology: A blueprint for the future of the discipline* (pp. 9–27). Washington, DC: American Psychological Association. http://dx.doi.org/10.1037/12063-001

McKay, V. C., & Rozee, P. D. (2004). Characteristics of faculty who adopt community service-learning pedagogy. *Michigan Journal of Community Service Learning, 10*(2), 21–33.

McMillan, D. W., & Chavis, D. M. (1986). Sense of community: A definition and theory. *Journal of Community Psychology, 14,* 6–23. http://dx.doi.org/10.1002/1520-6629(198601)14:1<6::AID-JCOP2290140103>3.0.CO;2-I

Millis, K. K. (2001). Comparing two collaborative projects in a cognitive psychology course. *Teaching of Psychology, 28,* 263–265. http://dx.doi.org/10.1207/S15328023TOP2804_06

Minkler, M., & Freudenberg, N. (2010). From community-based participatory research to policy change. In H. E. Fitzgerald, C. Burack, & S. D. Seifer (Eds.), *Handbook of engaged scholarship: Vol. 2. Contemporary landscapes, future directions. Community–campus partnerships* (pp. 275–294). East Lansing: Michigan State University Press.

Minkler, M., & Wallerstein, N. (2003). *Community-based participatory research for health.* San Francisco, CA: Jossey-Bass.

Mitchell, T. D. (2007). Critical service learning as social justice education: A case study of the citizen scholars program. *Equity & Excellence in Education, 40,* 101–112. http://dx.doi.org/10.1080/10665680701228797

Mitchell, T. D. (2008). Traditional vs. critical service-learning: Engaging the literature to differentiate two models. *Michigan Journal of Community Service Learning, 14*(1), 50–65.

REFERENCES

Moore, T. L., & Ward, K. (2008). Documenting engagement: Faculty perspectives on self-representation for promotion and tenure. *Journal of Higher Education Outreach and Engagement, 12*(4), 5–27.

Moore, T. L., & Ward, K. (2010). Institutionalizing faculty engagement through research, teaching, and service at research universities. *Michigan Journal of Community Service Learning, 17*(1), 44–58.

Mpofu, E. (2007). Service learning effects on the academic learning of rehabilitation services students. *Michigan Journal of Community Service Learning, 14*(1), 46–52.

Muenzinger, K. F. (1939). *Psychology: The science of behavior.* Denver, CO: World Press.

The National Task Force on Civic Learning and Democratic Engagement. (2012). *A crucible moment: College learning and democracy's future.* Washington, DC: Association of American Colleges and Universities.

Naudé, L. (2012). At the cultural crossroads: Intergroup psychology among students in a service-learning programme. *Current Psychology, 31,* 221–245. http://dx.doi.org/10.1007/s12144-012-9142-5

Nelson, G., Ochocka, J., Griffin, K., & Lord, J. (1998). "Nothing about me, without me": Participatory action research with self-help/mutual aid organizations for psychiatric consumer/survivors. *American Journal of Community Psychology, 26,* 881–912. http://dx.doi.org/10.1023/A:1022298129812

Nelson, P. D. (2004). *Civic engagement and scholarship: Implications for graduate education in psychology.* Retrieved from http://www.apa.org/education/undergrad/engage-nelson.pdf

Niehaus, E., & Crain, L. K. (2013). Act local or global?: Comparing student experiences in domestic and international service-learning programs. *Michigan Journal of Community Service Learning, 20*(1), 31–40.

Novak, J. M., Markey, V., & Allen, M. (2007). Evaluating cognitive outcomes of service learning in higher education: A meta-analysis. *Communication Research Reports, 24,* 149–157. http://dx.doi.org/10.1080/08824090701304881

O'Grady, C. R. (Ed.). (2000). *Integrating service learning and multicultural education in colleges and universities.* Mahwah, NJ: Erlbaum.

O'Meara, K. (2002). *Scholarship unbound: Assessing service as scholarship for promotion and tenure.* New York, NY: RoutledgeFalmer.

O'Meara, K. (2003). Reframing incentives and rewards for community service-learning and academic outreach. *Journal of Higher Education Outreach and Engagement, 8*(2), 201–220.

O'Meara, K. (2005). Effects of encouraging multiple forms of scholarship nationwide and across institutional types. In K. O'Meara & R. E. Rice (Eds.), *Faculty priorities reconsidered: Rewarding multiple forms of scholarship* (pp. 255–289). San Francisco, CA: Jossey-Bass.

O'Meara, K. (2013). Research on faculty motivation for service learning. In P. H. Clayton, R. G. Bringle, & J. A. Hatcher (Eds.), *Research on service learning: Conceptual frameworks and assessment, Vol. 2A: Students and faculty* (pp. 215–243). Sterling, VA: Stylus.

O'Meara, K., Lounder, A., & Hodges, A. (2013). University leaders' use of episodic power to support faculty community engagement. *Michigan Journal of Community Service Learning, 19*(2), 5–20.

O'Meara, K., & Niehaus, B. (2009). Service-learning is . . . : How faculty explain their practice. *Michigan Journal of Community Service Learning, 16*(1), 1–16.

Omoto, A. (2012). Social policy. In K. Deaux & M. Snyder (Eds.), *The Oxford handbook of personality and social psychology* (pp. 804–829). New York, NY: Oxford University Press.

Osborne, R. E., & Renick, O. (2006). Service learning. In W. Buskist & S. F. Davis (Eds.), *Handbook of the teaching of psychology* (pp. 137–141). Malden, MA: Blackwell. http://dx.doi.org/10.1002/9780470754924.ch23

O'Sullivan, M. J. (1993). Teaching undergraduate community psychology: Integrating the classroom and the surrounding community. *Teaching of Psychology, 20*, 80–83. http://dx.doi.org/10.1207/s15328023top2002_3

Ozorak, E. W. (2004). Integrating service learning into psychology courses. In B. Perlman, L. I. McCann, & S. H. McFadden (Eds.), *Lessons learned: Practical advice for the teaching of psychology* (Vol. 2, pp. 137–146). Washington, DC: American Psychological Society.

Pascarella, E., & Terenzini, P. (2005). *How college affects students: Vol. 2. A third decade of research.* San Francisco, CA: Jossey-Bass.

Penick, J. M., Fallshore, M., & Spencer, A. M. (2014). Using intergenerational service learning to promote positive perceptions about older adults and community service in college students. *Journal of Intergenerational Relationships, 12*, 25–39. http://dx.doi.org/10.1080/15350770.2014.870456

Perring, C. (2008). Ethical issues in teaching death and dying: Pedagogical aims in end-of-life ethics. In C. M. Moreman (Ed.), *Teaching death and dying* (pp. 33–48). Oxford, England: Oxford University Press. http://dx.doi.org/10.1093/acprof:oso/9780195335224.003.0004

Peters, S. J. (2010). *Democracy and higher education: Traditions and stories of civic engagement.* East Lansing: Michigan State University Press.

Peterson, C., & Seligman, M. E. P. (2004). *Character strengths and virtues: A handbook and classification.* Washington, DC: American Psychological Association and Oxford University Press.

REFERENCES

Petracchi, H. E., Weaver, A., Engel, R. J., Kolivoski, K. M., & Das, R. (2010). An assessment of service learning in a university living-learning community: Implications for community engagement. *Journal of Community Practice, 18*, 252–266. http://dx.doi.org/10.1080/10705422.2010.490743

Pierce, C. S. (1997). The fixation of belief. In L. Menand (Ed.), *Pragmatism: A reader* (pp. 7–25). New York, NY: Vantage Books. (Original work published 1878)

Porfilio, B., & Hickman, H. (Eds.). (2011). *Critical service learning as revolutionary pedagogy: A product of student agency in action.* Charlotte, NC: Information Age Publishing.

Porpora, D. V. (1999). Action research: The highest stage of service-learning? In J. Ostrow, G. Hesser, & S. Enos (Eds.), *Cultivating the sociological imagination: Concepts and models for service-learning in sociology* (pp. 121–133). Washington, DC: American Association for Higher Education.

Pribbenow, D. A. (2005). The impact of service-learning pedagogy on faculty teaching and learning. *Michigan Journal of Community Service Learning, 11*(2), 25–38.

Prilleltensky, I. (1997). Values, assumptions, and practices: Assessing the moral implications of psychological discourse and action. *American Psychologist, 52*, 517–535. http://dx.doi.org/10.1037/0003-066X.52.5.517

Prilleltensky, I. (2008). The role of power in wellness, oppression, and liberation: The promise of psychopolitical validity. *Journal of Community Psychology, 36*, 116–136. http://dx.doi.org/10.1002/jcop.20225

Putnam, H. (1962). What theories are not. In E. Nagel, P. Suppes, & A. Tarski (Eds.), *Logic, methodology and philosophy of science* (pp. 240–251). Stanford, CA: Stanford University Press.

Rajecki, D. W., Appleby, D., Williams, C., Johnson, K., & Jeschke, M. (2005). Statistics can wait: Career plans, activity, and course preferences of American psychology undergraduates. *Psychology Learning & Teaching, 4*, 83–89.

Ralph, R. O. (2005). Verbal definitions and visual models of recovery: Focus on the recovery model. In R. O. Ralph & P. W. Corrigan (Eds.), *Recovery in mental illness: Broadening our understanding of wellness* (pp. 134–145). Washington, DC: American Psychological Association. http://dx.doi.org/10.1037/10848-006

Reeb, R. N., Farmer, C. N., Glendening, Z. S., & Kinsey, R. (2014, August). *Application of psycho-ecological systems model: Behavioral activation in homeless shelters.* Poster presented at the meeting of the American Psychological Association, Washington, DC.

Reeb, R. N., & Folger, S. F. (2013). Community outcomes in service learning: Research and practice from a systems perspective. In P. H. Clayton, R. G. Bringle,

& J. A. Hatcher (Eds.), *Research on service learning: Conceptual models and assessment, Vol. 2B: Communities, institutions, and partnerships* (pp. 389–418). Sterling, VA: Stylus.

Reeb, R. N., Folger, S. F., Langsner, S., Ryan, C., & Crouse, J. (2010). Self-efficacy in service-learning community action research: Theory, research, and practice. *American Journal of Community Psychology, 46,* 459–471. http://dx.doi.org/10.1007/s10464-010-9342-9

Reeb, R. N., Glendening, Z. S., Farmer, C. N., & Kinsey, R. (2014, May). *Effects of behavioral activation in a homeless shelter for men.* Poster presented at the meeting of the Midwestern Psychological Association, Chicago, IL.

Reeb, R. N., Glendening, Z. S., Farmer, C. N., Snow, N. L., & Elvers, G. C. (2014, October). *Behavioral activation in a homeless shelter: An interdisciplinary service-learning community-based research project.* Paper presented at the meeting of the International Association for Research on Service-learning and Community Engagement, New Orleans, LA.

Reeb, R. N., Sammon, J. A., & Isackson, N. L. (1999). Clinical application of the service-learning model in psychology: Evidence of educational and clinical benefits. *Prevention & Intervention in the Community, 18,* 65–82. http://dx.doi.org/10.1300/J005v18n01_06

Reeb, R. N., Snow, N. L., Steel, A., Stayton, L., Mason, S., & Folger, S. F. (2014). *Psycho-ecological systems model for engaged scholarship and service-learning: Theory, research, and practice.* Manuscript submitted for publication.

Reich, J. N., & Nelson, P. D. (2010). Engaged scholarship: Perspectives from psychology. In H. E. Fitzgerald, C. Burack, & S. D. Seifer (Eds.), *Handbook of engaged scholarship: Contemporary landscapes, future directions. Volume 2: Community–campus partnerships* (pp. 131–147). East Lansing: Michigan State University Press.

Rice, D., & Stacey, K. (1997). Small group dynamics as a catalyst for change: A faculty development model for academic service-learning. *Michigan Journal of Community Service Learning, 4*(1), 464–471.

Rice, R. E. (1996). *Making a place for the new American scholar.* Washington, DC: American Association for Higher Education.

Roodin, P., Brown, L. H., & Shedlock, D. (2013). Intergenerational service-learning: A review of recent literature and directions for the future. *Gerontology & Geriatrics Education, 34,* 3–25. http://dx.doi.org/10.1080/02701960.2012.755624

Root, R., & Thorme, T. (2001). Community-based projects in applied statistics: Using service-learning to enhance student understanding. *The American Statistician, 55,* 326–331. http://dx.doi.org/10.1198/000313001753272295

Rosenthal, L. (2006). *2006 Action Teaching Award winner*. Retrieved from Social Psychology Network website: http://www.socialpsychology.org/action/2006winner.htm

Ruiz, A., & Warchal, J. (2013). Long-term impact of service-learning on alumni volunteer service activities. In P. Lin & M. Wiegand (Eds.), *Service-learning in higher education: Connecting the global to the local* (pp. 255–264). Indianapolis: University of Indianapolis Press.

Ruiz, A., Warchal, J., Chapdelaine, A., & Wells, C. (2011, April). *Service learning: New ethical goals and challenges for universities*. Retrieved from http://www.psychologytoday.com/blog/the-ethical-professor/201104/service-learning-new-ethical-goals-and-challenges-universities

Saltmarsh, J. (2005). The civic promise of service learning. *Liberal Education and the New Academy, 91*, 50–55.

Saltmarsh, J., & Hartley, M. (2011). *To serve a larger purpose: Engagement for democracy and the transformation of higher education*. Philadelphia, PA: Temple University Press.

Saltmarsh, J., Hartley, M., & Clayton, P. H. (2009). *Democratic engagement white paper*. Boston, MA: New England Resource Center for Higher Education.

Saltmarsh, J., & Zlotkowski, E. (2011). *Higher education and democracy: Essays on service-learning and civic engagement*. Philadelphia, PA: Temple University Press.

Saltmarsh, J., Zlotkowski, E., & Horowitz, K. (2010, April). *Students as colleagues in the next generation of civic engagement*. Paper presented at the meeting of the New England Regional Campus Compact, Burlington, VT.

Sandmann, L., & Plater, W. M. (2013). Research on institutional leadership for service learning. In P. H. Clayton, R. G. Bringle, & J. A. Hatcher (Eds.), *Research on service learning: Conceptual frameworks and assessment. Vol. 2B: Communities, institutions, and partnerships* (pp. 505–535). Sterling, VA: Stylus.

Sandmann, L., Saltmarsh, J., & O'Meara, K. (2008). An integrated model for advancing the scholarship of engagement: Creating academic homes for the engaged scholar. *Journal of Higher Education Outreach and Engagement, 12*, 47–64.

Sandy, L. R. (1998). The permeable classroom. *Journal on Excellence in College Teaching, 9*, 47–60.

Sandy, M., & Holland, B. A. (2006). Different worlds and common ground: Community partner perspectives on campus–community partnerships. *Michigan Journal of Community Service Learning, 13*(1), 30–43.

Sandy, M. G., & Franco, Z. E. (2014). Grounding service-learning in the digital age: Exploring a virtual sense of geographic place through online collaborative mapping and mixed media. *Journal of Higher Education Outreach and Engagement, 18,* 201–222.

Sarason, S. B. (1988). *The making of an American psychologist.* San Francisco, CA: Jossey-Bass.

Sax, L. J., & Astin, A. W. (1997). The benefits of service: Evidence from undergraduates. *The Educational Record, 78,* 25–32.

Schneider, S. F. (1990). Psychology at a crossroads. *American Psychologist, 45,* 521–529. http://dx.doi.org/10.1037/0003-066X.45.4.521

Seifer, S. D., & Connors, K. (Eds.). (2007). *Community campus partnerships for health. Faculty toolkit for service-learning in higher education.* Scotts Valley, CA: National Service-Learning Clearinghouse.

Sgoutas-Emch, S. A. (2013). Integrative learning and a community-based project in a health psychology course. *Journal for Civic Commitment, 20,* 1–14.

Shulman, L. (1998). Course anatomy: The dissection and analysis of knowledge through teaching. In P. Hutchings & L. Shulman (Eds.), *The course portfolio: How faculty can examine their teaching to advance practice and improve student learning* (pp. 5–12). Sterling, VA: Stylus.

Shupe, E. I. (2013). The development of an undergraduate study abroad program: Nicaragua and the psychology of social inequality. *Teaching of Psychology, 40,* 124–129. http://dx.doi.org/10.1177/0098628312475032

Sigmon, R. (1979). Service-learning: Three principles. *Synergist, 8,* 9–11.

Simons, L., Fehr, L., Hogerwerff, F., Blank, N., Georganas, D., & Russell, B. (2011). The application of racial identity development in academic-based service learning. *International Journal of Teaching and Learning in Higher Education, 23,* 72–83.

Skaggs, E. B. (1927). Dr. Schoen on "The elementary course in psychology." *American Journal of Psychology, 38,* 1S3–1S4.

Smith, B. L. (2001). The challenge of learning communities as a growing national movement. *AAC&U Peer Review, 4,* 4–8.

Smith, B. L. (2003). Learning communities and liberal education. *Academe, 89,* 14–18. http://dx.doi.org/10.2307/40252241

Smith, M. B. (1990). Psychology in the public interest. What have we done? What can we do? *American Psychologist, 45,* 530–536. http://dx.doi.org/10.1037/0003-066X.45.4.530

Smith, R. A. (2012). Benefits of using SoTL in picking and choosing pedagogy. In B. M. Schwartz & R. A. R. Gurung (Eds.), *Evidence-based teaching for higher education* (pp. 7–22). Washington, DC: American Psychological Association. http://dx.doi.org/10.1037/13745-001

Snow, N. L., & Reeb, R. N. (2013). Social stigma and homelessness. *Journal of Psychological Practice, 18,* 104–139.

REFERENCES

Sokol, B. W., & Kuebli, J. E. (2011). Psychological literacy: Bridging citizenship and character. In J. Cranney & D. S. Dunn (Eds.), *The psychologically literate citizen: Foundations and global perspectives* (pp. 269–280). New York, NY: Oxford University Press. http://dx.doi.org/10.1093/acprof:oso/9780199794942.003.0067

Stanton, T. K., Connolly, B., Howard, J., & Litvak, L. (2013). *Research university engaged scholarship toolkit* (4th ed.). Boston, MA: Campus Compact.

Stanton, T. K., Giles, D. E., Jr., & Cruz, N. I. (1999). *Service-learning: A movement's pioneers reflect on its origins, practice, and future.* San Francisco, CA: Jossey-Bass.

Steinberg, K. S., Bringle, R. G., & McGuire, L. E. (2013). Attributes of quality research in service learning. In P. H. Clayton, R. G. Bringle, & J. A. Hatcher (Eds.), *Research on service learning: Conceptual frameworks and assessment. Vol. 2A: Students and faculty* (pp. 27–53). Sterling, VA: Stylus.

Steinberg, K. S., Bringle, R. G., & Williams, M. J. (2010). *Service learning research primer.* Scotts Valley, CA: National Service-Learning Clearinghouse.

Steinberg, K. S., Hatcher, J. A., & Bringle, R. G. (2011). Civic-minded graduate: A north star. *Michigan Journal of Community Service Learning, 18*(1), 19–33.

Sternberg, R. J. (2010). *Defining a great university.* Retrieved from http://www.insidehighered.com/views/2010/11/29/sternberg

Sternberg, R. J., & Pardo, J. (1998). Intelligence as a unifying theme for teaching cognitive psychology. *Teaching of Psychology, 25,* 293–296. http://dx.doi.org/10.1080/00986289809709721

Steuer, F. B., & Ham, K. W., II. (2008). Psychology textbooks: Examining their accuracy. *Teaching of Psychology, 35,* 160–168. http://dx.doi.org/10.1080/00986280802189197

Stewart, T. (2008). Meta-reflective service learning poster fairs: Purposive pedagogy for pre-service teachers. *Journal of the Scholarship of Teaching and Learning, 8*(3), 79–102.

Stewart, T., & Webster, N. (2011). *Exploring cultural dynamics and tensions within service-learning.* Charlotte, NC: Information Age Publishing.

Stoecker, R., Beckman, M., & Min, B. H. (2010). Evaluating community impact of higher education civic engagement. In H. E. Fitzgerald, C. Burack, & S. D. Seifer (Eds.), *Handbook of engaged scholarship: Volume 2. Community–campus partnerships* (pp. 177–196). East Lansing: Michigan State University Press.

Stoecker, R., Tryon, E. A., & Hilgendorf, A. (2009). *The unheard voices: Community organizations and service learning.* Philadelphia, PA: Temple University Press.

Stoloff, M., McCarthy, M., Keller, L., Varfolomeeva, V., Lynch, J., Makara, K., . . . Smiley, W. (2010). The undergraduate psychology major: An examination of structure and sequence. *Teaching of Psychology, 37,* 4–15. http://dx.doi.org/10.1080/00986280903426274

Stoloff, M. L. (2010). Addressing the multiple demands of teaching Introductory Psychology. In D. S. Dunn, B. C. Beins, M. A. McCarthy, & G. W. Hill, IV, (Eds.), *Best practices for teaching beginnings and endings in the psychology major* (pp. 15–29). New York, NY: Oxford University Press.

Stoloff, M. L., Curtis, N. A., Rodgers, M., Brewster, J., & McCarthy, M. A. (2012). Characteristics of successful undergraduate psychology programs. *Teaching of Psychology, 39,* 91–99. http://dx.doi.org/10.1177/0098628312437721

Stoloff, M. L., & Feeney, K. J. (2002). The major field test as an assessment tool for an undergraduate psychology program. *Teaching of Psychology, 29,* 92–98. http://dx.doi.org/10.1207/S15328023TOP2902_01

Strage, A. A. (2000). Service learning: Enhancing student learning outcomes in a college-level lecture course. *Michigan Journal of Community Service Learning, 7*(1), 5–13.

Strait, J., & Sauer, T. (2004). Constructing experiential learning for online courses: The birth of e-service. *EDUCAUSE Quarterly, 1,* 62–65.

Strand, K. J., Cutforth, N., Stoecker, R., Marullo, S., & Donohue, P. (2003). *Community-based research and higher education: Principles and practices.* San Francisco, CA: Jossey-Bass.

Stukas, A. A., Snyder, M., & Clary, E. G. (1999). The effects of "mandatory volunteerism" on intentions to volunteer. *Psychological Science, 10,* 59–64. http://dx.doi.org/10.1111/1467-9280.00107

Taylor, S. E. (2015). *Health psychology* (9th ed.). New York, NY: McGraw-Hill.

Teaching Tolerance Project. (n.d.). *Service-learning and prejudice reduction.* Retrieved from Teaching Tolerance website: http://www.tolerance.org/service-learning

Toro, P. A., & Janisse, H. C. (2004). Homelessness, patterns of. In D. Levinson (Ed.), *Encyclopedia of homelessness* (pp. 244–250). Thousand Oaks, CA: Sage. http://dx.doi.org/10.4135/9781412952569.n69

Tress, B., Tress, G., & Fry, G. (2006). Defining concepts and the process of knowledge production in integrative research. In B. Tress, G. Tress, G. Fry, & P. Opdam (Eds.), *From landscape research to landscape planning: Aspects of integration, education, and application* (pp. 13–26). Dordrecht, The Netherlands: Springer.

Trochim, W. M. K., & Donnelly, J. P. (2006). *The research methods knowledge base* (3rd ed.). Mason, OH: Atomic Dog.

United Nations General Assembly. (1948). *Universal declaration of human rights.* Retrieved from http://www.ohchr.org/EN/UDHR/Documents/UDHR_Translations/eng.pdf

United Nations General Assembly. (2000). *United Nations millennium declaration.* Retrieved from http://www.un.org/millennium/declaration/ares552e.pdf

United Nations Human Rights. (2014a). *International covenant on civil and political rights.* Retrieved from http://www.ohchr.org/en/professionalinterest/pages/ccpr.aspx

United Nations Human Rights. (2014b). *International covenant on economic, social, and cultural rights.* Retrieved from http://www.ohchr.org/EN/ProfessionalInterest/Pages/cescr.aspx

U.S. Department of Education. (2003). *Identifying and implementing educational practices supported by rigorous evidence: A user-friendly guide.* Washington, DC: Author.

Vanags, T., George, A. M., Grace, D. M., & Brown, P. M. (2012). Bingo! An engaging activity for learning physiological terms in psychology. *Teaching of Psychology, 39,* 29–33. http://dx.doi.org/10.1177/0098628311430639

Van de Ven, A. H. (2007). *Engaged scholarship: A guide for organizational and social research.* New York, NY: Oxford University Press.

Wade, A., & Demb, A. (2012). A conceptual model to explore faculty community engagement. *Michigan Journal of Community Service Learning, 15*(2), 5–16.

Waldner, L. S., McGorry, S. Y., & Widener, M. C. (2012). E-service-learning: The evolution of service-learning to engage a growing online student population. *Journal of Higher Education Outreach and Engagement, 16,* 123–150.

Walker, T. (2000). A feminist challenge to community service: A call to politicize service-learning. In B. J. Balliet & K. Heffernan (Eds.), *The practice of change: Concepts and models for service-learning in women's studies* (pp. 25–45). Washington, DC: American Association for Higher Education.

Walshok, M. L. (1999). Dialogue and collaboration as keys to building innovative educational initiatives in a knowledge-based economy. *New Directions for Adult and Continuing Education, 81,* 77–86. http://dx.doi.org/10.1002/ace.8108

Wandersman, A., & Florin, P. (2000). Citizen participation and community organizations. In J. Rappaport & E. Seidman (Eds.), *Handbook of community psychology* (pp. 247–272). New York, NY: Kluwer Academic/Plenum. http://dx.doi.org/10.1007/978-1-4615-4193-6_11

Wang, Y., & Rodgers, R. (2006). Impact of service-learning and social education on college students' cognitive development. *NASPA Journal, 43,* 316–337. http://dx.doi.org/10.2202/1949-6605.1642

Warren, J. L. (2012). Does service-learning increase student learning?: A meta-analysis. *Michigan Journal of Community Service Learning, 18*(2), 56–61.

Weinreb, L., Gelberg, L., Arangua, L., & Sullivan, M. (2007). Health problems. In D. Levinson & M. Ross (Eds.), *Homelessness handbook* (pp. 188–198). Great Barrington, MA: Berkshire.

Welch, M. (2006). *Reflecting on why we choose to take the path of service-learning.* Providence, RI: Campus Compact.

Wells, C., Warchal, J., Ruiz, A., & Chapdelaine, A. (2011). Ethical issues in research on international service learning. In R. G. Bringle, J. A. Hatcher, & S. G. Jones (Eds.), *International service learning: Conceptual frameworks and research* (pp. 319–343). Sterling, VA: Stylus.

Wergin, J. F. (2003). *Departments that work: Building and sustaining cultures of excellence in academic programs.* Bolton, MA: Ankar.

Whitbourne, S. K., Collins, K. J., & Skultety, K. M. (2001). Formative reflections on service-learning in a course on the psychology of aging. *Educational Gerontology, 27*, 105–115. http://dx.doi.org/10.1080/036012701750069076

White, F. A. (2011). The social psychology of intergroup harmony and the education of psychologically literate citizens. In J. Cranney & D. Dunn (Eds.), *The psychologically literate citizen: Foundations and global perspectives* (pp. 56–71). New York, NY: Oxford University Press. http://dx.doi.org/10.1093/acprof:oso/9780199794942.003.0025

Wilkenfeld, B., Lauckhardt, J., & Torney-Purta, J. (2010). The relation between developmental theory and measures of civic engagement in research on adolescents. In L. R. Sherrod, J. Torney-Purta, & C. A. Flanagan (Eds.), *Handbook of research on civic engagement in youth* (pp. 193–219). Hoboken, NJ: Wiley. http://dx.doi.org/10.1002/9780470767603.ch8

Wilson, E. O. (1999). *Consilience: The unity of knowledge.* New York, NY: Vintage Books.

Winnicott, D. W. (1953). Transitional objects and transitional phenomena: A study of the first not-me possession. *The International Journal of Psychoanalysis, 34*, 89–97.

Wolfle, D. (1942). The first course in psychology. *Psychological Bulletin, 39*, 685–712. http://dx.doi.org/10.1037/h0057510

Wood, R. J. (1990). Changing the educational program. *New Directions for Higher Education, 71*, 51–58. http://dx.doi.org/10.1002/he.36919907107

Wurr, A. J. (2002). Service learning and student writing. In S. H. Billig & A. Furco (Eds.), *Service learning through a multidisciplinary lens* (pp. 103–121). Greenwich, CT: Information Age Publishing.

Yorio, P. L., & Ye, F. (2012). A meta-analysis on the effects of service-learning on the social, personal, and cognitive outcomes of learning. *Academy of Management Learning & Education, 11*, 9–27. http://dx.doi.org/10.5465/amle.2010.0072

Young, C. A., Shinnar, R. S., Ackerman, R. L., Carruthers, C. P., & Young, D. A. (2007). Implementing and sustaining service-learning at the institutional level. *Journal of Experiential Education, 29*, 344–365. http://dx.doi.org/10.1177/105382590702900306

REFERENCES

Zechmeister, J. S., & Zechmeister, E. B. (2000). Introductory textbooks and psychology's core concepts. *Teaching of Psychology, 27*, 6–11. http://dx.doi.org/10.1207/S15328023TOP2701_1

Zhao, C. M., & Kuh, G. D. (2004). Adding value: Learning communities and student engagement. *Research in Higher Education, 45*, 115–138. http://dx.doi.org/10.1023/B:RIHE.0000015692.88534.de

Zlotkowski, E. (Series Ed.). (1997–2006). *Service-learning in the academic disciplines.* Sterling, VA: Stylus.

Zlotkowski, E. (2000). Service-learning in the disciplines. *Michigan Journal of Community Service Learning, Special Issue* (1), 61–67.

Zlotkowski, E., & Duffy, D. K. (2010). Two decades of community-based learning. *New Directions for Teaching and Learning, 123*, 33–43. http://dx.doi.org/10.1002/tl.407

Zlotkowski, E., & Saltmarsh, J. (2006). The engaged department in the context of academic change. In K. Kecskes (Ed.), *Engaging departments: Moving faculty culture from private to public, individual to collective focus for the common good* (pp. 278–289). San Francisco, CA: Jossey-Bass.

Zucchero, R. A. (2011). A co-mentoring project: An intergenerational service-learning experience. *Educational Gerontology, 37*, 687–702. http://dx.doi.org/10.1080/03601271003723487

Zuiches, J. J. (2008). Attaining Carnegie's Community Engagement Classification. *Change, 40*(1), 42–45. http://dx.doi.org/10.3200/CHNG.40.1.42-45

Index

Abnormal psychology courses, 95–99, 103–106
  benefits of service learning in, 96–97
  reflection in, 103–106
  service learning project examples for, 97–99
Academic and Student Affairs departments, 181
Academic credit, for service learning, 10
Academic knowledge, 12, 32
  assessment of, 188–1189
Adams, B., 173–174
Advocacy service learning
  in abnormal psychology service learning project examples, 99
  in behavioral neuroscience service learning project examples, 133
  as civic skill, 30
  in cognition service learning project examples, 132
  in community psychology service learning project examples, 101
  in cultural psychology service learning project examples, 112
  in developmental psychology service learning project examples, 122, 123
  in health psychology service learning project examples, 100
  in introductory psychology service learning project examples, 87
  in learning service learning project examples, 133
  as participatory community action research, 50–52
  in participatory community action research service learning project examples, 49
  in personality psychology service learning project examples, 110
  in scientific methods service learning project examples, 141
  as service learning, 10
  in service learning courses, 57–58
  and social justice, 13
  in social psychology service learning project examples, 111
Alexander, P. A., 83–84
Allen, M., 12

INDEX

Altman, I., 25–26
American Psychological Association (APA)
   APA Guidelines for the Undergraduate Psychology Major (Version 2.0). *See APA Guidelines for the Undergraduate Psychology Major* [Version 2.0]
   Board of Educational Affairs, 169
   educational initiatives of, 4
   Ethical Principles of Psychologists and Code of Conduct, 48, 69
   founding of, ix
   Learning Goals and Inferred Attributes, 203–206
   Learning Goals and Outcomes Indicators, 201–202
   National Conference on Undergraduate Education, 176
   Public Interest Directorate. *See* Public Interest Directorate [APA]
Analysis. *See also* Assessment
   learning different levels of, 108
   of research capstone projects, 148–149
Ansburg, P. I., 83–84
APA. *See* American Psychological Association
APA Guidelines for the Undergraduate Psychology Major (Version 2.0; APA)
   in abnormal, health, and community psychology courses, 96
   civic growth assessment with, 189
   and civic learning, 9, 26, 33–34
   in cognition, learning, and behavioral neuroscience courses, 134–135
   curricula assessment with, 191
   in developmental psychology courses, 124–125
   in health psychology service learning example, 102–103
   in introductory psychology courses, 85
   and participatory community action research, 50
   personal growth assessment with, 190, 191
   in personality psychology courses, 108
   psychology program assessment with, 182
   in research capstone courses, 143, 146–148
   in service learning course design, 60–63
   service learning used to meet, 5–6, 15
   in social psychology service learning projects, 115, 118
   and student assessment, 187
Application, scholarship of, 38
Arbitrage, 45
Articulate learning stage (DEAL model), 70, 72
Ash, S. L., 12
Assessment. *See also* Student assessment
   of administrators and staff, 195
   of community impact, 195–196
   of curricula, 191–192
   of engaged psychology departments, 182–184
   of faculty, 194–195
   formative, 187
   of partnerships, 196
   self-report measures as, 188
   by students, in service learning example, 88, 91
   summative, 187
Association of American Colleges and Universities, 96
Astin, A. W., 15

INDEX

Barr, R. B., 13
Battistoni, R. M., 28, 29, 31, 177
Behavior, as theme of service learning projects, 108, 110
Behavioral neuroscience courses, 129–131, 133–138
    educational fair as service learning in, 131, 134–138
    service learning in, 130–131
    service learning project examples for, 133
Benson, L., 14
Bloom, B. S., 72
Bloom's taxonomy, 72, 80, 187, 190, 191
Board of Educational Affairs (APA), 169
Bowman, N. A., 14
Boyer, Ernest, 25, 37–38, 172, 175
Brandenberger, J. W., 115, 120
Bringle, K. E., 193
Bringle, R. G., 3–4, 8, 32, 35, 60, 70, 120, 158, 159, 170, 176–177, 193, 196, 197
Bronfenbrenner, U., 35–36
Brown, M. A., 14, 199

Campus administrators
    service learning research including, 194, 195
    as stakeholders in service learning courses, 64
Campus Compact, 60, 177
Carnegie Foundation, 182
Chalmers, A. F., 41
Chapdelaine, A., 48–49, 158–159
Chavis, D. M., 152
Checkoway, B., 174
Child development, assessment of, 88, 91
Civic engagement
    community involvement vs., 8
    defined, 176–177
    democratic. *See* Democratic civic engagement
    in education, 175–176
    as outcome of higher education, 32
    in service learning, 6–8
Civic internships, 157–158
Civic knowledge, 28
Civic learning, 21–36
    and *APA Guidelines for the Undergraduate Psychology Major* (Version 2.0; APA), 33–34
    assessment of, 189
    and civic-minded graduates, 32–33
    as collaboration, 31
    conceptual frameworks for, 27–31
    and educational theories, 35–36
    as intentional, 27
    in psychology, 25–27
    for public good, 21–25
    in service learning, 9–10
    taught through service learning, 6
Civic-minded graduates (CMGs), 32–33
Civic professionalism, 29
Civic skills, 29–31
Civic values, 31
Classroom learning communities, 152
Clayton, P. H., 3, 8, 12, 35, 176–177, 193, 194, 196, 197
Clinical psychology, 95
CMGs (civic-minded graduates), 32–33
Cobb, S., 97
Codes of conduct. *See* Conduct codes
Cognition courses, 129–132, 134–138
    educational fair as service learning in, 131, 134–138
    service learning in, 130–131
    service learning project examples for, 132
Collaboration
    barriers to, 179–180
    civic learning as, 31
    in classroom learning communities, 152

Collaboration (*continued*)
    of community partners and
        students, 118
    in engaged psychology departments,
        179–180
    enhanced with service learning, 86
    learning outcomes and emphasis
        on, 97
    in research capstone courses, 146
Collaborative Institutional Training
    Initiative Program, 49, 69, 147
Commodification, of education, 22
Communication skills
    and Mode 2, 43
    as outcome of higher education, 32
    in research capstone projects, 148
    service learning contributing to,
        32, 34, 50, 103, 115, 125,
        134, 135, 148, 160, 191
Community. *See also specific types*
    of practice, 168, 170–171
    sense of, 152
Community action research, 39
Community-based research, 39, 46–47
Community Engagement Elective
    Classification (Carnegie
    Foundation), 182
Community impact assessment,
    195–196
Community involvement
    civic engagement vs., 8
    as co-educators, 16, 28, 64, 65,
        177, 193
    defined, 7
    as result of service learning, 15
Community members
    service learning research including,
        194–196
    as stakeholders in service learning
        courses, 28, 64, 65
Community partners
    in research capstone projects, 149
    in service learning course design, 167

    service learning research including,
        194, 196
    as stakeholders in service learning
        courses, 64
    in study design, 147
Community psychology courses,
    95–98, 101–106
    benefits of service learning in,
        96–97
    reflection in, 103–106
    service learning project examples
        for, 98, 101–102
Community Service Self-Efficacy
    Scale, 106
Companionship
    to individuals with brain disorders,
        131
    to relatives of persons receiving
        hospice care, 121, 124–128
Conduct codes, 48–49, 66–70
Connected knowing, 30
Connors, K., 171
Conscious pluralism, 43
Consensus-building skills, 32
Consilience, 45
Constructive strategy, 198
Contact strategies, 102
Coping
    assessment of, in service learning
        example, 91
    as theme of service learning
        projects, 97–99
Corrigan, P. W., 102
Council for the Advancement of
    Standards in Higher Education,
    157
Course objectives, in service learning
    course design, 60–63
Crain, L. K., 160
Critical realism, 41
Critical reflection, 3, 30, 36, 56, 70–72,
    135, 142, 187
Critical service learning, 50–51

INDEX

Critical thinking, 34
    service learning contributing to, 9, 29, 34, 50, 56, 81, 103, 125, 143, 158, 164, 186, 191
A Crucible Moment (National Task Force on Civic Learning and Democratic Engagement), 22–23
Cultural psychology courses, 107, 112–114, 118
    service learning in, 113–114
    service learning project examples for, 112
Curricula
    assessment of, 191–192
    of engaged psychology departments, 181–182
Curricular learning communities, 152
Cutforth, N., 39

Das, R., 153
DEAL model
    in abnormal psychology courses, 104–105
    assessing curricula with, 192
    in cognitive, learning, and behavioral neuroscience courses, 136–137
    in death and dying courses, 126–127
    in developmental psychology service learning example, 125–127
    in direct service project example, 103–106
    in educational fair example, 136–137
    in introductory psychology service learning example, 89–90
    for reflection, 70–72, 80
    sample reflection prompts for, 73–79
    in social psychology service learning example, 115–117
    in statistics, research methods, and research capstone courses, 144–145
    student assessment including, 80–81
    in student assessments, 190
Death and dying psychology courses, 121, 124–128
Demb, A., 165
Democratically sound partnerships, 11, 14
Democratic civic engagement
    in engaged psychology department, 177
    as rationale for service learning, 14
    in scientific methods courses, 142
Description stage (DEAL model), 70, 72
Developmental psychology courses, 119–128
    in service learning example, 121, 124–128
    service learning in, 120–121
    service learning project examples for, 122–123
Dewey, John, 14, 31, 35, 41, 196
Diamond, R., 173–174
Direct service learning
    in abnormal psychology service learning project examples, 99
    in behavioral neuroscience service learning project examples, 133
    in cognition service learning project examples, 132
    in community psychology service learning project examples, 101
    companionship as, 121
    in cultural psychology service learning project examples, 112

Direct service learning (*continued*)
  in developmental psychology
    service learning project
    examples, 122, 123
  in health psychology service learning
    project examples, 100
  in introductory psychology
    service learning project
    examples, 87
  in learning service learning project
    examples, 132
  in participatory community action
    research service learning
    project examples, 49
  in personality psychology service
    learning project examples,
    110
  in scientific methods service learning
    project examples, 141
  as service learning, 10
  in service learning courses, 57
  in social psychology service learning
    project examples, 111
Disciplinary learning, 12
Discipline support, for faculty
  development, 171–172
Discovery, scholarship of, 37
Dismantling strategy, 198
Diversity
  in abnormal, health, and community
    psychology courses, 96
  benefits of exposure to, 14
  in cultural psychology service
    projects, 113–114
  and personality psychology
    courses, 108
  in service learning, 86
  service learning contributing to
    knowledge of, 34
  skills in dealing with, 32
  as theme of developmental
    psychology service projects,
    122–123

Donohue, P., 39
Dossiers, 173
Dostilio, L. D., 11
Dovidio, J. F., 109
Driscoll, A., 172
Duffy, D. K., 3–4, 13, 60

Education
  commodification of, 22
  evolution of, 21–23
  history of college, viii–x
  purpose of, 175
Educational fair, 131, 134–138
Educational initiatives, of APA, 4
Educational theories, 35–36
Education strategies, 102
Educators. *See also* Faculty
  implementation of service learning
    by, 56
  nontraditional, 28, 43
Efficacy, of service learning, 12, 15, 56,
  85–86
Elvers, G. C., 154
Engaged Department Institutes, 177
The Engaged Department Toolkit
  (Campus Compact), 177
Engaged psychology departments,
  175–184
  assessment of, 183–184
  curricula of, 181–182
  departmental collaboration in,
    179–180
  importance of, 176–178
  infrastructure of, 181
  leadership in, 178–179
  rewards in, 180–181
Engaged scholarship
  as civic skill, 30–31
  Mode 2 as, 42–45
  and tenure, 172–173
Engaged Scholarship for Homelessness,
  154–155
Engagement, scholarship of, 38

Engaging Departments (Kecskes), 178
Engel, R. J., 153
Epistemology, 37
Esses, V. M., 109
Ethical Principles of Psychologists and Code of Conduct (APA), 48, 69
Ethic of caring, 30
Ethics
    implementing service learning, 44, 69–70, 113, 124, 158–159
    service learning contributing to, 34, 48–49, 50, 69–70, 124, 144–145, 146–148, 191
Examine stage (DEAL model), 70, 72
Experiential learning, 170
Experimental College Program (University of Wisconsin), 152
Extreme e-service learning, 156
Eyler, J. S., 15

Faculty
    career stages of, 169–170
    characteristics of, 165–166
    collaboration among, 179–180
    educating, about service learning, 167–168
    resources for, 59–60
    service learning research including, 194–195
    as stakeholders in service learning courses, 64
Faculty development, 163–174
    and faculty characteristics, 165–166
    faculty programs as, 169–171
    and faculty recruitment strategies, 166–168
    graduate training as, 168–169
    institutional and discipline support for, 171–172
    for introductory psychology courses, 84
    and tenure/promotions, 172–174
Faculty programs, 169–171

Faculty recruitment strategies, 166–168
Faculty Toolkit for Service Learning in Higher Education (Seifer & Connors), 171
Farmer, C. N., 154
Feedback, on educational fair project, 138
Finkelstein, M. A., 118
Fitch, P., 12
Folger, S. F., 196
Folkman, S., 97
Formative assessment, 187
Franco, Z. E., 156
Franz, N. K., 174
Freudenberg, N., 39, 51–52
Friedman, T. L., 45
Fry, G., 153–154
Furco, A., 171

Gazley, B., 196
Gent, P. J., 114
Gibbons, M., 42–44
Glassick, C. E., 173
Glendening, Z. S., 154
Gottlieb, K., 61
Graduate training, 168–169
Grant money, and collaboration, 179
Gurecka, L. E., 114
Gurung, R. A. R., 83–84, 200

Hakel, M. D., 60
Hall, K., 31
Halpern, D. F., 4, 60, 181–182
Harkavy, I., 14
Harvard University, viii
Hatcher, J. A., 8, 32, 70, 158, 159, 170, 176–177
Health care access, as theme of service learning projects, 98, 100
Health psychology courses, 95–98, 100, 102–106
    benefits of service learning in, 96–97
    reflection in, 103–106

INDEX

Health psychology courses (*continued*)
   in service learning example, 102–103
   service learning project examples for, 98, 100
Hesser, G., 164
Higher Education Research Institute Faculty Survey, 165
High-road study abroad programs, 158
HIV/AIDS community services, 114–118
Homelessness
   in health psychology service learning example, 102–103
   service learning projects involving, 98
   studied in interdisciplinary courses, 154–155
   as theme of service learning projects, 100
Homeless shelter
   designing service learning courses that include, 58
   participatory community action research service learning project at, 49
   studied in interdisciplinary courses, 154–155
Hou, S. I., 166–167
Hovey, R, 158
Hudson, T. D., 12
Hybrid online service learning, 155–156

Incentives. *See* Rewards
Indirect service learning
   in abnormal psychology service learning project examples, 99
   in behavioral neuroscience service learning project examples, 133
   in cognition service learning project examples, 132
   in community psychology service learning project examples, 101
   in cultural psychology service learning project examples, 112
   in developmental psychology service learning project examples, 122, 123
   in health psychology service learning project examples, 100
   in introductory psychology service learning project examples, 87
   in learning service learning project examples, 132
   in participatory community action research service learning project examples, 49
   in personality psychology service learning project examples, 110
   in scientific methods service learning project examples, 141
   as service learning, 10
   in service learning courses, 57
   in social psychology service learning project examples, 111
Institutional review board (IRB) approval, 147–148
Institutional support, for faculty development, 171–172
Integration, scholarship of, 37–38
Intellectualism, public, 30
Interdisciplinary courses, 153–155
Interdisciplinary service projects, 152
International Bill of Human Rights, 159
International service learning (ISL), 158–160

Introductory psychology courses, 83–93
   content of, 83–84
   service learning course design for, 87–92
   service learning example in, 88–92
   service learning in, 85–87
   service learning project examples for, 87
IRB (institutional review board) approval, 147–148
Isackson, N. L., 96–97
ISL (international service learning), 158–160

Jacoby, B., 156–157, 171
James, W., 41
Jameson, J. K., 12, 171, 192
Janisse, H. C., 98
Janke, E. M., 196
Johns Hopkins University, viii
Johnson, D. E., 83–84
Jones, S. G., 158, 170

Kecskes, K., 178–179, 183
Keen, C., 31
Kiely, R., 159–160
Knowledge
   academic, 32
   civic, 28
   service learning contributing to, 33–34, 50, 103, 124, 134, 146
   social trusteeship of, 33
   transdisciplinary, 43
Knowledge translation boundary conversations, 43
Kolb, D. A., 170
Kolivoski, K. M., 153
Kremer, J. F., 120
Kuh, G. D., 152, 153

Lagemann, E. C., 35
Land Grant Act (1862), viii, 22
Lauckhardt, J., 197

Lawrence, N., 83–84
Lazarus, R., 97
Leadership
   assessing growth in, 190
   in engaged psychology departments, 178–179
   public, 30
Learning. *See also* Civic learning; Service learning
   assessment of, in service learning example, 88
   disciplinary, 12
   experiential, 170
   student-centered, 13
Learning-centered orientation, 13
Learning communities, 152–153
   classroom, 152
   curricular, 152
   residential, 152–153
   student-type, 153
Learning courses, 129–138
   educational fair as service learning in, 131, 134–138
   service learning in, 130–131
   service learning project examples for, 132–133
Learning Goals and Inferred Attributes (APA), 203–204
Learning Goals and Outcomes Indicators (APA), 201–202
Learning objectives. *See* Course objectives
Levine, P., 14, 31
Lewin, L., 41
Lightfoot, C., 35
Lincoln, Abraham, viii
Lisman, C. D., 13–14
Listening skills, 32
Literature review, in research capstone courses, 146
Littlepage, B., 196
Low-road study abroad programs, 158

Markey, V., 12
Marullo, S., 39
Matthews, D., 21
McGorry, S. Y., 155–156
McGovern, T. V., 4, 176, 200
McMillan, D. W., 152
MDGs (Millennium Development Goals), 159
Measurement, in service learning research, 199
Metacognitive skills, 157
Millennium Development Goals (MDGs), 159
Minkler, M., 38–39, 51–52
Mission creep, 179
Mitchell, T. D., 13, 50–51
Mode 2 Production of Knowledge, 42–45
Moely, B. E., 171
Moore, T. L., 172
Morrill, Justin, viii
Muthiah, R., 70

National Conference on Undergraduate Education (APA), 176
National Review Board for the Scholarship of Engagement, 174
National Task Force on Civic Learning and Democratic Engagement, 22–23
Nelson, P. D., 6, 17, 25, 169
The New Production of Knowledge (Gibbons et al.), 42
Next Generation Engagement Project, 169
Niehaus, B., 166
Niehaus, E., 160
Nonprofit organizations, 32
Nontraditional educators, 28, 43
Novak, J. M., 12

O'Meara, K., 166, 169, 195
Omoto, A., 109
Online service learning courses, 155–157
Ontology, 37
O'Shaughnessy, J. R., 102

Package strategy, 198
Parametric strategy, 198–199
Participatory action research, 39
Participatory community action research (PCAR), 37–52
  benefits of, 47–48, 49–52
  compared to traditional research, 46–47
  defining, 38–39
  Engaged Scholarship for Homelessness as, 154–155
  and philosophies of science, 40–45
  principles of, 45–48
  in scientific methods courses, 142
  as service learning, 48–52
Partnerships
  as coeducators, 28, 118
  democratically sound, 11, 14
  in participatory community action research, 45, 47
  reciprocal, 3, 8, 11, 61, 64–65, 113
  in service learning, 10–11
  service learning research including, 196
  transformational, 64–65
PCAR. *See* Participatory community action research
Personal growth
  assessment of, 189–191
  enhanced through service learning, 56, 61, 70, 72, 92, 106, 124–125, 134, 135
Personality
  assessment of, in service learning example, 91–92
  study of, 108

Personality psychology courses, 107–110
   service learning in, 108–109
   service learning project examples for, 110
Peterson, C., 197
Petracchi, H. E., 153
Pierce, C. S., 40–41
Plater, W. M., 35, 195
Porpora, D. V., 39
Positivism, 40
Postpositivism, 41–42
Pragmatism, 40–41
Prejudice, reducing, 115, 118
Prilleltensky, I., 52
Professional development
   of faculty, 168–172
   in research capstone courses, 148
   service learning contributing to, 34, 50, 103, 125, 134, 135, 146, 148, 190
Professionalism, civic, 29
Promotions (of faculty), 172–174
Protest strategies, 102
Psychologically literate citizen(s)
   and civic-minded graduates, 33
   defined, 4, 176
   importance of developing, x, 4, 26
Psychopolitical validity, 52
Psychotherapy outcome research, 198
Public good
   civic learning for, 21–25
   defined, 21
   and education, 21–22
   enhanced by higher education, x
   responsibility to use knowledge for, 33
Public intellectualism, 30
Public Interest Directorate (APA), 24–25
   in abnormal, health, and community psychology courses, 96
   and cultural psychology, 114
   and Millennium Development Goals, 159
   in participatory community action research, 51
   in service learning course design, 60
Public leadership, 30
Public policy, 51–52
Public scholarship, 30–31. *See also* Engaged scholarship
Puckett, J., 14

Quality control, 44

Ralph, R. O., 97
Random assignment, in service learning research, 199
Realism, 41
Reciprocal partnerships, 61, 64–65
Recovery, concepts of, 97–98
Reeb, R. N., 96–97, 102, 154, 196
Reflection
   in abnormal psychology courses, 103–106
   in community psychology courses, 103–106
   to connect course work to service learning, 97
   design of, 11–12
   in developmental psychology service learning example, 125–127
   in educational fair example, 135–138
   in health psychology courses, 103–106
   importance of, for service learning, 86
   in international service learning, 158, 159
   learning generated by, 70
   meeting APA learning goals with, 33–34

INDEX

Reflection (*continued*)
  in Mode 2, 44
  in online courses, 155, 156
  in scholarly teaching, 186
  in service learning course design, 70–80
  and social justice, 30
  in social psychology service learning example, 115–117
  in statistics, research methods, and research capstone courses, 143–145
  in student assessment, 190
Reich, J. N., 6, 17, 25
Relationships, 114. *See also* Partnerships
Relativism, 40
Relevance, of research, 43
Research. *See also* Participatory community action research
  on administrators and staff, 195
  and civic engagement, 7
  on community impact, 195
  conduct codes for, 69
  as engaged scholarship, 30–31
  on faculty, 194
  Mode 2, 42–45
  on partnerships, 196
  relevance of, 43
  on service learning, 12, 15, 196–199
  traditional, 40–42
  traditional vs. community-based, 46–47
  training for, 49
Research capstone courses, 139, 143, 146–149
Research design, 198–199
Research methods courses, 139–143, 149
  service learning in, 140, 142–143
  service learning project examples for, 141
Research questions, formulation of, 143, 146

Research service learning
  in abnormal psychology service learning project examples, 99
  in behavioral neuroscience service learning project examples, 133
  in cognition service learning project examples, 132
  in community psychology service learning project examples, 101
  in cultural psychology service learning project examples, 112
  in developmental psychology service learning project examples, 122, 123
  in health psychology service learning project examples, 100
  in introductory psychology service learning project examples, 87
  in learning service learning project examples, 133
  in participatory community action research service learning project examples, 49
  in personality psychology service learning project examples, 110
  in scientific methods courses, 140, 142
  in scientific methods service learning project examples, 141
  as service learning, 10
  in service learning courses, 57
  in social psychology service learning project examples, 111
Residential learning communities, 152–153

Resources
    for engaged psychology
        departments, 181–182
    for service learning course design,
        59–60
Rewards, in engaged psychology
    departments, 180–181
Rice, D., 173
Riddle, A., 14
Robinson, G., 61
Rodgers, R., 30
Ruiz, A., 48–49, 158–159

Saltmarsh, J., 31, 177, 178
Sammon, J. A., 96–97
Sandmann, L., 195
Sandy, M. G., 156
Scholarly teaching, 186
Scholarship
    of application, 38
    different types of, 37–38
    of discovery, 37
    engaged or public. *See* Engaged
        scholarship
    of engagement, 38
    evaluation of, 173–174
    of integration, 37–38
    of teaching, 38
Scholarship of teaching and learning
    (SoTL), 186, 192–200
Scholarship Reconsidered (Boyer), 37–38
School-age children, 130
Schwartz, B. M., 200
Scientific method courses, 139–143, 149
    service learning in, 140, 142–143
    service learning project examples
        for, 141
Seifer, S. D., 171
Self-efficacy, as outcome of education,
    32
Self-report measures, as assessments,
    188
Self-stigma, 102

Seligman, M. E. P., 197
Sense of community, 152
Service learning, 3–16
    in abnormal psychology courses,
        59, 102–103, 182, 192, 200
    in behavioral neuroscience
        courses, 130–131
    benefits of, 5–6
    as civic engagement, 8
    civic engagement in, 6–8
    in civic internships, 157–158
    civic learning in, 9–10
    in cognition courses, 130–131
    in community psychology courses,
        96–98, 101
    in cultural psychology courses,
        113–114
    defined, 3, 8
    in developmental psychology
        courses, 120–121
    educating faculty about, 167–168
    efficacy of, 15–16
    faculty characteristics, 165–166
    in health psychology courses,
        95–98, 100
    history of, viii–x
    in interdisciplinary courses, 153–155
    international, 158–160
    in introductory psychology
        courses, 85–87
    in learning communities, 152–153
    in learning courses, 130–131
    low incidence of, 165–166
    in online courses, 155–157
    participatory community action
        research as, 48–49
    partnerships in, 10–11
    pedagogical rationales for, 12–14
    in personality psychology courses,
        108–109
    reflection in, 11–12
    in research methods courses, 140,
        142–143

INDEX

Service learning (*continued*)
   in scientific method courses, 140, 142–143
   in sequences of courses, 102–103
   in social psychology courses, 109, 113
   in statistics courses, 140, 142–143
Service Learning Code of Ethics (Chapdelaine et al.), 48–49
Service learning course design, 55–81
   barriers to, 166–167
   course objectives in, 60–63
   for introductory psychology courses, 87–92
   reciprocal partnerships in, 61, 64–65
   reflection in, 70–80
   resources for, 59–60
   student orientation in, 65–70
   types of courses, 57–59
Service-Learning Essentials (Jacoby), 171
Service learning example(s)
   in abnormal psychology courses, 99, 103–106
   in behavioral neuroscience courses, 131, 133, 134–138
   in cognition courses, 131, 132, 134–138
   for community psychology courses, 101
   for cultural psychology courses, 112
   in death and dying psychology courses, 121, 124–128
   in developmental psychology courses, 121, 122–123, 124–128
   in health psychology courses, 98, 100, 102–103
   in introductory psychology courses, 87–92

   in learning courses, 131, 132–133, 134–138
   for personality psychology courses, 110
   in research capstone courses, 143, 146–149
   for research methods courses, 141
   for scientific method courses, 141
   in social psychology courses, 111, 114–118
   for statistics courses, 141
"Service-Learning in the Disciplines" (Zlotkowski), 12
Service learning research, 185–186, 192–200
   measurement in, 199
   populations in, 193–196
   problems with, 196–197
   research design of, 198–199
   on theory, 197–198
Shulman, L., 55
Sigmon, R., 10, 61, 64
Skills
   civic, 29–31
   communication. *See* Communication skills
   consensus-building, 32
   diversity, 32
   listening, 32
   metacognitive, 157
   technical, 32
Smith, R. A., 196
Snow, N. L., 102, 154, 196
Social issues, 85
Social justice
   as civic skill, 29–30
   as rationale for service learning, 13–14
   as theme of social psychology service learning projects, 111, 113
Social policy, 123
Social psychology, assessment of, 91

Social psychology courses, 107, 109, 111, 113–118
   in service learning example, 114–118
   service learning in, 109, 113
   service learning project examples for, 111
Social responsibility
   as civic skill, 29
   in Mode 2, 44
   service learning contributing to, 4, 29, 34, 36, 50, 86, 97, 103, 108, 124, 135, 146, 159, 191
Social stigma, 98, 101–102
Social support, 97–98
Social trusteeship, of knowledge, 33
Society for the Study of Social Issues, 23
SoTL (scholarship of teaching and learning), 186, 192–200
Stacey, K., 173
Statistics courses, 139–143, 149
   service learning in, 140, 142–143
   service learning project examples for, 141
Steinberg, K., 32
Steinke, P., 12
Stoecker, R., 39
Stoloff, M. L., 85
Strand, K. J., 39, 45, 47
Stress, assessment of, 91
Students, as stakeholders, 64
Student assessment, 80–81, 185–192, 200
   civic growth in, 189
   of community service self-efficacy, 106
   curricular assessment in, 191–192
   in developmental psychology service learning example, 127–128
   of educational fair project, 138
   personal growth in, 189–191
   in service learning example, 92
   types of evidence in, 188–189
Student-centered learning, 13
Student e-portfolios, 192
Student orientation
   in developmental psychology service learning example, 124
   in service learning course design, 65–70
Student-type learning communities, 153
Study abroad, 158–160
Study design, 146–147
Study execution, 148
Stukas, A. A., 199
Summative assessment, 187

Tagg, J., 13
Tampa AIDS Network (TAN), 118
Teaching
   and civic engagement, 7
   scholarly, 186
   scholarship of, 38
Teaching-centered orientation, 13
Teaching Tolerance Project, 114
Technical skills, 32
Tenure, 172–174
Theory, research based on, 197–198
Thorndike, Edward L., 35
Torney-Purta, J., 197
Toro, P. A., 98
Traditional research, 40–42, 46–47
Transactional relationships, 64
Transdisciplinary courses, 153–154
Transdisciplinary knowledge, 43
Transformational partnerships, 64–65
Tress, B., 153–154
Tress, G., 153–154
Triangulation, 44–45
Truman Commission on Higher Education, 22
Tutoring, as service learning, 88

INDEX

Type I online service learning, 155
Type II online service learning, 155–156
Type III online service learning, 156
Type IV online service learning, 156

United Nations, 159
University of Wisconsin, 152
U.S. Department of Education, 23, 196

Values
    altered, as result of service projects, 124
    civic, 31, 33
    as outcome of higher education, 32
Van de Ven, A. H., 39–41, 43–45
Volunteering
    as outcome of higher education, 32
    service learning vs., 9, 10

Wade, A., 165
Waldner, L. S., 155–156
Walker, T., 29–30

Wallerstein, N., 38–39
Wang, Y.,
Warchal, J., 48–49, 158–159
Ward, K., 172
Weaver, A., 153
Weinberg, A., 158
Weinreb, L., 98
Welch, M., 164
Wells, C., 48–49, 158–159
Weltanschauung, 40
Wergin, J. F., 179
White, F. A., 115
Widener, M. C., 155–156
Wilkenfeld, B., 197
"Wisconsin Idea," viii
With Service in Mind (Bringle and Duffy), 3–4
Wolfe, D., 85
Wood, R. J., 178

Zhao, C. M., 152, 153
Zlotkowski, E., 12, 13, 178

About the Authors

Robert G. Bringle, PhD, received his doctorate in social psychology from the University of Massachusetts–Amherst. He is the Kulynych/Cline Visiting Distinguished Professor of Psychology at Appalachian State University; Chancellor's Professor Emeritus of Psychology and Philanthropic Studies, and Senior Scholar, Center for Service and Learning at Indiana University–Purdue University Indianapolis (IUPUI). From 1994 to 2012, he served as executive director of the IUPUI Center for Service and Learning. He has published *With Service in Mind: Concepts and Models for Service-Learning in Psychology* (with D. Duffy), *The Measure of Service Learning* (with M. Phillips & M. Hudson), *International Service Learning* (with J. Hatcher & S. Jones), and *Research on Service Learning: Conceptual Frameworks and Assessment. Vol. 2A: Students and Faculty,* and *Vol. 2B: Communities, Institutions, and Partnerships* (with P. H. Clayton & J. A. Hatcher). Dr. Bringle received the Thomas Ehrlich Faculty Award for Service Learning, the IUPUI Chancellor's Award for Excellence in Teaching, and the Legacy of Service Award from Indiana Campus Compact. In 2004, he was recognized at the International Service-Learning Research Conference for his outstanding contributions to the service learning research field. The University of the Free State, South Africa, awarded him an honorary doctorate for his scholarly work on civic engagement and service learning.

ABOUT THE AUTHORS

Roger N. Reeb, PhD, received his doctorate in clinical psychology from Virginia Commonwealth University. He is a professor of psychology and Roesch Endowed Chair in the Social Sciences at University of Dayton. At this institution, he served as Director of Graduate Programs in Psychology (2006–2014), received awards (Alumni Award in Teaching, 2012; Outstanding Faculty Service-Learning Award, 1997; Service-Learning Faculty Research Award, 1998), and was nominated for the national Ehrlich Faculty Award for Service Learning (1998). From the American Psychological Association, he received the Dissertation Award (1991) and the Springer Award for Excellence in Research in Rehabilitation Psychology (Division 22; 1994). Dr. Reeb's research focuses on homelessness, psychopathology, and service learning outcomes for students and community. With approximately 30 publications and 80 conference presentations, he published *Community Action Research: Benefits to Community Members and Service Providers* (2006), edited a service learning research section for *American Journal of Community Psychology* (2010), and developed the *Community Service Self-Efficacy Scale.* He serves on numerous editorial boards (e.g., *Michigan Journal of Community Service Learning*). As a licensed clinical psychologist, Dr. Reeb serves on the Homeless Solutions Board and the National Alliance on Mental Illness Board (Montgomery County, Ohio).

Margaret A. Brown, PhD, received her doctorate in social psychology from the University of Washington. She is a professor of psychology at Seattle Pacific University. She is an experienced service learning practitioner and has won multiple awards for excellence in teaching, including the Distinguished Teaching Award from the University of Washington and the endowed Patricia M. Bentz Teacher of the Year Award from Seattle Pacific University. She was recently nominated by her institution for the CASE/Carnegie Foundation's U.S. Professor of the Year Award. In addition, she is the recipient of a National Science Foundation fellowship. Dr. Brown's research interests are self-psychology and the intersection of prosocial behavior and intergroup relations. She is the author of numerous journal articles and book chapters and has coauthored a text on self-psychology. Dr. Brown has conducted rigorous theory-based, experimental research on service learning. Her examinations of service learning as a form of counternormative helping behavior have revealed its impact on social justice attitudes. This line of research has also identified multiple mediators and moderators of this relationship, such as empathy, generosity, and intergroup contact.

Ana I. Ruiz, PhD, received her doctorate in developmental psychology from Cornell University. She is a professor of psychology at Alvernia University. Her publications include the book *Service-Learning Code of Ethics*, chapters and articles on ethical issues in international service learning and research on international service learning, the impact of service on alumni career development, and teaching ethics to undergraduate psychology students. Dr. Ruiz is the cocreator of the online resource "Teaching Ethics to Undergraduate Psychology Students" (https://de.alvernia.edu/teachingpsychethics/). Her scholarship has been funded by grants from Campus Compact, the Association for Psychological Science (Fund for Teaching and Public Understanding of Psychological Science), and the American Psychological Association (Division 2, Instructional Resource Award from the Society for the Teaching of Psychology). She has presented at numerous national and international conferences. Dr. Ruiz has successfully completed service learning projects in several undergraduate psychology courses, served on several ethics boards, and consulted on adoption and implementation of service learning.